806

Geoffrey A. Pe
Denby
6.2.15.

'A BROTHER KNOCKING AT THE DOOR'

The Malines Conversations 1921–1925

'A brother knocking at the door'

The Malines Conversations 1921–1925

by

BERNARD BARLOW OSM

Foreword by Geoffrey Rowell

The Canterbury Press
Norwich

© Bernard F. Barlow OSM 1996
First published 1996 by The Canterbury Press Norwich
(a publishing imprint of Hymns Ancient & Modern Limited,
a registered charity)
St Mary's Works, St Mary's Plain,
Norwich, Norfolk, NR3 3BH

All rights reserved. No part of this publication which is copyright may be reproduced, stored in a retrieval system, or transmitted, in any form or by any means, electronic, mechanical, photocopying, recording, or otherwise, without the prior permission of the publisher.

Bernard F. Barlow has asserted his right under the Copyright, Designs and Patents Act, 1988, to be identified as Author of this Work

British Library Cataloguing in Publication Data

A catalogue record for this book is available
from the British Library

ISBN 1-85311-135-X

*Typeset by David Gregson Associates
Beccles, Suffolk and
Printed and bound in Great Britain by
Biddles Ltd.
Guildford and King's Lynn*

In memory of my parents
Daniel and Mary Anne Barlow

'I would never in this world allow it to be said that one of our separated brothers came knocking at the door of a Roman Catholic bishop, and that that bishop refused to answer'

Cardinal D. J. Mercier,
Pastoral Letter of 18th January 1924.

Foreword

by The Rt Revd Dr Geoffrey Rowell, Bishop of Basingstoke

In January 1924 *Punch* published verses written by Dean Norris of Westminster 'with apologies to A.A. Milne.' Their subject was the Malines Conversations and their Anglican participants, Bishop Herbert Hensley Henson as an opponent of any official Anglican countenancing of this ecumenical encounter, and Archbishop Randall Davidson's very cautious endorsement of it, so that:

> Armitage Armitage, Robinson, Gore,
> Halifax, Frere and Kidd
> are constantly seen on the
> way to Malines
> and no longer try to be hid.

The conversations which took place at Malines in Belgium between Anglicans and Roman Catholics during the years 1921–1925 seemed significant at the time, and in retrospect have come to have an even greater significance as the harbinger of the more sustained ecumenical theological work of the Anglican-Roman Catholic International Commission and the agreed statements that have been its fruit. The ecumenical vision of Lord Halifax, and Abbé Portal, and Cardinal Mercier, and the cautious support of Archbishop Davidson, enabled this first significant exchange of views to occur, and trust between traditionally suspicious churches to grow. The first steps across ancient barriers are always hard to take, and it is often difficult in an age when ecumenical exchange is so much more taken for granted to realise just how significant a step it was when Halifax enthusiastically accepted Portal's suggestion that they should together visit Cardinal Mercier to talk with him about the reunion of Christendom. It was even more significant that the second conversation took place with the formal endorsement of a letter from Davidson to Mercier.

It is not surprising, given the difficulties that the more recent ARCIC conversations encountered in relation to Primacy, that Davidson was concerned to remind Mercier of the ambiguity of the term 'primacy', which had both 'an historical meaning' which Anglicans could accept without difficulty, and a more problematic meaning (from an Anglican perspective) if it implied 'that the Pope holds *jure divino* the unique and solemn position of sole Vicar of Christ on earth, from whom as Vicar of Christ must come directly or indirectly the right to minister validly within the Church'. How significant that latter understanding of primacy

FOREWORD

is as an ecumenical stumbling block is in a measure acknowledged by the invitation in the recent papal encyclical, *Ut unum sint*, to non-Roman Catholic Christians to engage in a dialogue about the exercise of the Petrine ministry.

It was in the context of the Malines conversations that the celebrated phrase *L'Eglise Anglicaine unie non absorbée* appeared in a paper by Dom Lambert Beauduin utilised by Mercier, which proposed a kind of Uniate status for Anglicans. By stressing unity, as opposed to either absorption or separation, the ecclesiological discussion, however unsatisfactory uniate models may now be recognised as being, was moved into a relational context, which may not unfairly be considered as foreshadowing the contemporary emphasis on κοινωνια in ecumenical ecclesiology.

At the time it seemed that Malines had not led to the unity for which Halifax in particular longed, yet in the longer perspective there is no doubt that the conversations made a notable breach in the walls of division, isolation and hostility, and remained as a prophetic sign of where the ecumenical journey of Anglicans and Roman Catholics might lead. The conversations were as symbolically significant in their way and at their time as was Archbishop Fisher's visit to Pope John XXIII in 1960.

In their important survey of relations between Anglicans and Roman Catholics, *Rome and Canterbury through four centuries* (1974), Bernard and Margaret Pawley note that although there have been many accounts of the Malines conversations 'none has so far been definitive'. Bernard Barlow's painstaking and scholarly work provides us with the fullest account so far of the conversations and their context, drawing on original source material and showing both the political, and to some extent personal, complexities surrounding the conversations. No one now doubts the need for dialogue and patient exploration of deeply held convictions in the course of ecumenical dialogue. More and more the churches are being forced, for both cultural and ecumenical reasons, to ask serious ecclesiological questions. All concerned with the unity of Anglicans and Roman Catholics as a necessary part of our obedience to Christ's command that his church should be one can be encouraged by this detailed and moving account of a pioneering ecumenical encounter. We can be thankful for what Malines showed to be possible; we can be even more thankful that the degree of trust, understanding, and theological agreement, if not yet perfect, is infinitely more than the Malines' participants—and even more the churches from which they came—would have believed possible.

GEOFFREY BASINGSTOKE

Contents

Foreword by Bishop Geoffrey Rowell   vii

1. **Introduction to the topic, and brief history of remote beginnings.**   1
   - (i) The Oxford Movement.   5
   - (ii) The efforts of Ambrose Phillipps and the idea of a Uniate Church of England using the Sarum liturgy.   10
   - (iii) The influence of Frederick George Lee, 'The Union' newspaper, and the A.P.U.C.   12
   - (iv) The reaction of Dr Manning to Phillipps and Lee, and the consequences of the strong Ultramontane attitude then existing in the Roman Catholic Church in England.   16
   - (v) The social and political situation in England in 1800-1880, with its large Irish immigrant population, and its effects on the attitude of the English Roman Catholic Church.   20

2. **Immediate forerunner to Malines – the issue of Anglican Orders.**   24
   - (i) The meeting of Lord Halifax and Fr Portal in Madeira, their friendship, and the search for common ground in matters of reunion.   24
   - (ii) Decision to initiate an approach through continental Roman Catholics rather than those in England.   27
   - (iii) The provocative pamphlet of 'M. Fernand Dalbus'.   30
   - (iv) The reactions in Rome and consequent initiatives.   33
   - (v) Change of attitude in Rome, the Pontifical Commission of Enquiry and the resulting publication of *Apostolicae Curae*, declaring Anglican Orders null and void.   38

3. **Renewed attempts at reunion – the Conversations at Malines**   45
   - (i) Publication of the Lambeth Appeal of 1920. Church of England's openness to accepting a commissioning from other Churches as a way to reunion.   45
   - (ii) Cardinal Mercier's own interest and involvement in ecumenism.   50

CONTENTS

  (iii) The Cardinal agrees to 'informal conversations' at his palace in Malines. 53

4. **The first Conversation of Malines in December 1921, its participants, and the consequences of the election of a new Pope in February 1922.** 57
   - (i) Lord Halifax chooses the Anglican members, and visits Cardinal Bourne to keep him informed. 57
   - (ii) The first Conversation, and content of discussion. 64
   - (iii) Important changes which affected the progress of the Conversations. 71
   - (iv) Publication of Cardinal Mercier's Pastoral Letter to his diocese, and his request to Halifax to translate and publish it in English. 82
   - (v) Mercier's request to Pope Pius XI for support for the Conversations, and his receipt of the letter of authorization. 87
   - (vi) The beginnings of adverse reaction, both from Cardinal Bourne and from the Anglicans. 89

5. **The second and third Conversation – some intermediary problems.** 93
   - (i) Preparation of the Agenda for the second meeting. 93
   - (ii) The discussions of the second Conversation. 96
   - (iii) Concerns of Archbishop Davidson after the second Conversation, and his suggestions for future discussions. 102
   - (iv) The choice of additional members for the third Conversations. 110
   - (v) The third Conversation – November 1923. 115

6. **Controversy grows as the Conversations are made public.** 121
   - (i) The Conversations are made public – Archbishop Davidson's Christmas Letter. 121
   - (ii) Initial reaction of English Roman Catholics to the news of Malines. 124
   - (iii) Cardinal Bourne's reactions 125
   - (iv) Cardinal Mercier's Pastoral Letter. 133
   - (v) The Malines Conversations – official or not? 136

CONTENTS

7. **The fourth Conversation and an examination of the discussion papers.** 139
   (i) The fourth Conversation gets under way. 139
   (ii) Cardinal Mercier's surprise presentation. 146
   (iii) Genesis of the Cardinal's Paper. 147
   (iv) Examination of the Cardinal's Paper. 149
   (v) Concluding presentations by Dr Gore. 151
   (vi) The human factor versus the official. 157

8. **Preparations for a fifth Conversation. Mercier's interventions against Woodlock. The death of Mercier and then of Portal, and the effect on the fifth and final Conversation.** 159
   (i) Preparations for a fifth Conversation. 159
   (ii) Fr Woodlock enters the scene again. 161
   (iii) The death of Cardinal Mercier in January 1926, and Portal in June 1926. 167
   (iv) Problems which hindered the publication of the two Reports. 171

9. **Reflections on the importance of the Conversations in the history of Anglican/Roman Catholic ecumenical relations, their contemporary context, and the particular influences of the personalities involved.** 178
   (i) Objectives of the Conversations. 178
   (ii) The historical context and theological stance of both Churches. 179
   (iii) The differences in character and structure of the Anglican and Roman Catholic Churches. 183
   (iv) Important assumptions in the methodology of the Conversations, the themes chosen for discussion, and the points approaching agreement and points of disagreement. 187
   (v) Points of major difficulty and disagreement. 193
   (vi) The role of powerful individuals, and contemporary issues which impinged on the Conversations. 198

CONTENTS

Conclusions
Towards drawing a conclusion on the Malines Conversations – success or failure?   211
(i)   The primary objectives of Halifax, Portal and Mercier.   211
(ii)   Consequential successes.   213

Appendix 1
Unpublished letter of Cardinal Merry del Val to
Fr Francis Woodlock SJ, 16th January 1930.   215

Appendix 2
Compte rendu of the second Conversation –
15th March 1923.   221

Appendix 3
Speech of the Archbishop of Canterbury in the Upper
House of Convocation, 6th February 1924.   227

Appendix 4
Memoire read by Cardinal Mercier at the fourth
Conversation entitled *L'Église anglicane unie non absorbée*.   233

Bibliography   247

Index   263

1

Introduction to the topic, and brief history of remote beginnings.

When the Vatican *Response to The Final Report of ARCIC I*[1] was eventually published in December 1991,[2] a good nine years after the Report had been presented to Rome for consideration, the initial reaction of many observers was a rather mixed one of disappointment and hope, disappointment with some of the negative aspects of the Vatican response, whilst at the same time acknowledging that there were some strongly positive elements and that, on the whole, the language used was one of encouragement rather than discouragement.

The first Anglican-Roman Catholic International Commission (ARCIC-I) had published its Final Report in 1982, following its final meeting at Windsor, in 1981. The members of this first Commission submitted that they had reached 'substantial agreement' on the doctrine of the Eucharist and on the ordained ministry, and had reached 'a degree of convergence' in their discussions on authority in the Church. *The Final Report* was then submitted to the authorities of both Churches for their evaluation.

The official Anglican reaction was given in a resolution of the Lambeth Conference of 1988, which stated that the ARCIC statements on eucharist and ordination were 'consonant in substance with the faith of anglicans' and that the statement on authority was considered 'a firm basis for the direction and agenda of the continuing dialogue'[3].

The Roman Catholic Church's initial reaction was to issue in 1982 a set

---

1. A.R.C.I.C., *The Final Report,* (Anglican-Roman Catholic International Commission), London, C.T.S./S.P.C.K., 1982.
2. *L'Osservatore Romano*, 6th December 1991, p. 10. Also published under the title: "Rome and Canterbury" in *The Tablet*, 7th December 1991, pp. 1521–1524.
3. *'The Truth Shall Make You Free'*, The Lambeth Conference 1988: The Reports, Resolutions and Pastoral Letters from the Bishops, London: Church House, 1988, pp. 210–212.

of observations made by the Congregation for the Doctrine of the Faith, and to invite National Episcopal Conferences to submit their observations on the *Final Report* as part of the process of arriving at a considered judgement. The Pontifical Council for Promoting Christian Unity also collaborated in the assessment of the replies from the various Episcopal Conferences and in preparing an official declaration, but the Congregation for the Doctrine of the Faith was the organ of final authority in issuing the final *'Response'*. This *'Response'* was published in *'L' Osservatore Romano'* in December 1991. *The Response* issued by the Roman Catholic Church warmly welcomed the *Final Report*, commending its achievements, but also drew attention to the fact that 'there still remain between anglicans and catholics important differences regarding essential matters of catholic doctrine'[1].

Typifying the Anglican reaction was a comment from Christopher Hill, former ecumenical affairs secretary of the Archbishop of Canterbury: 'Now that it (the Response) has appeared, Anglicans of whatever school will at best be able to raise one cheer out of three. Some few Anglicans will be relieved at its implicit assumption that they are really Protestants, rather than reformed catholics, whatever they say and however they worship. Others will say *sotto voce*, "I told you so, let's get on with the main agenda without ecumenical diversion". Yet others will be saddened at the very uncertain signals Rome is sending to all engaged in ecumenical dialogue, not only to Anglicans'.[2]

Roman Catholic commentators such as Fr Edward Yarnold SJ, who himself played a leading part as a member of the ARCIC-I commission from the beginning, tried to paint a more positive picture, highlighting the points of progress which the *Response* had indicated: 'Despite its reservations, its overall emphasis is positive.' *The Final Report* of ARCIC-I is praised as 'a significant milestone not only in relations between the Catholic Church and the Anglican communion but in the ecumenical movement as a whole'. *The Report* is said to be evidence of 'very consoling' areas of convergence and agreement which many would have thought impossible to establish. The progress made is said

---

1. *L'Osservatore Romano*, 6th December 1991, p. 10.
5. Christopher Hill, *Response to the Response: 2, The Tablet*, 7th December 1991, pp. 1525–1527.

INTRODUCTION AND BRIEF HISTORY OF REMOTE BEGINNINGS

to be 'notable' (twice) and 'quite remarkable'. Fr Yarnold noted also that the commitment to the restoration of visible unity made by Pope John Paul II and the Archbishop of Canterbury, Robert Runcie, during the visit of the latter to Rome in 1989 was endorsed.[1]

Whatever the outcome of the present difficulties are, one really remarkable element which people take for granted these days is the fact that Anglicans and Roman Catholics are actually sitting down together and seriously discussing the differences between the two Churches, to see if such difficulties can at least be elucidated if not actually resolved by examining both the language of presentation and the meanings of the words used in presenting each Church's doctrine and beliefs. The goal of these meetings is specifically the restoration of unity, based on the Second Vatican Council's *Decree on Ecumenism*,[2] and as proclaimed by Archbishop Michael Ramsey, Archbishop of Canterbury, and Pope Paul VI, during their historic encounter in Rome in March 1966. This meeting between the two heads of the respective Churches laid the foundation of this theological dialogue between the Roman Catholic and Anglican Church.

This enormous ecumenical step was not undertaken, however, as a single leap. In the four centuries since Henry VIII declared himself the head of the Church of England and the consequent changes and differences in emphasis brought about under the influence of the various Reformers, there had been several tentative initiatives at dialogue between certain Anglicans and Catholics with a view to bringing about a reunion. These initiatives, although unsuccessful, were vitally important in slowly if imperceptibly changing attitudes in both Churches and in preparing the ground for the serious dialogue at present underway in the ARCIC discussions.

1. Edward Yarnold SJ, *Response to the Response: 1*, *The Tablet*, 7th December 1991, pp. 1524–1525, and in *Anglicans and Roman Catholics: The Search for Unity*, (London: SPCK/CTS: 1994), pp. 237–251.
Note: Other Roman Catholic commentators are less kind than Fr. Yarnold. Bishop Alan Clark of the Diocese of East Anglia, who was himself co-chairman for 12 years of the ARCIC I Commission, in an interview with the Italian religious magazine *'Il Regno'* (Attualità, (Bologna), No. 6, 15th March 1992, pp. 135/138), makes quite cutting comments on the attitude of the Congregation for the Doctrine of the Faith, and suggests a growing influence on the Congregation by such right-wing Church groups as *Opus Dei* and 'all those other groups in Rome who speak badly about us (sparla di noi)'.
2. Walter M. Abbott SJ (Ed.), *The Documents of Vatican II*, (Herder: New York 1966), *Decree on Ecumenism* (Unitatis Redintegratio), No. 13, pp. 355/356.

Internal developments within each of the Churches themselves, especially in how they perceived the *nature and mission* of the Church in a rapidly changing and increasingly industrial society, contributed greatly towards a progressive change of attitudes particularly towards the beginning of the 20th century and, despite the many religious confrontations, jealousies and fears which the previous century had engendered, there was evidence also of a growing desire to work for and promote that unity of the Church of Christ for which Jesus prayed. Many other Churches and ecclesial communions were also engaged radically in this search for unity, notably since the 1910 World Missionary Conference at Edinburgh. The concentrated efforts to carry the Gospel to foreign parts which emanated especially from the Evangelicals, led also to practical experiences of co-operation and inter-denominational fellowship in overseas mission areas, an experience which became a common ground to a new generation of Church leadership. The subsequent efforts of Bishop Brent[1] to organise an International and Inter-Church Conference to discuss questions related to 'Faith and Order' gave added impetus to what eventually became known simply as 'the Ecumenical Movement'.[2]

In the history of relationships between Anglicans and Roman Catholics, it has been frequently postulated that one of the key factors in this changing of attitudes was the series of informal and yet semi-official meetings which were held in Belgium between the years 1921 and 1925. These meetings, known as the Malines Conversations, were conducted between invited representatives of both Churches to discuss in a friendly and informal manner some of the major differences of doctrine and

---

1. Bishop Charles Henry Brent (1862–1929). Born in Newcastle, Ontario, a missionary bishop in the Philippines, eventually becoming Protestant Episcopal Bishop of Western New York. In later years his chief work was for the Ecumenical (Faith and Order) Movement of which he was President. His initial inspiration came from the Edinburgh Conference of 1910.
2. Invitations to participate in the proposed international conference had been sent. (in Latin) to the cardinals and bishops of the Roman Church, but no reply was forthcoming. It was only in 1919 that a delegation from North America, who were actively promoting the conference, were able to discuss the proposal personally with Pope Benedict XV and his Secretary of State, Cardinal Gasparri. However, as the members of the deputation later reported, 'the word "discussed" was perhaps too strong a word, for the audience with his Holiness, though cordial throughout, was not what is sometimes called an "ecumenical discussion". To borrow a classical 'Irishism', "the reciprocity was all on one side". The contrast between the Pope's *personal* attitude towards us and his *official* attitude towards the Conference was very sharp. One was irresistibly benevolent, the other irresistibly rigid'. Norman Goodall, *The Ecumenical Movement (what it is and what it does)*, (London: Oxford Univ. Press, 1961), p. 49.

INTRODUCTION AND BRIEF HISTORY OF REMOTE BEGINNINGS

practice of the Anglican and Roman Catholic Church. The initiative for these Conversations, however, did not emanate from the authorities of either church, but rather from dedicated apostles of unity such as Lord Halifax and Fr Ferdinand Portal. By involving Cardinal Mercier, Archbishop of Malines, and through the persistent efforts of Halifax in England, they succeeded in extracting a certain guarded measure of semi-official approval from both Rome and Canterbury. The agenda which was discussed during these Malines Conversations was almost identical to the one being discussed today by the members of ARCIC - the sacraments, especially the eucharist and the ordained ministry; the history, nature and exercise of papal authority and jurisdiction; the nature and meaning of dogma. It is these series of meetings or 'conversations' which will be the subject of our present study, and we shall attempt to place them in the perspective of the on-going process of ecumenical relations between the Church of England and the Roman Catholic Church and to evaluate their importance *vis-à-vis* current inter-church dialogue.

(i) The Oxford Movement and Tractarians.

The Oxford Movement of the mid-nineteenth century was not properly speaking a new movement, but rather a flowering and re-birth in thought and activity of the old High Church[1] party which had been in existence in the Church of England since the break with Rome in the 16th century. This 'High Church' tendency was highlighted at various moments in such figures as Bishop Andrewes and the Caroline Divines. During the reign of King Charles I, the notion of reunion with the Church of Rome came to the surface again, particularly in discussions regarding the nature of the church. It was an idea which was actively proposed during the mission of the Benedictine Dom Leander a Sancto Martino (otherwise known as Dom Leander Jones) and Fr Gregorio Panzani to England[2]. These two Roman Catholic priests came to England on a papal mission in 1634 to try to settle differences between the Roman secular and religious clergy, but were encouraged by the prevailing eirenic situation to widen their mission to include an ecumenical

---

1. A description of the initial development and impact of the High Church 'party' can be found in Peter B. Nockles, *The Oxford Movement in Context*, (Cambridge: Cambridge Univ. Press, 1994).
2. Henry R.T. Brandreth, *The Ecumenical Ideals of the Oxford Movement*, (London: S.P.C.K., 1947), p. 2.

perspective with regard to the Church of England. Dom Leander Jones, in particular, made contact with Archbishop Laud who had been a contemporary at Oxford, and this influenced greatly his subsequent reports to Rome. In his reports he emphasised the similarities with the Church of England rather than the differences, and was himself in favour of English Catholics taking the oath of allegiance.[1] With the accession of King William and Queen Mary, however, and the consequent requirement of the oath of allegiance to the new royal family, many of the 'High Church' clergy being strong Jacobite supporters, refused to take the oath and either left or were ejected from the State Church. These non-jurors carried with them their Caroline Unionist tradition, and in the course of time were impelled by their own 'schismatic' position into gradually clarifying and evolving a clearer doctrine of Catholic unity, though more on a theoretical than a practical level. This group of marginalised non-jurors consequently preserved those principles and usages which the rest of the Church of England gradually abandoned, and the restoration of which became the focus of the Oxford Movement.

In the course of the eighteenth century, another external factor intervened in English history which led to an amelioration in the general public's view of Roman Catholics. The persecution of members of the Roman Catholic Church in France who were suffering from the attacks of the anti-clerical philosophers of the French Revolution, and the subsequent flood of Catholic refugees to England in 1792, including some eight thousand bishops and priests, led to a growing sympathy for Catholics.[2] Moreover, the witness of the patient suffering of these refugee clergy, together with a growing admiration for their piety and ascetic lifestyle, made the ordinary Englishman aware that Catholics were not as bad as they had been led to believe. The influence of these

1. Elizabeth B. Stuart, *R.C. reactions to the Oxford Movement and Anglican schemes for reunion, from 1833 to the condemnation of Anglican Orders in 1896*, D. Phil Diss., Oxford 1987, pp. 20–21.
2. It is interesting to note the extent of the generous British Government assistance to these French exiles – during the period 14th February 1794 till 14th February 1805, a total of £2,192,226 17s. 7½ d. in grants were administered on behalf of 'relief of suffering clergy and laity of France'.
Margery Weiner, *The French Exiles 1789–1815*, (London: John Murray, 1960): (Source: Annual Register).

Dom Dominic Bellenger OSB points out however, that there were several negative aspects for the English Roman Catholics caused by this massive intake of clergy from France: (i) the immediate need for charitable assistance which strained the resources of the

INTRODUCTION AND BRIEF HISTORY OF REMOTE BEGINNINGS

refugee clergy on those in the Anglican ministry who were active in their assistance was considerable. This change of tone was typified by Dr Shute Barrington, the Bishop of Durham, who in 1810 stated that there was no public duty of greater magnitude than the restoration of peace and union to the Church by the reconciliation of two so large a portions of it as the Churches of Rome and England.[1] Dr. Barrington had been one of those active in assisting the refugee clergy.

The years 1833 to 1860 saw the main thrust of the Oxford Movement encapsulated in the publication of the *Tracts for the Times*, a series of papers whose writers subsequently were known as the 'Tractarians'. The authors were principally Oxford men, such as Edward Pusey, John Keble, John Henry Newman, Hurrell Froude, William Palmer of Magdalen College,[2] Isaac Williams and Frederick Oakeley. The movement was not primarily directed towards an objective of reunion, but of the internal reform of the Church of England through seeking a return to the original sources of the early Church. Indeed one of the professed aims of the Tractarians was to 'combat popery and dissent'[3]. The Tractarians urged faithfulness to the beliefs and customs of the ancient and undivided Church, a heritage which they saw as the Church of England's own catholic heritage, and in so doing, encouraged the restoration and renewal of lost practices such as some of the medieval hymns, prayers for the dead, respect for the ideals of religious and monastic life, the eucharist as sacrifice, and even the real presence. It soon became obvious to the writers of the *Tracts* that one of the fundamental and distinctive marks of the early Church was that it was a

---

local Catholic communities, (ii) the French clergy's request to distinguish between the jurors and non-jurors (to the Civil Constitution of 1791) among themselves, (iii) the problem which arose concerning whether these immigrant clergy owed obedience to their French bishops who came with them or to the English Vicars Apostolic, and (iv) the '*foreigness*' of the French clergy which eventually gave rise to an anti-French sentiment among some English Catholics. Dominic Bellenger, *The French exiled clergy in the British Isles after 1789*, (Bath: Downside Abbey, 1986), pp. 48–50.

1. Dr Shute Barrington, *Grounds of Union between the Churches of England and Rome considered, in a Charge delivered to the Clergy of the Diocese of Durham*, (London: William Bulmer & Co., 1811) pp. 11/12.
2. There were two noted academics by the name of William Palmer at Oxford at this time, and they are distinguished by the addition of the names of their College. The other William Palmer was of Worcester College, and this latter was noted for his fanatical antagonism towards the Church of Rome.
3. Brandreth, *The Ecumenical Ideals of the Oxford Movement*, p. 14.

visible unity in its organization and structure (catholicity), and consequently fidelity to the principles of the early church (apostolicity) also included inevitably a search for christian reunion.

In 1841, there appeared the famous *Tract XC, Remarks on certain Passages in the Thirty-Nine Articles*, written by John Henry Newman. His intention was to try to show that the Thirty-Nine Articles of the Church of England were not inconsistent with Catholic beliefs. With the publication of this Tract, a storm broke out within the Church of England, and a series of pamphlets produced both by supporters and opponents of Newman's thesis. The opposition of the Anglican bishops in particular, for whose authority Newman had a very reverential regard, was a most painful experience, and led him to re-examine his theory of the Church of England as a *via media* between England and Rome. This controversy and the continuing development of his studies finally led to the conclusion that the Church of Rome was the legitimate successor of the apostolic Church, and ended with Newman's secession to the Roman Church in 1845.[1]

The departure of Newman from the Church of England acted as a catalyst for other prominent members of the Oxford Movement, in that it forced them to clarify their own position as regards the Church of England and the Church of Rome. The various strands of theological thought and opinion which had sheltered under the single umbrella of the Oxford Movement diversified into roughly three distinct strands. Dr Edward Pusey[2] became the acknowledged head of the Anglican Catholic or High Church party (eventually to be succeeded by Lord Halifax, one of the central figures in later ecumenical efforts and in the Malines Conversations) after Newman's departure, and continued to write in support of church reunion. Both Pusey and Keble re-aligned the movement away from doctrinal polemics and back to the surer ground of pastoral and liturgical matters, and many adherents of the movement concentrated their efforts on promoting the Catholic tradition in the slums of mid-Victorian England. The opposition which led to the seces-

---

1. A. R. Vidler, *The Church in an Age of Revolution – 1789 to the Present Day*, (London: Penguin Books, 1971, pp. 53–54.
2. In 1865 Pusey published *Eirenicon* in which he defended the catholic heritage of the Church of England, and at the same time addressed an appeal for Christian unity to the gallican elements within the Roman Church.

INTRODUCTION AND BRIEF HISTORY OF REMOTE BEGINNINGS

sion of Newman really signaled the end to Tractarianism as an intellectual movement, and it developed into a form of ritualism which was manifested in the parochial life of the Church of England. Consequently, the focus of the Movement was shifted away from the now unfriendly terrain of Oxford University into the cities and towns of England. William G. Ward and Frederick Oakeley, on the other hand, saw nothing inconsistent in the logic of Newman's position, and Ward wrote strongly in defence of Tract XC in the following terms: '... that the Roman Church and ours *together* make up so far more adequate a representation of the early church (our several defects and practical corruptions as it were protesting against each other) than either separately'.[1] Both Ward and Oakeley believed that it was possible to accept completely the Roman position within the Church of England, but when they found opposition and rejection of their views from the bishops and Anglican Divines, they followed Newman in making their individual submission to the Holy See. A third strand can be drawn from those like William Palmer of Magdalen College, Oxford. Palmer, who was actively involved in the Oxford Movement although never a really representative Tractarian, remained consistently hostile towards the Church of Rome and any would-be 'romanizers'.[2]

The real ecumenical importance of the Oxford Movement was in its educating of the intellectual classes, particularly the rising generation of Anglican clergy, many of whom bought and avidly read the *Tracts*, as to what the Roman Church actually believed and taught. In seeking to retrace the primitive roots of the Church of England in the undivided Catholic Church through the publication of the Tracts of the Times, it brought a realization of the importance of reunion with Rome to the forefront of theological discussion. Another important development was its influence in the re-introduction of many catholic practices and rituals in parish churches throughout England, hence touching the lives of many of the ordinary English christians who would have otherwise been bypassed by the academic controversies. Many of the more protestant churches were similarly influenced to some degree by this catholic

---

1. William G. Ward, *A Few Words in support of Number 90 of the Tracts for the Times*, p. 33.
2. For a fuller description of the nature of these diverse trends within the Oxford Movement after Newman's departure in 1845, cf. Brandreth, *The Ecumenical Ideals of the Oxford Movement*, pp. 14–30.

movement, as evidenced by the introduction of organ music and liturgical vestments in their liturgies.

(ii) The efforts of Ambrose Phillipps and the idea of a Uniate Church of England using the Sarum liturgy.

A further constituent to the cause of union was added by the distinguished layman, Ambrose Phillipps de Lisle, a convert to Roman Catholicism in pre-Tractarian times, who was to be for some 35 years involved in various ecumenical initiatives. Phillipps was the squire of Grace Dieu in Leicestershire, whose generosity included the gifting of 250 acres of land for the foundation of the Trappist Monastery of Mount St Bernard at Charnwood, part of his estate.[1] Dr Elizabeth Stuart notes concerning Phillipps that, 'a staunch Tory, he feared that the Oxford Movement heralded the destruction of the Church of England and that the Establishment would fall with it, leaving the country in the hands of dissenters and revolutionaries. This could only be prevented by the absorption of the disintegrating Church of England into the ever-powerful Catholic Church which could then support the Establishment'.[2]

In 1840, Ambrose Phillipps initiated a correspondence with Dr John Rouse Bloxam, a Fellow of Magdalen College, who had been till recently (1837-1840) a curate of Newman's at Littlemore. They had met by chance at the site of the new Mount St Bernard Monastery, and this led to an ongoing correspondence throughout the following year, a correspondence in which Phillipps described his vision of how the reunion of the Churches of England and Rome could be effected. In essence he proposed that the Church of England should expel all Protestants from its midst, and that the remainder of the Church (principally the High Church groups) should, with the English Roman Catholics, form a Uniate Church such as existed in eastern Christianity. 'You shall lay aside your modern common Prayer, we our Roman Rite,

---

1. The estates owned by the de Lisle family had originally belonged to the Cistercian Order, confiscated and sold to the family following the dissolution of the monasteries by Henry VIII. Margaret Pawley notes: 'He (Ambrose) saw it as an act of reparation for the dissolution of the earlier foundation and purchase into lay hands by his ancesters'.
Margaret Pawley, *Faith and Family: The Life Circle of Ambrose Phillipps de Lisle*, (Canterbury Press, Norwich: 1993), p. 89.
2. Elizabeth B. Stuart, *R.C. reactions to the Oxford Movement and Anglican schemes for reunion*, p. 37.

INTRODUCTION AND BRIEF HISTORY OF REMOTE BEGINNINGS

and let the antient (sic) rites of Sarum and York resume their place'.[1] Phillipps proposed that Latin should be the language of the old rites, but that some English would be allowed in parish churches. The English clergy would be permitted to retain their wives, and future clergy would also be allowed to marry. The Holy See might sanction the omission of the invocation of the saints from public liturgies, and the Church in England would be permitted to make its own decisions regarding the use of images and statues. Phillipps was of the opinion that there would be no real difficulty with such doctrines as transubstantiation. His conclusion was that such a Uniate Church as he proposed would add some 9 million faithful to the Church of Rome, smooth if not heal the political and religious divisions between England and Ireland, and present a powerful resistance to the Dissenters[2]. Phillipps expressed his certainty that 'the Holy See would give every *facility* for the restoration of catholick (sic) unity in England'.[3]

Phillips' rather novel if naive proposals took Bloxam by surprise, and the reaction of friends to whom he showed the letter (among whom was Newman[4]) was generally sceptical, although not by any means all of them. What is interesting to us is that some of these same ideas of a Uniate Church of England re-surfaced some 80 years later in the fourth session of the Malines Conversations, when Cardinal Mercier presented the famous *memoire* on 'L'Église Anglicane, Unie non Absorbée'

---

1. Letter of Phillips to Bloxam of 25th January 1841, published in R.D. Middleton, *Newman and Bloxam – an Oxford Friendship*, (Oxford: Univ. Press, 1947), pp. 102–111.
2. Phillips had been much impressed by the Armenian Church which he had encountered during his visits to Venice. The fact that the Armenians, with their own language and liturgies, lived and worshipped side by side with the Latin Church in Venice was surely an important element in his idea and proposal of a Uniate Anglican Rite. John Henry Newman was not so impressed, as he stated in his note to Bloxam on 6th February 1840: 'As to the instance of the Armenians at Venice, *they* act with *leave* of the bishop of the place, and are in communion with him but the R.C.s in England are not acting with permission of our bishops. However, I have never called R.C.s schismatics in England'. Middleton, *Newman and Bloxam*, p. 113.
3. Middleton, *Newman and Bloxam*, p. 106.
4. Newman's reaction to Phillipps' proposals was extremely cautious. He wrote an anonymous letter to Phillipps commenting on his proposals and asked Bloxam to deliver it. Newman's attitude at this time was that while reunion with Rome was *desirable*, it was in fact *impossible* until the Church of Rome had reformed itself.At this stage of his life Newman held to the theory dear to the Tractarians of distinguishing between the two Romes, that of the Councils and early Christianity which the Anglicans felt close to, and the other of the Council of Trent and more popular romanism.
c.f. J.A. Dick, *The Malines Conversations Revisited*, (Leuven: Univ. Press, 1989) p. 23.

(written, in fact, by a Belgian Benedictine). Phillipps' scheme also brought to the fore another difficult and delicate problem. In the case of reunion, would the Roman Catholic Church unite with the whole of the Church of England, or only with that part which was evidently nearest to it in beliefs and practices, namely the High Church? Did 'corporate reunion' really mean the whole of the *corpus*, or simply one part of it? The reaction of Roman Catholics to Phillipps' proposition was understandably mostly negative, he having publicized his proposals by sending a copy of his letter for publication in *The Tablet*, but there was encouragement from the Jesuits of Stonyhurst and from a Fr B.F. Crosbee, who, in a letter to the same publication on the 17th February 1840, urged him 'to continue to speak and write on the subject'.

(iii) The Influence of Frederick George Lee, 'The Union' newspaper, and the A.P.U.C.

In December 1856, Dr Frederick George Lee (1832-1902) founded an Anglican newspaper called *The Union* (changed in 1862 to *Union Review*). Dr Lee was an Anglican priest, just two years out of theological college, and, at the time, a curate at the Berkeley chapel in London. He was an able theological writer with a genuine and enthusiastic desire for reunion, but his style of writing was sharp and tended to polemic. While the self-proclaimed purpose of *The Union* was to promote the corporate reunion of the Church of England to the Holy See, the sometimes offensive nature and language of some of the articles belied its principal goal. Phillipps de Lisle quickly became a contributor to the new newspaper, content to have found and be able to work with others for the cause of reunion. His contributions, however, resulted in strong criticism from his fellow Roman Catholics, and he decided to seek approval from higher authority. As he explained in a letter to Newman on 2nd July 1857,

> 'Now it having been officially intimated to me, who, as you know, have for many years cherished the hope that by means of a reunion of the Churches the great breach of the 16th century might be healed, that there was now a powerful party in the Established Church ready to take definite steps towards the realization of such a measure, I was induced in the early part of the year to write the letters which appeared in The Union, and when subsequently these letters occasioned a strong outburst of remonstrance in some of the organs of the

INTRODUCTION AND BRIEF HISTORY OF REMOTE BEGINNINGS

catholic body, I felt we could take no further step, until we had ascertained from the voice of authority how far we could with safety proceed on our course.'[1]

As a consequence, de Lisle wrote to Cardinal Barnabo, who was the Cardinal Prefect of Propaganda Fide,[2] the Roman Congregation which was responsible for England and Wales before the restoration of the English Roman Catholic hierarchy in 1850.

Almost contemporaneously, de Lisle published in the Spring of 1857 a pamphlet of some 69 pages entitled 'On the future unity of Christendom', in which he postulated that the church consisted of three great bodies: Greek, Roman and Anglican, and that the Church of England was in essence both Orthodox and Catholic. He insisted that the Oxford Movement had exposed the dominant and underlying catholic nature of the Church of England, and that charity among all would now lead progressively towards union.[3] Phillipps de Lisle called for a congress in Paris of theologians of all three Churches to prepare the ground for a possible ecumenical council to restore unity. The pamphlet caused some considerable sensation, especially when it became known that Fr William Lockhart, a respected Roman Catholic theologian, had revised the pamphlet and presumably given his approbation. Dr Lee considered that

'No treatise has been published for many years in England of greater interest, nor has any statement from a member of the Roman

---

1. From the original letter of the 2nd July 1857 in the Birmingham Oratory, as cited in Bernard & Margaret Pawley, *Rome and Canterbury through Four Centuries*, (London: Mowbray, 1981), p. 171.
2. Cardinal Barnabo consulted with Cardinal Nicholas Wiseman, Archbishop of Westminster, in considering his reply to Phillipps de Lisle. Wiseman's detailed letter pointed out that de Lisle was both naive and mistaken about the numbers of Anglicans whom he thought were strongly favourable to reunion (de Lisle had cited 2000 priests and 10 Bishops among the High Church groups desirous of reunion), but his strongest criticism was for de Lisle's theory of the 'three great denominations' of the Church. This, he said, presupposed that all three Churches were on an equal footing, and he was opposed to any suggestion that heterodox and schismatical bishops of England should be considered as participating Fathers of any proposed Council.
c.f. Wilfred Ward, *Life and Times of Cardinal Wiseman*, (London: Longmans & Green, 1897), Vol. 2, pp. 380–381.
3. Owen Chadwick, *The Church of England and the Church of Rome from the beginning of the nineteenth century to the present day*, p. 80.

'A BROTHER KNOCKING AT THE DOOR'

Communion received such general and respectful attention from members of the Church of England.'[1]

In the summer of 1857, Phillipps de Lisle, Dr Lee and Alexander Forbes[2], Bishop of Brechin, met to discuss how best to continue their efforts for reunion. Bishop Forbes, in a letter to Dr Lee, wrote that:

'I have, as you may imagine, thought of little else since my conversation with yourself and Mr Phillipps. Although the difficulties seem enormous, by God's help they are not insurmountable, and though the British mind is not prepared for an immediate proposition for a union, yet it is something, if in our days that mind be so far awakened to a sense of its wants, as to begin to pray for their supply. Yet I need not impress upon you how much I feel the necessity for caution. An ill-advised expression may ruin the whole good work, and therefore I do not think it would be wise to do more now than to put forth the prayer, and to furnish to the Curia all the documents we can in support of our undoubtedly valid Orders ...'[3]

On the 8th September 1857, both Phillipps de Lisle and Dr Lee, together with a group of like-minded friends, gathering in Dr Lee's apartments in London, decided to found a society – the Association for the Promotion of the Unity of Christendom, which became known as the A.P.U.C. for short. This Association had one very simple stated goal – to pray daily for christian unity. The foundation charter emphasized that no principles needed to be compromised, and its appeal was made to all who lamented and decried the state of disunity in Christendom. In practice, however, things were not quite so simple. The prayer which was chosen for recitation by all was modelled principally upon one in the Roman Missal and, together with one Our Father, was to be recited daily. Priest members of the Association, in addition, were requested to offer one Mass every three months for the intention of Christian unity.

---

1. *Union Review*, Vol. 1, p. 27.
2. Alexander Penrose Forbes (1817–1875), Bishop of Brechin in the Scottish Episcopal Church. Promotor of the Tractarian movement in Scotland. Among many writings, he published at the suggestion of Pusey two volumes entitled *An Explanation of the 39 Articles*.
3. MS. Letter cited by Brandreth, *The Ecumenical Ideals of the Oxford Movement*, pp. 31–32.

INTRODUCTION AND BRIEF HISTORY OF REMOTE BEGINNINGS

The A.P.U.C. expanded rapidly, and from its foundation in 1857 till 1864 counted some 7000 members, including approximately 1000 Roman Catholics and 300 eastern Orthodox. Initially its formation and ideals were looked upon in a friendly manner by Cardinal Wiseman and some Roman Catholic bishops, and even Pope Pius IX commented to an Anglican visitor (Revd George Nugee, Vicar of Wymering, Cosham, Portsmouth, and one of the Anglican secretaries of the A.P.U.C.) that he had high hopes for the Association.[1] Cardinal Wiseman was, however, increasingly incapable, because of his poor health, of managing the affairs of the archdiocese of Westminster, and depended more and more on the assistance of the Provost of Westminster, Dr. Henry Manning, a former Anglican himself who had left the Church of England in disagreement with the Privy Council's ruling on baptism in the Book of Common Prayer. He was no supporter of corporate reunion, and the latter's effective opposition to the A.P.U.C. grew as Wiseman's energies declined.

Although established before the foundation of the A.P.U.C. and, in reality, separate from it, *The Union* newspaper quickly became the mouthpiece of the new Association. With Dr Lee as editor, its polemical style continued but, despite contributions from good writers, the newspaper folded in 1862. A letter from John Keble to the editor typifies the reaction of some of the early subscribers: 'Mr Keble presents his compliments to the editor of the *Union* and requests to be no longer considered as a subscriber to that paper ... the amount of support promised by him to the Revd F.G. Lee being that he would try the paper for half a year *if he found it dutiful to the Church of England.*[2] He is sorry to say that he cannot consider the publication, so far as he has examined it, such as to answer this description; though he readily allows there is some very good writing in it, and he is far from questioning the motives (whatever he may think of the *judgement*) of its conductors.'[3] Another contributor who quickly withdrew from the newspaper was Bishop Forbes of Brechin, one of the Association's founders.

One year later, in 1863, the newspaper rose again like a phoenix, but this

---

1. H.R.T. Brandreth, *Dr Lee of Lambeth*, (London: S.P.C.K., 1951), p. 104.
2. Italics by author.
3. MS. Letter in possession of Brandreth, as cited in his work *The Ecumenical Ideals of the Oxford Movement*, p. 33.

time under the title of the *Union Review*. The principal difference between this new *Union Review* and the old 'Union' newspaper was that the majority of articles were now of a more scholarly and solid character, but the editor was the same Dr Lee, and the polemical tone of the publication continued. It was this which led to its eventual demise in 1865.

(iv) The reaction of Dr Manning to Phillipps and Lee, and the consequences of the strong Ultramontane attitude then existing in the Roman Catholic Church in England.

Henry Edward Manning (1808-1892) was a convert from Anglicanism. Coming from a middle-class background, he was first ordained as an Anglican priest, having been educated at Oxford, but without being really an active participant in the Oxford Movement. He was received into the Roman Catholic Church in 1851, and ordained a Catholic priest by Cardinal Wiseman less than a year after his conversion. Wiseman sent him to Rome to study at the *Accademia dei Nobili Ecclesiastici*, and he received a Doctorate of Divinity degree in 1854. Under Wiseman's tutelage, Dr Manning rapidly became an important personage in the archdiocese of Westminster, eventually succeeding Cardinal Wiseman as Archbishop on the latter's death in 1865. Because of his background, Dr Manning was considered one of the leading supporters in Britain of papal authority and all things 'Roman' in terms liturgical and devotional. As a convert and prominent Ultramontane figure in the Roman Catholic Church in England[1], Manning's rapid rise within the hierarchical structure in England was viewed with some concern by the Old Catholic families of England, who tended on the whole to sympathize with those Anglicans engaged in efforts of reunion.

Dr Manning's sympathies lay in entirely the opposite direction. He was opposed to the notion of 'corporate reunion' with the Church of England, and consequently had no time for either the A.P.U.C. or for the *Union Review*. The difference between Cardinal Wiseman's approach to

---

1. The vast majority of individual converts to the Roman Catholic Church during this period were regarded as 'Ultramontane', that is, strongly attached to all things Roman, particularly Italian devotional practices, liturgical styles and modes, and especially the supremacy of the Pope in things spiritual and even temporal. Later they proved themselves the strongest supporters of Papal Infallibility at Vatican I.

INTRODUCTION AND BRIEF HISTORY OF REMOTE BEGINNINGS

the reunion efforts and that of Dr Manning is accurately described by Manning's biographer:

'The difference between Wiseman's treatment of the question of reunion and Manning's was not so much a difference of principle as of temperament. Wiseman's heart was touched, his warm imagination fired by the fact that for the first time since the Reformation a large number of clergymen of the Church of England were inspired by God's grace with an active desire for reunion with Rome ... Deeply as he desired such a reunion, Manning had no belief in the movement, no great trust in its advocates, no hope of its success.'[1]

The *Union Review* continued throughout this period to publish articles on reunion in a lively manner, including a number of letters by some Roman Catholic priests of the 'Old Catholic' groups, attacking among other things clerical celibacy and the attitudes of some of their bishops. One of these articles, written by an ex-Anglican convert, E.S. Ffoulkes (who eventually returned to the Anglican Church), and entitled 'Experiences of a "vert" ', was particularly notorious. The English bishops were already concerned at the *Union Review*'s constant support for the 'Branch' theory, and these latest criticisms eventually spurred them to action. At the bishops' annual meeting in Low Week in April 1864, the Roman Catholic bishops discussed the A.P.U.C. and the question of allowing Catholic membership of the Association. Bishop Ullathorne of Birmingham was delegated to write to the Holy See, to describe the A.P.U.C. and its goals and practices, and to request a decision on two points: (a) whether Catholics should be permitted to join such an Association and, (b) whether priests should be allowed to offer Holy Mass for the intention of the Association.[2] In addition to Ullathorne's official letter on behalf of the English hierarchy, Dr Manning himself wrote two letters to Cardinal Barnabo at Propaganda Fide adding his own negative opinion about the A.P.U.C., and being very scathing about Dr Lee in particular. In the first letter, dated 10th June 1864, Manning warned that Dr. Lee was on his way to Rome to seek some measure of approbation from the authorities there:

1. E.S. Purcell, *Life of Cardinal Manning*, 2 Vols., (London: Macmillan & Co., 1895), Vol. 2, p. 277.
2. Letter of 26th April, 1864, in the archives of Propaganda Fide (Scritt. Refer, nei Congress: 1864–1866. Anglia 17, No. 156), as cited by Bernard & Margaret Pawley, *Rome and Canterbury through Four Centuries*, pp. 174–175.

'He is a very wily person and the least indication or recognition of the Anglican church, its priesthood and catholicity, or that of the Greek schismatic Church will be much exaggerated and publicised.'[1]

In a second communication with Roman authorities, Manning also warned about Phillipps de Lisle, whom he described as 'that excellent man', although he personally believed that de Lisle was only half a Catholic.

Phillipps de Lisle himself could see trouble looming, and he tried to warn Dr Lee about the probably adverse effect on readers of some of the more critical articles. He wrote that

'a poison was introduced ... by some bad and factious Catholic priests in the North of England. These men were at open war with their bishops, were tired of the restraints of clerical celibacy and other Catholic ascetic practices, and in their wickedness and folly they flattered themselves that by means of Reunion they could overthrow the discipline of the Church, as laid down by the first Council of Nicea ... I knew what would be the end of this and I wrote to warn the editor of the *Review*, a most excellent Anglican clergyman. He entirely agreed with me, but others were too much for us, and he allowed, against his own wish, the *Review* to continue as the channel for their miserable articles. The result was, what I had feared it would be. Some of our bishops from England complained of the thing, and represented to the authorities at the Holy See, that the working of the Association, especially thro' its official organ the *Union Review*, instead of promoting union among the separated fragments of the christian church was spreading disunion and disaffection in the ranks of that portion of the Baptised Body which alone remained faithful to catholic principles and catholic unity.'[2]

On the 16th September, 1864, the Holy Office in Rome issued a Decree addressed to the English Catholic bishops which clearly condemned the 'Branch' theory of there being three Christian communities, and hence-

---

1. Letter of 10th June, 1864, in Archives of Propaganda Fide, Scritt. Refer., nei congress; 1864–1866. Anglia 17, No. 279, as cited by Bernard & Margaret Pawley, *Rome and Canterbury*, p. 175.
2. E.S. Purcell, *Life and Letters of Ambrose Phillipps de Lisle*, (2 vols.), (London: Macmillan & Co., 1900), Vol. 1, p. 415.

forth forbade Catholics from being members of the A.P.U.C. The Decree added a further warning when it continued:

'A further reason why the faithful ought to keep themselves entirely apart from the London Society (i.e. the A.P.U.C.) is this, that they who unite in it both favour *Indifferentism* and introduce scandal. That Society, at least its founders and directors, assert that Photianism and Anglicanism are two forms of one and the same true Christian religion, in which equally, as in the Catholic Church, one can please God; and that the active dissensions between these christian communities do not involve any breach of faith, inasmuch as their faith continues one and the same. Yet this is the very essence of that most pestilential indifference in matters of religion, which is at this time especially spreading in secret with the greatest injury to souls. Hence no proof is needed that Catholics who join this Society are giving both to Catholics and non-Catholics an occasion of spiritual ruin.[1]'

The Decree concluded with the curiously phrased sentence that Catholics should 'not be carried away by a delusive yearning for such newfangled christian unity'.[2]

The members of the A.P.U.C., and in particular Phillipps de Lisle and Dr Lee, were stunned by the condemnation which, they protested, was based on misrepresentation of the Association to Rome, and in a mistranslation of the Association's aims. The Holy Office letter, in rejecting the Branch theory of the Christian Church, quoted the Association as claiming all three branches had 'an equal right to claim the title catholic'.[3] This, de Lisle asserted, was not what the A.P.U.C. had stated in its aims and objectives, but rather had appealed to those of the three great Christian communities which 'claim for themselves the inheritance of the priesthood, and the name of Catholic'. The Latin and French translations of the original English were not correct. It is clear that Dr Manning was aware of the mistake in translation, but he nevertheless confirmed to Rome that the A.P.U.C. had been in no sense misrepresented.[4] Despite an appeal to the Holy Office by de Lisle and Lee, no notice was taken of the corrected texts and explanations given, and the

1. E.C. Messenger, *Rome and Reunion*, (London: Burns & Oates, 1934), pp. 91–95.
2. Messenger, *Rome and Reunion*, p. 95.
3. Messenger, *Rome and Reunion*, p. 92.
4. Purcell, *Life of Cardinal Manning*, Vol. 1, p. 281.

disapproval of the Holy See was confirmed in a further communication from Rome on the 8th November 1865. Dr Manning was also involved in this reply to de Lisle's appeal, as he was consulted by Mgr George Talbot, the Pope's English consultant in Rome. Although Manning wrote to Rome against the A.P.U.C., Margaret Pawley notes that it was more likely Archbishop Ullathorne who was the originator of the process which led to the condemnation.[1]

Ambrose Phillipps de Lisle resigned from the A.P.U.C. in obedience to the instruction of the Holy See, but continued to assert that a great mistake had been made. Despite this setback, de Lisle continued to work diligently for the cause of reunion for the next fifteen years or so, but in loyalty to the Holy See confined his efforts to mostly private meetings and discussions with others interested in the unity of Christendom.

There seems little doubt that with the accession to positions of authority in the English Roman Catholic hierarchy of such Ultramontane figures as Cardinal Manning, any initiatives for reunion in the direction of 'corporate reunion' would encounter similar renewed difficulties, and that more and more such ecumenical attempts as might arise from members of the Church of England would be directed away from the English bishops and to the continental Catholic Church which was perceived to be more sympathetic to the cause of reunion.

(v) The social and political situation in England in 1800/1880, with its large Irish immigrant population, and its effects on the attitude of the English Roman Catholic Church.

The industrial revolution in England in the early 19th century created a great demand for cheap labour, the nearest source of which was Ireland. This, together with the increasing poverty in Ireland caused in part by British political policies and finally by the devastation of that country by the famine of 1847, brought considerable numbers of destitute Irishmen and their families to Britain. The Roman Catholic population consequently underwent an enormous increase in a fairly short period of time, with large concentrations of Irish Catholic immigrants centered principally around the great cities of Liverpool, London and Birmingham.[1]

1. M. Pawley, *Faith and Family*, p. 311.
2. John Bossey, *The English Catholic Community 1570–1850* (London: Darton, Longman & Todd, 1975), pp. 295–322.

INTRODUCTION AND BRIEF HISTORY OF REMOTE BEGINNINGS

This in turn led to increasing pressures on the Roman Catholic Church authorities and structures in trying to cope with the spiritual needs of this new Irish urban population. A series of Religious Toleration statutes, culminating in the Catholic Emancipation Act of 1829, had allowed Catholics to worship openly again and to participate in almost all public offices, but this did not spell an end to extensive expressions of anti-Catholicism throughout England. The Irish Catholics in England were mostly poor labourers who tended to congregate together in ghettos, and did not assimilate quickly or easily with the local populations. Moreover, their religion was regarded by many Englishmen as 'disloyal', being accused of acknowledging a foreign ruler (the Pope) in preference to the King.[1] All these elements, together with their own history and experiences in Ireland itself, were contributory factors in producing a defensive attitude on the part of the Irish Catholics, and a distrust among them of British governmental and ascendancy power. By 1880, moreover, Roman Catholics of Irish origin accounted for almost 80% of all Catholics in England, and this constant increase had already begun to cause tensions between the Catholic newcomers and the 'Old Catholics' of native English stock. There tended to be more support among the Old Catholics for a type of Gallican Catholic church, whereas the incoming Irish Catholics and the spate of converts from Anglicanism were almost completely Ultramontane (with the notable exception of John Henry Newman), rejecting any suggestion that compromises be made with the Church of England even for the sake of unity. Hence we see a steady movement within the Roman Catholics in England, from about 1800 onwards, in favour of a more centralized, Roman, and distinctly Ultramontane character.

The Church of England, on the other hand, was moving in the opposite direction. The influx of French Roman Catholic refugees from the French Revolution had elicited much sympathy from Anglicans, who were both impressed and edified by the asceticism and devotion of the refugee clergy. The French clergy had prayed and worshipped openly in England, and the English people with whom they had come into contact had begun to learn more about the Roman Church and its beliefs and practices. This openness of the French Catholics was in sharp contrast

---

1. An excellent treatment of this area can be found in Robert J. Klaus, *The Pope, the Protestants, and the Irish: Papal Aggression and Anti-Catholicism in Mid-19th-Century England*, (New York & London: Garland Publishing, 1987).

'A BROTHER KNOCKING AT THE DOOR'

with the subsequent secretiveness and defensive attitude of the Irish Catholics, who carried with them the consequences of their penal history of oppression and suppression in Ireland. The Oxford Movement and the Tractarians aroused further interest in and study of the Roman Catholic Church, and when the members of the Movement eventually spread into the town and country parishes of Victorian England, their presence initiated and encouraged a return to liturgical and devotional practices which were little different from those of Roman Catholic practice. This ritualistic revival did not pass unopposed within the Church of England, both Evangelicals and Dissenters protesting vigorously against such 'popish' practices.

The British Parliament and Government were inevitably mirrors of these divisions, and yet in its foreign affairs and particularly during the wars with Napoleon the Government had to strive to maintain good diplomatic relations with the Pope whose help had been essential in re-supplying the British Mediterranean Fleet in 1794. The Papacy was also anxious to maintain good relations with Britain, especially following the capture of Rome by Napoleon, firstly in 1797 and again in 1808. The British government and the Pope had considerable mutual interests in the negotiations leading to the Congress of Vienna in 1814. A Papal envoy, Cardinal Erskine, was already established in Britain, attached to the court of George III. Thus, in many ways, inter-governmental relations between Britain and the Holy See in the early nineteenth century were better than they had been for many years, although based principally on self-interest. This improved contact helped to prepare the ground for the Catholic Emancipation Bill of 1829.

In 1850 Pope Pius IX re-established the Roman Catholic hierarchy of England and Wales, naming Cardinal Wiseman as Archbishop of Westminster and Metropolitan, and thus began an important re-structuring of the administration of the Roman Catholic Church in England. Wiseman's initial concerns were to concentrate on creating a parish system and to build churches and schools for his catholic congregations. Little thought was given to questions of proselytization. In some ways, the Oxford Movement and its consequences represented a distraction from the principal task of building-up the Catholic Church in England and Wales, although the Cardinal was sympathetic with the aims and vision of the Tractarians for a united Christendom. When Wiseman's health began to fail, George Errington, Bishop of Plymouth, was appointed in

INTRODUCTION AND BRIEF HISTORY OF REMOTE BEGINNINGS

1855 as his co-adjutor, but Errington was of old Catholic origin and Wiseman found him increasingly difficult to work with and consequently turned more and more to Henry Manning for advice and support. It was Manning who was eventually appointed to succeed Wiseman in preference to Errington.

The restoration of the English hierarchy was not universally welcomed by English catholics. Generally speaking, the old Catholics were not in favour of the change. They considered that having endured the difficulties of penal times, they had, nevertheless, emerged with their faith intact despite the many years of persecution. It is clear also that they remained very English, proud not only of their faith but also of their national institutions and monarchy.[1] By their endurance they had proved to the world that one could be a Catholic and an Englishman, loyal to both Pope and King. The restoration of the hierarchy by Rome caused uneasiness among many, especially when the new cardinal and some of the younger convert clergy exhibited overtly Roman or Italian tendencies. Ultra sensitive to the prejudice and mistrust of their fellow citizens, the old Catholics were both offended and socially embarrassed by the activities of the converts, and saw them as introducing an overly ritualistic and pietistic zeal into Roman Catholic worship. In a real sense they felt that the liberty from 'foreigners' which they had gained during the times of the Vicars Apostolic was being taken away, and they now found themselves facing conflicting loyalties. This led them to recognise much common ground with the Anglican 'Romanists' who wanted unity, but with conditions. Cardinal Wiseman's initial exuberance as expressed in his Pastoral Letter from Rome dated 7th October 1850[2] on the restoration of the hierarchy caused much indignation among Catholics and non-Catholics alike. In its tactlessness, the Cardinal's Pastoral Letter marked the beginning of a period of strengthening Ultramontanism within the English Roman Catholic Church, a mood which built on the foundation of the large number of new immigrant Irish Catholics, and came eventually to dominate the Gallican tendency of the small number of indigenous English Catholics.

---

1. Klaus, *The Pope, the Protestants, and the Irish*, pp. 14–15.
2. For a brief summary of the reactions to Cardinal Wiseman's Pastoral Letter from the Flaminian Gate of Rome, dated 7th october 1850, cf. Bernard & Margaret Pawley, *Rome and Canterbury through Four Centuries*, pp. 146–154.

2

Immediate forerunner to Malines – the issue of Anglican Orders.

(i) The meeting of Lord Halifax and Fr Portal in Madeira, their friendship, and the search for common ground in matters of reunion.

In December 1889, Charles Lindley Wood, the 2nd Viscount Halifax,[1] learned that his eldest son Charles, who had just gone up to Oxford, was suffering from tuberculosis and needed to spend the winter in a warm climate. Having already experienced the loss of two children through chest diseases (Henry Paul in June 1886 and Francis in February 1889), Lord Halifax lost no time in tidying up his affairs and leaving with all his family for the town of Funchal on the island of Madeira.

Although his family had a strong tradition of service in the field of politics (his grandfather had been Prime Minister and his father Chancellor of the Exchequer), Halifax, greatly influenced from his student days at Oxford by the High Church Movement, and in particular by Edward Bouverie Pusey and Henry Parry Liddon, had decided – to the great consternation of his traditionally Whig and Low Church family – to dedicate his time and energies to the cause of High Church Anglicanism[2] and to the goal of reunion of the Christian Church. He held firmly to the principle of the 'Branch' theory, namely that the Church of England was one of the three great branches of Christendom, and was truly the recipient of apostolic teaching and sacraments. During the difficult period of the late 1850s when the Anglo-Catholics were under attack, the English Church Union was formed as a vehicle of

---

1. Lord Halifax inherited his title on the death of his father, the 1st Viscount Halifax, on 8th August, 1885. The best biography of the 2nd Viscount Halifax is by J.G. Lockhart, *Charles Lindley Viscount Halifax*, 2 Vols., (London: Centenary Press, 1935).
2. After Halifax had taken his seat in the House of Lords, he was asked by Lord Granville at the Foreign Office it he would accept any office: Halifax replied that 'apart from what I might feel it my duty to do under special circumstances, my Church work rather demanded that I should keep myself free – and that he would understand that as things were, it was better for me to remain as I was'.
Lockhart, *Charles Lindley Viscount Halifax*, Vol. II, p. 3.

FORERUNNER TO MALINES – THE ISSUE OF ANGLICAN ORDERS

defence (1859), and in 1868 the young Charles Wood was elected President.

Two months previously, in September 1889, after preaching a retreat at the orphanage run by the Sisters of Charity at Grenade, Fr Ferdinand Portal, a priest of the Congregation of the Missions (Vincentian), was requested by his superiors to go to the island of Madeira, to replace one of the chaplains at the hospice of Maria Amelia, run by the same congregation of Sisters of Charity. Of the two chaplains assigned to the hospice there, one had become ill and the other could not manage on his own. Portal had barely begun his temporary chaplaincy duties when the other priest made a rapid recovery, and this left him with virtually nothing to do. On the verge of boredom, he learned one morning that an English nobleman who was greatly interested in such works of charity wanted to visit the hospice. Through such an accidental encounter, there thus began a long and deep friendship between Halifax and Portal.

They began to walk together, and after some days of polite conversation, they began to discuss religious matters. Portal's initial motivation was undoubtedly that of leading this English heretic to conversion,[1] but he rapidly came to like his companion of numerous walks around the island, and was surprised at the depth and piety of his companion. He offered to teach French to Halifax's son Charles, but Halifax would only consent if he promised not to try to convert the young man. Once a week the two men went for long walks in the hills above Funchal, discussing deep religious topics and discovering each other's humanity. Portal began to study the Latin edition of the Prayer Book which Halifax had brought with him, encouraged by Halifax to see how largely the revision of the Breviary by Cardinal Quinones had influenced the English Offices for Matins and Evensong, and how closely, apart from the dislocation of the Canon, the Anglican communion service followed the rite of the Mass in the Roman Missal.[2] When, eventually, it was time for Abbé Portal to leave Madeira, it was in a state of some confusion that he quit the island as he was convinced that their friendship would be a

---

1. Régis Ladous, *Monsieur Portal et les siens (1855–1926)*, (Paris: Éditions du Cerf, 1985), p. 48.
'As a Priest, I would have naturally hoped to convert this Anglican who had come of his own accord to discuss religious matters'.
2. Lord Halifax, *Leo XIII and Anglican Orders*, (London: Longmans & Green, 1912), p. 9.

lasting one and that it would lead one day to a common effort to extend the comprehension and rapprochement which had been built up between them.[1]

The following year, 1890, was a difficult one for Abbé Portal. His great ambition had been, as a priest of the Mission,[2] to work in missionary lands. His assignment till this point in his life had been as professor of moral theology at the Grande Séminaire at Cahors, in the south of France, a post which he had regarded as being temporary whilst awaiting a missionary assignment. Now, in the autumn of 1890, the newly re-elected superior general of the Vincentians offered him his wish, to serve as a missionary in Quito, Ecuador. He turned down the offer of a mission and requested that he return to Cahors, a request which was eventually granted. One of the reasons for his decision he explained to Lord Halifax in a letter of 22nd November 1890,[3] was that he had reached the conclusion that their meeting in Funchal was providential and that God wished him to continue to seek the path of unity with the Church of England. This required the abandonment of his long-held ambition to be a missionary. At Cahors, he plunged into a study of the Church of England, with ample books and other material being supplied by the willing Lord Halifax. In July 1891, Portal joined Halifax and his family on holiday at Roscoff in Britanny, recommencing their custom of long walks and discussions. It was during this holiday that Portal convinced Halifax that the time for action had arrived, and together they planned a campaign of information directed at the French Catholic Press to place the project of reunion at a higher level of consciousness. They planned a series of articles which Halifax was to write and which Portal would assure of publication.

Despite the plans they had jointly conceived, Halifax found on his return to England that he could not settle down to accomplish his part in writing the required articles. His son Charles had died on the 6th September 1890, and his friend and spiritual confidant Henry Liddon had died the week following. Consequently, Halifax found himself

1. Ladous, *Monsieur Portal*, p. 50.
2. The official title of Abbé Portal's religious congregation was 'Priests of the Mission', but this group, founded by St Vincent de Paul in 1632, were also known as 'Vincentians' (after their founder) or 'Lazarists' (their first house was in the St Lazare area of Paris).
3. Ladous, *Monsieur Portal*, p. 52.

without the energy or enthusiasm to concentrate. Despite the encouragements of Portal, all the noble lord could reply was: '*Mea culpa, mea culpa, mea maxima culpa!* The only word I can find to answer you is "pity" '.[1]

During a subsequent visit of Halifax to Portal at the seminary at Cahors, the two friends decided that they would re-launch their information campaign, but this time on a specific theme – the theme of the validity of Anglican Orders. This theme that they chose was an important one, one which was central to many of the proselytising arguments of Roman Catholics in England, and which had been used by some Catholic controversialists to ridicule and hurt those members of the Anglican communion who sincerely believed in both the validity and efficacy of their sacramental life. The sacrament of baptism in the Church of England was already recognized by Rome, both on account of the common trinitarian formula and also because it could be administered by any Christian, lay or cleric, but all the other sacraments depended on the legitimacy and validity of the celebrant's ordination, and whether there was an unbroken succession in fact and in intention between the early Anglican bishops of the Reformation times and the Apostles, a succession claimed by Rome as vital for validity.

More important for both Halifax and Portal, however, was the fact that the information campaign could be a vehicle to bring together theologians and authorities of both communions, a meeting-point where exchanges could take place, without argument and polemic, and where good-will would be allowed to work in establishing a real brotherly reconciliation between the two groups of Christians. In practice, neither Halifax nor Portal envisaged provoking a decision on the tricky question of Anglican Orders.[2]

(ii) Decision to initiate an approach through continental Roman Catholics rather than those in England.

The decision to commence their initiative on the Continent rather than in

1. Letter of Halifax to Portal, 12th December 1891, Portal Papers, Paris.
Note: The personal library, together with the unclassified letters of Abbé Ferdinand Portal are in the care of the community of *Congrégation des Oblates de l'Assomption*, 203 rue Lecourbe, 75015 Paris.
2. Ladous, *Monsieur Portal*, pp. 58–59.

England is rather easier to understand when looked at from the diverse points of view of the individuals involved. For Halifax there had been the history of opposition to any idea of corporate reunion by Cardinal Manning of Westminster during the height of the Oxford Movement and its aftermath. Since the re-establishment of the English hierarchy in 1850, the Roman Catholic Church in England had been predominantly engaged in building up its structures, developing its parish system, constructing its schools and establishing a sound catholic education system. Its energies were absorbed in these matters, together with the difficulty of integrating the influx of Catholic emigrants from Ireland and from continental countries, and there was little time, energy or reflection available for the matter of ecumenism or for developing relations with the Church of England.

In January 1892 a new Archbishop of Westminster, Herbert Vaughan, had been appointed to succeed Cardinal Manning. Vaughan came from a long established Catholic family which had endured the persecutions of the centuries since the Reformation, and entered his charge like a missionary seeking new souls to save. In later years, he was to demonstrate this by founding the missionary College and Congregation of Mill Hill in London. In matters of reunion he followed very much the line of his predecessor, and when Halifax went to see him on the 4th July 1892 to speak about the proposed project on Anglican Orders, he got fairly short shrift. From a comment made at the time, Vaughan's opposition is crystal clear:

> 'Halifax and his party are anxious to get some kind of recognition – anything that can be twisted into a hope of recognition will serve their purpose. They wish to keep people from becoming Catholics individually and tell them to wait for a Corporate Reunion. This will never be till after the Last Judgement – and all the poor souls that will be born and will die in heresy before Reunion must suffer in their own souls for this chimera of Corporate Reunion.'[1]

---

1. J.G. Snead-Cox, *Life of Cardinal Vaughan*, 2 Vols., (London: Burns & Oates, 1910), Vol. II, p. 182
Note: John J. Hughes in his book *Absolutely Null and Utterly Void*, (Washington: Corpus Books, 1968), p. 38 footnote 24, points out that Snead-Cox has softened the phrase 'anything that can be twisted into a hope of recognition' into 'anything that can suggest a hope of recognition.'

About the same time some deep-rooted Catholic versus Protestant rivalries were aroused when the British East Africa Company, at the instigation of the Church Missionary Society, expelled the Catholic Vicar Apostolic from Uganda and imprisoned a group of French Catholic missionaries, the White Fathers. The times were not auspicious in England for a new ecumenical initiative. In a speech to a group of French editors and writers in February 1896, Halifax noted that,

> 'the last time I had seen Cardinal Newman I had discussed the question of the possibility of reunion with him, and he had then said I should probably find more sympathy among the French clergy than among the English, and had advised me to interest them in the subject.'[1]

For Portal things were much clearer. Being French himself, his mentality, background and contacts were Continental and Francophone. His vision was on a wider scale than Halifax, drawing into his scheme the additional prospect of reunion with the Eastern Orthodox Churches. He knew of Pope Leo XIII's interest in the Eastern Churches of Russia, the Balkans, Turkey, Armenia, Egypt and Ethiopia. The Pope had already made clear his good regard for the Eastern Christians, who already held many things in common with the Roman Church, and he had sent his Apostolic Delegate to visit Joachim IV, the Patriarch of Turkey, at his residence at Phanar. Portal's reasoning was clear. If the Holy See was seeking better relations with Constantinople, why not with Canterbury? He saw his prime purpose as to open up the way for such an eventuality.

Portal felt himself very much in line with the new and dynamic sense of mission which Leo XIII had ushered in with his social encyclical *'Rerum Novarum'* (15th May, 1891). In his defence of the working classes and his vision of their rights, whether political, moral or spiritual, the Pope had kindled a flame which affected the whole Church and which transformed it from a defensive attitude to one of action. In a 1909 manuscript, Portal describes this Catholic movement as:

---

1. Lord Halifax, *Leo XIII and Anglican Orders*, pp. 251/252.
Halifax also pointed out at the same time that the annoyance felt in England (as reflected in *The Tablet*) was probably due to the belief that foreign ecclesiastics were not likely to be as well-informed on such subjects as Englishmen.

'characterized, despites its vigour, by a spirit of reconciliation which emanated directly from Leo XIII's pacifying genius.'[1]

In his enthusiasm Portal tended to forget that before his election as pope, Leo XIII had been one of the supporters of the *Syllabus of Errors*, and that he was just as strongly anti-Modernist and anti-liberal as his predecessor Pope Pius IX. The major difference was that he was not going to sit passively warning against such things, but was determined to move on to the attack. There was, nevertheless, a definite change of attitude and signs of more openness and receptivity in Rome and on the Continent than had previously been apparent, but this attitude stopped abruptly at the English Channel.

(iii) The provocative pamphlet of 'M. Fernand Dalbus'.

In view of Lord Halifax's inability to concentrate on writing, Abbé Portal himself had commenced work on a paper on Anglican Orders. The main purpose of his paper was to arouse interest and provoke reaction, and to this end he designed his paper as though he were initially in favour of the validity of Anglican Orders by attacking the strongest traditional arguments of canonists against them, but finally concluding as to their invalidity on the grounds of the weakest objection. He was trying to provoke the reader to reject the final argument, and hence lead him to draw his own conclusion as to the genuine validity of Church of England Orders. The paper duly presented one by one the strong traditional arguments against Anglican validity; the insufficiency of the rite, the break in apostolic succession, the intention of the consecrating bishops. These objections, he argued, were not justified because they were not true, and he sought to prove this in the first twenty-nine pages with his own counter-arguments.[2] However, when it came to the question of the 'instruments', that is, when the ordaining prelate hands to the new priest a chalice and paten, symbols of the eucharistic sacrifice, then this was a tradition evidently not kept by the Church of England. The reformers of the XVIth century had replaced the chalice and paten with a bible, and so, citing a decree of Pope Eugenius IV against the Armenians in which the Pope had emphasized the necessity of this

---

1. Abbé Portal, *De l'union des Églises*, Manuscript, 1909. Portal Papers, Paris.
2.. Fernand Dalbus, *Les Ordinations anglicanes*, (Arras & Paris, 1894).

gesture of the 'instruments', the author of the paper then concluded that Anglican Orders were indeed invalid on this point.

The problem with the conclusion which was thus arrived at was that any discerning reader who knew anything about Church history would realize that the Latin Church herself had excluded this ritual gesture of the 'instruments' over a long period of time, and that the Eastern Orthodox Church, whose Orders had always been held as valid by Rome, had never used this symbol of 'instruments'. It was by reasoning like this that Portal hoped to lead the reader to reject the conclusion that the writer was proposing.

One problem about the paper (or pamphlet as it later became) was that the arguments against the traditional hostile objections had to be strong and convincing, and Portal felt that it needed someone from a High Church Anglican background, someone who was used to the cut and thrust of arguing the case for Anglican Orders to give the document a final editing. Lord Halifax undertook to find such a person, eventually persuading his old Eton schoolfriend, the Revd Frederick William Puller, now a religious of the Anglican Society of St John the Evangelist, to edit the pamphlet. Puller was an erudite scholar, a theologian, a student of patristics, but, equally importantly, familiar with French theological thinking and sympathetic towards Gallican Catholicism. The finished pamphlet was presented under the pseudonym of 'Fernand Dalbus', and was published initially in two parts in the review *La Science catholique* on the 15th December 1893 and the 15th January 1894, and eventually as a unified pamphlet under the title: *Les Ordinations anglicanes.*

If Portal was expecting an immediate reaction in France to the publication of his articles, then he was surely disappointed. In any case the death of his mother in February 1894 gave him other preoccupations of a more personal nature. In England, on the contrary, Halifax was using his contacts with the Anglican bishops in the House of Lords and his influence with the Press, and on the 21st February *The Guardian* newspaper published a full-page summary of the Dalbus article. On the 3rd April, the French newspaper, *L'Univers*, took up the theme of *The Guardian*, praising Dalbus as 'a servant of papal thinking' and inviting scholars to reopen the investigation of Anglican Orders. Two other Paris newspapers took up the story, *Le Monde* and *La Vérité*, and the French clergy and academics began to take notice. Most important of these French academics, the Abbé Louis Duchesne, the great historian of the Institut Catholique in Paris, added his support in a letter of the 13th April 1894 in which he avowed that in finding himself in agreement with the arguments of Dalbus, 'I must go further and, on the basis of this premise, I must deduce the validity of Anglican Orders'.[1]

Halifax circulated this letter among his clerical and other High Church friends, including the Archbishops of Canterbury and York. They suggested that the learned Bishop of Salisbury, John Wordsworth, renowned on the Continent for his work on the Vulgate, should write a public letter to Dalbus inviting him to discuss the matter in a dialogue without rancour or preconditions. In this letter, published in *The Guardian*, Wordsworth declared that,

> 'it is certain that in dropping the formulas and rites of the roman church at certain points in our liturgies, we believed ourselves authorized by the freedom of the National Churches, but we never wanted to separate ourselves from the catholic church.'[2]

This letter of the Anglican Bishop of Salisbury was subsequently reproduced by *L'Univers, Le Monde, La Verité* and *Le Moniteur de Rome*.

A concurrent event which both Portal and Halifax saw as providential was the publication on the 20th June, 1894, of the Encyclical Letter, *Praeclara Gratulationis*,[3] of Pope Leo XIII, addressed 'to all the princes and peoples of the universe'. The main thrust of this encyclical was one of 'unity', the unity of all mankind without distinction of nation or race, a call for unity in the divine faith. For the first time all Protestant groups were included in this papal appeal, and the perjorative term of 'sect', normally used in describing all Protestant groups, disappeared in favour of the more friendly and neutral name of 'communions'. The only group

---

1. Letter of Duchesne to Portal, 13th April 1894, Portal Papers, Paris.
2. Text reproduced in Fernand Dalbus, *Les Ordinations anglicanes*, 2nd edition, (Paris: 1894), pp. II–IV.
3. Full text of *Praeclara Gratulationis* to be found in Messenger, *Rome and Reunion*, pp. 3–13.
Note: This Encyclical was written to celebrate the occasion of the completion of Pope Leo XIII's fifty years as a bishop.

still tagged as a 'sect' were the Freemasons. Particularly explicit was the Pope's call to the 'communions' of the Reformation;

> 'Let us all come together in the unity of faith and the knowledge of the Son of God (Eph.4,13). Suffer us to invite you to that unity which has ever existed in the Catholic Church, and can never fail; suffer us lovingly to hold out our hand to you [...] the Catholics of the world await you with brotherly love, that you may render holy worship to God together with us, united in perfect charity by the profession of one Gospel, one faith, and one hope.'[1]

(iv) The reactions in Rome and consequent initiatives.

When Portal returned to Cahors in August 1894 to resume his teaching post, he was informed that the Secretary of State at the Vatican, Cardinal Mariano Rampolla, wished to see him urgently, but asked him to make his visit secretly. Leaving his moral theology classes in the hands of the Rector of the seminary, Portal went post-haste to Paris pleading urgent family business. In Paris he met with Lord Halifax, whom he had informed immediately of the call to Rome, and although filled with hope, Halifax was also filled with anxiety – an anxiety which he had already expressed in a letter of 3rd September to Portal.[2] Halifax's fear was that things seemed to be going too well. Portal left for Rome on the 8th September, where, in the space of ten days, he was received twice by the Pope and eight times by Cardinal Rampolla.

What surprised and delighted Portal in particular was the urgency with which the subject of reunion was examined. There was no doubt that Pope Leo XIII was anxious for a rapprochement with the Church of England, perhaps in an even more specific way than that apparent in his appeal to all non-Catholics of good will made in the encyclical *Praeclara Gratulationis*. Pontifical diplomacy, particularly since Cardinal Rampolla had become Secretary of State in 1887, also dictated closer relations between the United Kingdom and the Vatican. Rome's attitude on the Irish question had softened, and the British Government had responded by sending to Rome a British representative, a '*chargé de mission*'. A papal representative had been present at the jubilee celebra-

---

1. *Praeclara Gratulationis*, Encyclical Letter of Pope Leo XIII, 20th June, 1894; in Messenger, *Rome and Reunion*, p. 11.
2. Letter of Halifax to Portal, 3rd September 1894, Portal Papers, Paris.

tions of Queen Victoria, and there was talk of a permanent exchange of ambassadors.

The Pope told Portal that he was considering making an appeal to the members of the Church of England similar to the one he had just prepared for Christians of the Eastern Churches. In that apostolic letter, ***Orientalium Dignitas*** (30th November 1894), the Pope promised to respect the hierarchy, the liturgy, the discipline and local customs of the oriental Churches, and declared his willingness to renounce any attempt at 'Latinization'. There seemed no reason why a similar offer could not be made to the Church of England. But the Pope wanted to address the whole of the Church of England, and not just the High Church section. Reunion in his mind was on a grander scale than simply those Anglicans who were closest to the Roman Church. To this effect, he revealed his intention to enter into contact with the Archbishops of Canterbury and York. What was the best way to do this? The Pope did not want his offer to be rebuffed, and so it was proposed to test the ecumenical waters by addressing a letter to Abbé Portal and signed by Cardinal Rampolla which would in reality be intended for the two Anglican archbishops. This letter would contain some outline proposals for possible direct discussions between the two Churches. If the response from the Anglican archbishops was open and positive, then direct contact could be established between the Pope and the Archbishop of Canterbury. The Pope would also compose an official Apostolic Letter addressed to all the English peoples. The first letter was duly consigned to Portal on the 19th September 1894, and in April 1895 the Apostolic Letter ***Ad Anglos***[1] proposed Christian unity in England to all who sought the kingdom of Christ in that land. The principal purpose of the first letter was to initiate some sort of dialogue with the English Established Church,[2] and really discounted the other more Protestant-minded Christian communions in Britain.

1. A good account of the history and development of *Ad Anglos* can be found in the unpublished Masters dissertation at the University of Louvain entitled: *An Unheard of Thing: An Historical Study of the Apostolic Letter Ad Anglos*, by Dom Kentigern Connolly OSB, Louvain 1967.
2. Cardinal Rampolla expressed his hope for dialogue thus: 'a friendly exchange of ideas and a deeper study of ancient cults and practices ... to prepare the way for this desired union. All this must be conducted without bitterness or recrimination, without any preoccupation of earthly interests, being held in an atmosphere where one breathes only the spirit of humility and christian charity ...'. Letter of Cardinal Rampolla to Abbé Portal, 19th September 1894, published in *Revue anglo-romaine*, Paris 1896, Vol. I, p. 393.

FORERUNNER TO MALINES – THE ISSUE OF ANGLICAN ORDERS

The second letter constituted an appeal to all baptized Christians in the kingdom. In one of Portal's audiences with the Pope already the practicalities of dialogue were discussed. The Pope acknowledged that Anglican ordinations would have to be the starting point, but should be quickly enlarged to embrace other points of divergence. He asked Portal for suggestions as to where such meetings should take place, and the names that should be proposed.

This unexpected urgency on the part of the Pope impressed itself deeply on Portal, and could not be explained simply by the pontiff's advanced age (he was 85 years old). Nor was it a case of ill-informed optimism. The Pope had listened to other voices less enthusiastic than Portal's, and even some that were strongly contrary. The Rector of the Scottish seminary told him it would be easier to re-unite with the Presbyterians than with the Anglicans as the former were not bound up in relation to the civil power of the State. One Anglican even told him that the Established Church of England would never unite with Rome because it believed that it was already Catholic.

As is abundantly clear from his *Letter to the English Peoples*, Pope Leo was aware of the many difficulties which lay in the path of reunion:

> '... no doubt the many changes that have come about, and time itself, have caused the existing divisions to take deeper root. But is that a reason to give up all hope of remedy, reconciliation, and peace? By no means if God is with us'.[1]

Both the Pope and his Cardinal Secretary of State knew that humanly speaking they were perhaps asking the impossible, but Leo believed that prayer would be more effective than all the negotiations and political manoeuvring which would inevitably be involved, and in *Ad Anglos* he exhorted a crusade of prayer for unity, and for the Rosary in particular:

> 'Care should be taken that the prayers for unity already established amongst Catholics on certain fixed days should be made more popular and recited with greater devotion and especially that the pious practice of the Holy Rosary, which we ourselves have so strongly

---

1. Apostolic Letter of Pope Leo XIII to the English People (*Amantissima Volntatis*), 14th April 1895; English translation in Messenger, *Rome and Reunion*, p. 24.

recommended, should flourish, for it contains as it were a summary of the Gospel teaching, and has always been a most salutary institution for the people at large.'[1]

Encouraged by his visit to Rome, Abbé Portal hurried back to France and immediately on to England, where Halifax was awaiting him. On the 28th September at 10.00 am, led by his noble friend, Portal was received by Dr Benson, the Archbishop of Canterbury. To the Archbishop, the Abbé explained the purpose of his visit, the contacts and opinions which had been expressed in Rome by both the Pope and the Cardinal Secretary of State, and produced the Cardinal's letter, which, he recounted, was in reality addressed to the Anglican archbishops. Despite Portal's obvious sincerity and the good import of his communications, Dr Benson was not at all moved, and, in fact, received the French priest very coldly. The reason is not difficult to discover, as, only two weeks previously, Cardinal Vaughan had embarked on a virulent speech against the Church of England while addressing a meeting of the Catholic Truth Society in Preston. What weight was the Archbishop of Canterbury to give to a letter addressed to a French priest by an Italian Cardinal when at the same time his Church was publicly being attacked by the Pope's official representative in Westminster? Portal and Halifax were politely but firmly dismissed after a very short interview. It seems clear that, according to Dr Benson's son, the Archbishop thought he was being compromised by some subtle scheme connived at by the Roman Church: 'The Archbishop's view from the first was that an attempt was being made from Rome, working through the sincere and genuine enthusiasm of Lord Halifax and the Abbé Portal, to compromise the official chief of the Anglican Church'.[2] Under the urging of the Archbishop of York, Dr Benson did nevertheless write a letter on the 24th October 1894 addressed to Lord Halifax, but it merely called on all branches of the Church of Christ to stand 'side by side against the forces of evil'. Dr Benson refused to agree to or encourage the idea of any form of contact or conference with the Vatican until Vaughan ceased his fulminations. The Archbishop's letter was considered in Rome neither a good basis for direct contact nor justification for continuing to seek one.

---

1. Apostolic Letter of Pope Leo XIII to the English People (*Amantissima Voluntatis*), 14th April 1895; in Messenger, *Rome and Reunion*, p. 27.
1. A.C. Benson, *The Life of Edward White Benson – Sometime Archbishop of Canterbury*, 2 Vols., (London: Macmillan, 1899), Vol. II, p. 593.

FORERUNNER TO MALINES – THE ISSUE OF ANGLICAN ORDERS

The Roman Catholic Archbishop of Westminster, Cardinal Herbert Vaughan, meanwhile was marshalling his forces of opposition. His speech in Preston was merely the opening salvo in the engagement, and he continued vigorously to oppose any proposed meetings or conferences between Roman Catholics and Anglicans on the question of reunion. His concept of reunion was the complete submission of the Church of England, and he was totally opposed to the idea of 'corporate reunion', believing that such a notion would stem the flow of individual converts to catholicism. Further, he felt that Rome was in danger of compromising in some way if this path of joint discussion were allowed to proceed: 'English Ultramontanes were as determined in 1895 as in 1865 that their claim to Catholicity should not be weakened by a half-recognition of Anglican Catholicity. They believed that such recognition impeded conversions. It allowed Anglicans nervous of their present Catholicity to feel less insecure. It hinted that after all their sacraments were good'.[1]

For Lord Halifax in particular the times were painful. He saw them as a great opportunity being missed by the authorities on both sides, Anglican and Roman Catholic. It was Cardinal Vaughan, however, that bore the brunt of Halifax's criticism. Halifax had never had any intention of excluding the English Roman Catholic bishops from any proposed discussions, and had, in fact, been to Vaughan in July 1893 to seek his approval and support for re-examining the issue of Anglican Orders. In giving his guarded support, Vaughan had proposed that the issue of papal supremacy should be considered before that of Anglican Orders. Halifax had continued to try to keep Vaughan informed, but eventually even he had been forced to admit defeat:

> 'I say it with regret: the whole of Cardinal Vaughan's conduct, as I think the correspondence makes sufficiently clear, was unworthy of him ... On Cardinal Vaughan's shoulders rests the chief responsibility for the failure of all that was attempted, but a share of that responsibility must also rest on the shoulders of Archbishop Benson.'[2]

In January 1895 Vaughan went to Rome where he told the Pope that

---

1. Chadwick, *The Church of England and the Church of Rome*, p. 89.
2. Viscount Halifax, *Leo XIII and Anglican Orders*, p. 386/388.

Portal and Halifax had misrepresented the actual situation in England. He also submitted his view that all talk of reunion should be presented as submission to the Church of Rome and warned of the danger of losing converts with all the talk of 'corporate reunion'. Vaughan found strong support from two of the English clerics then in Rome, Monsignor Rafael Merry del Val and the Benedictine Dom Francis Aidan Gasquet OSB. Merry del Val in particular kept Vaughan informed of how things were proceeding in Rome, writing to warn Vaughan in July 1895 about Cardinal Rampolla's sympathy for Halifax: 'The Cardinal is an earnest upholder of H[alifax]. He has to my mind been completely hoodwinked by him and he evidently has no grasp of the situation in England'.[1]

By the spring of 1895 there was obviously no further hope for any sort of joint commission being established to examine Anglican Orders, but perversely, many of those involved wished to see some kind of declaration on the issue: the Anglicans, while not desiring to commit themselves to or be involved in any kind of official enquiry, at the same time hoping for a favourable outcome if such an investigation took place, and those Roman Catholics in Westminster and Rome who were hostile to the corporate reunion quest wanting a declaration of nullity to bring to an end any further discussion. In April 1885 when the apostolic letter *Ad Anglos* appeared, its content reflected the strength of the opposition which had been posed, and mentioned nothing about Anglican Orders. It was at this point that Rome decided to set up a commission to investigate Anglican Orders, a commission which would be composed exclusively of Roman Catholics.

(v) Change of attitude in Rome, the Pontifical Commission of Enquiry and the resulting publication of *Apostolicae Curae*, declaring Anglican Orders null and void.

In March 1896 a Commission of Enquiry was set up to examine the question of Anglican Orders. Under pressure from Cardinal Vaughan, the Pope decided that it should be based in Rome, thereby avoiding the possibility of a strong influence by French experts (whom Vaughan saw as a major threat) on the members of the commission. Cardinal Rampolla tried to ensure that the commission had a balanced membership

---

1. Letter from Merry del Val to Vaughan, 24th July 1895, cited in Hughes, *Absolutely Null and Void*, p. 296.

between those in favour and those against Anglican validity, but although still Secretary of State he was now rapidly losing influence with the Pope who listened increasingly to others like Merry del Val. Those members thought generally to be in favour of validity were Fr Aemilius M. de Augustinis SJ (Rector of the Gregorianum University in Rome), Abbé Louis Duchesne, Fr T.B. Scannell from Sheerness in England and Mgr (later Cardinal) Pietro Gasparri; those thought to be opposed were Dom (later Cardinal) Francis Aidan Gasquet, Fr David Fleming, Canon James Moyes and the Spanish Capuchin, Fr Calasanzio de Llevaneras. However the president of the commission, Cardinal Camillo Mazzella, and the secretary, Merry del Val, were both ultra conservative and were utterly opposed to validity. Mazzella arranged the timetable, and even the questions which should be addressed, and imposed a strict injunction on the members of the commission - that it was forbidden to question or put in doubt the 1704 declaration of nullity by Pope Clement XI in the case of Dr John Clement Gordon, the Anglican Bishop of Galloway. This had been the case which had established the grounds for previous declarations of nullity.[1] Mgr Gasparri and Abbé Duchesne protested vigorously at this restriction, but to no avail. Two Anglican clerics came to Rome to be available for consultation by the commission members if needed; Canon Thomas Alexander Lacey,[2] a Cambridge professor and latinist, who was a council member of the English Church Union, and Revd Frederick William Puller (the person who had helped Abbé Portal edit the original pamphlet on Anglican Orders under the name 'Dalbus'). Their presence in Rome was officially recognized by Canterbury but they had no official mandate from the Anglican primate. Mgr Gasparri was the only commission member who seems to have consulted regularly with them about Anglican viewpoints during the twelve sessions held by the commission. The commission contented itself with deliberating for a mere three months on an issue which had been in discussion for over three centuries.

After the final meeting on the 7th May 1896, the commission's consultative recommendations were handed over to the Holy Office, and

---

1. A brief and succinct presentation of Dr Gordon's case can be found in Hughes, *Absolutely Null and Void*, pp. 280–293.
2. Dr Lacey later wrote an account of his period spent in Rome at this time, entitled, *A Roman Diary and Other Documents relating to the Papal Inquiry into English Ordination*, (London: Longman Green, 1910).

thence to a meeting of all the cardinals in Rome presided over by the Pope himself (but with Cardinal Rampolla absent). This meeting took place in July 1896. Two principal items presented by the commission seem to have carried much weight in the minds of the assembled Cardinals – the strong and clear opposition of the English Roman Catholic hierarchy to any semblance of recognition of Anglican claims, and a previously unknown document from the Reformation period found in the register of Pope Paul IV which dealt with delegated powers given to Cardinal Pole concerning the re-admission of those ordained under the Edwardian Ordinal. The Cardinals were unanimous in giving a negative response to the possibility of the validity of Church of England Orders. The decision of previous centuries was confirmed.

Before the July meeting of the Cardinals, but shortly after the commission had finished its work, the final decision seemed to be presaged by the appearance of another papal document on the 29th June, 1896, entitled *Satis Cognitum*, which elucidated that the only basis on which Christendom could be re-united was that of recognition of the Pope as sole source of authority and jurisdiction in the Church.

On the 13th September, 1896, Pope Leo XIII issued his bull *Apostolicae Curae*, the document which declared Anglican Orders 'absolutely null and utterly void',[1] the grounds being defect of intention and lack of apostolic continuity in episcopal succession. The initial draft of this bull was composed by a delighted Merry del Val, aided by Dom Gasquet. In a private and unpublished letter[2] some 35 years later, Cardinal Merry del Val explained some of his reactions at the time of *Apostolicae Curae*. It was not the English Catholics who wanted the issue raised, he said,

> 'but a section of Anglicans raised the question and appealed to the Holy See for a fresh examination. With the Holy See English Catholics had always held Anglican Orders to be invalid and only defended their conviction when it was clamorously questioned by Lord Halifax and his followers. They were anxious in view of the

---

1. Text published in English in Messenger, *Rome and Reunion,* pp. 110–126. The best and fullest treatment of the whole subject of Anglican Orders at this period can be found in J.J. Hughes, *Absolutely Null and Utterly Void*, (Washington: Corpus Books, 1968).
2. Letter dated 16th January, 1930, from Cardinal Merry del Val to Fr Francis Woodlock SJ, Jesuit Archives, Farm Street, London, BH/6.

controversy that the Pope should speak again ... When the commission ended its debates, the minutes and reports were handed to the Holy Office, where they were examined. And then came the solemn meeting of all the cardinals of the Holy Office at the Vatican in the Holy Father's presence. It was what we call a *Feria Quinta*. Short of an ecumenical Council and a definition '*ex cathedra*', I suppose there is no more solemn form of procedure ... Policy or expediency played no part in the decision. Certainly not on our side. Indeed, if policy had come into the matter it would have been in the opposite direction, for the Pope would have been only too glad to remove an obstacle to reunion and the conversion of those who believed in the validity of their orders.'[1]

Even after a lapse of time of some 35 years the strength of Merry del Val's opposition to the notion of anything suggesting compromise with the Church of England on Anglican Orders comes through very clearly, although it must be pointed out that at the time of writing this letter in 1930 he had just come through another ecumenical skirmish with Halifax and Portal, this time because of the Malines Conversations.

Even before the publication of *Apostolicae Curae* in September 1896, both Portal and Halifax suspected what the decision would be. When it was finally promulgated on the 13th September, Portal wrote in a letter to Halifax on the 19th of the same month expressing the depth of his sorrow;

'May Our Lord have mercy on us. May he grant us at least the consolation of seeing with our own eyes that we have not done more harm than good.'[2]

Lord Halifax's response was equally moving;

'We tried to do something which, I believe, God inspired. We have failed, for the moment; but if God wills it, His desire will be accomplished, and if He allows us to be shattered, it may well be because He means to do it Himself ... I prefer, many thousand times, to suffer with you in such a cause, than to triumph with the whole world.'[3]

---

1. Full text of this important elucidation of the process by the then Cardinal Secretary of the Holy Office is given in full as Appendix 1 in this volume.
2. Letter of Portal to Halifax, 19th September 1896, Portal Papers, Paris.
3. Letter of Halifax to Portal, 21st September 1896, Portal Papers, Paris.

Deeply disappointing as the papal proclamation was to both Halifax and Portal, its effect on the Church of England as a whole was nowhere nearly as drastic. A more widespread reaction was one of anger and indignation that the Church of Rome should dare to pronounce on an issue intrinsic to the internal structure of the Church of England. Lord Halifax knew that he represented only a comparatively small group within the Church of England, and that not all Anglo-Catholics or even all the members of the Church Union would agree totally with his views.[1] He acknowledged to Portal in March 1896 that in considering the Church of England as a whole, the proportion of those who desired reunion with Rome was small, but he saw his role as one of forming public opinion and sowing the seeds for future reunion of the two Churches. The immediate issue had been the validity of Anglican Orders, but the ultimate goal was reunion with Rome and Halifax was aware that the more Protestant elements of the Church of England were opposed to this.

Portal returned to Paris and continued to work with the ecumenical publication which he had founded less than a year previously (the first issue appeared on Saturday 7th December 1895), the *Revue anglo-romaine*. He was informed unofficially that the Holy See wished him to continue his work for reunion,[2] and then officially his religious superior, Abbé Fiat, was informed by Cardinal Rampolla of the great work which Portal could still render to the cause of reunion with the Church of England.[3] But the *Revue anglo-romaine* also seemed to have lost much of its heart. Two of its principal contributors, Duchesne and Loisy, decided they could no longer diplomatically continue to contribute

---

1. William S.F. Pickering in his book on Anglo-Catholicism, clearly draws out the historical development of the various threads of the Anglo-Catholic movement from the Tractarians of the Oxford Movement. He describes Anglo-Catholicism as a movement within a movement (Tractarianism), which itself was a minority grouping within the Church of England.
W.S.F. Pickering, *Anglo-Catholicism – A Study in Religious Ambiguity*, (London: S.P.C.K., 1991), pp. 15–40.
2. Letter of Portal to Halifax, 1st Octrober 1896. 'Here is the letter I received from the Nunciature: "His Excell. the cardinal Secretary of State has asked me to let you know that, on behalf of the Holy Father the Pope, you may continue with your good relations with the anglicans in which you have been particularly occupied, trying to bring them closer to the doctrine of the Roman Church, whilst holding strictly to the two documents on the unity of the church and on anglican ordinations. In adhering to the instructions of the Holy See you will usefully collaborate in the conversion of England which the Pontiff has so much at heart" '.
3. Letter of Portal to Halifax, 19th October 1896, Portal Papers, Paris.

articles, but Portal himself was convinced that although the decision about Anglican validity had been made, it was not an absolutely irreformable one, and this theme appeared now in the *Revue*. This, in turn, caused displeasure in Rome, and the Pope duly wrote a letter on the 5th November 1896[1] addressed to Cardinal Richard, the Archbishop of Paris, complaining that the decisions of *Apostolicae Curae* were being put in doubt by the *Revue anglo-romaine*. The letter noted that the Anglicans themselves had asked for a decision on the validity of their Orders and now were unwilling to accept it, aided and abetted by 'a certain religious' (Portal). For Portal this was manifestly untrue. It was not the Anglicans who had requested a declaration of the validity of their Orders, and, consequently, they were not bound to accept the papal decision. Portal did not mind taking the blame on himself, but he refused to sign a declaration that the Anglicans had requested a decision with a view to accepting whatever was decided.[2] He did agree, however, to the request of the Archbishop of Paris for the immediate suppression of the *Revue anglo-romaine*.

In England, the Anglican bishops at the Lambeth Conference of 1897, now under the leadership of the new Archbishop of Canterbury Frederick Temple, issued a statement regretting the publication of the papal bull, and concluded that it was impossible to consider reunion with the Church of Rome under the present conditions. Cardinal Vaughan, on the other hand, through his public speeches and publications, faithfully reported in *The Tablet* (Vaughan had purchased *The Tablet* outright in 1868), made no secret of his jubilation at the decision from Rome and missed no opportunity to denounce those who still believed in the possibility of corporate reunion.

We can see from this whole episode of Anglican Orders how the vision of two convinced Christians, Halifax and Portal, to bring the two Churches together in a process of ecumenical dialogue went badly

---

1. Letter of Pope Leo XIII to Cardinal Richard, Archbishop of Paris, (on the authority of the Bull *Apostolicae Curae*), 5th November 1896. Text in Messenger, *Rome and Reunion*, pp. 127–128.
2. In fact the *Revue anglo-romaine* could not have continued anyway. After the publication of the Papal Bull on Anglican Orders, many contributors and subscribers in England were reluctant to continue to support the *Revue*. Lord Halifax, writing to Portal, stated that the enthusiasm was gone, and 'one person who had previously given me £100 for the *Revue* now refused to give anything'. Letter of Portal to Halifax, 19th November 1896, Portal Papers, Bound volume of letters Halifax to Portal, letter no. 251, Paris.

wrong. The conditions seemed right: a Pope who was well-disposed and eager for rapprochement; a Cardinal Secretary of State who was willing to promote and encourage Portal and Halifax and their efforts towards reunion; a growing interest on the Continent and particularly in France in the question of Christian union and a gradual (if short-lived) lessening of ignorance of each other's positions through the *Revue anglo-romaine*. On the other hand there were the two archbishops in England, Westminster and Canterbury, who had little interest in the matter, and in the case of the Roman Catholic one, increasingly bitter opposition to it. As the matter developed, we can see a change in the attitudes of the authorities in Rome, and particularly the growing influence of the young Anglo/Spanish cleric, Mgr Merry del Val, in advising the Pope on English affairs. His advice and opinions were often in contradiction to Cardinal Rampolla, who was officially the second highest authority in the Roman Church, but it was Merry del Val who succeeded in gaining the ear of the aging Pope Leo. But it was finally the strength of opposition of Cardinal Vaughan of Westminster, in conjunction with the other conservatives in Rome, who forced through the one-sided commission of enquiry and the publication of its negative decision. There was no need for Rome to re-examine Anglican Orders yet again – that issue had already been long ago decided. When the commission reached its unfavorable decision on validity, there was no need for the results to be published as they were in the manner of a formal promulgation. It would seem, therefore, that the prevailing Ultramontane spirit in England had demanded and finally received support from Rome in its tussle with Modernism and Liberalism, but had also quenched the growing spirit of ecumenism which they either failed to perceive or saw as being tainted. Perhaps also a comment from the Bishop of Peterborough, the historian Mandell Creighton, comes near to the heart of the matter as he reflects on the whole process,

'First the conception of a higher duty, then endless diplomacy; in its course expediency creeps into the foremost place, the original point disappears, and the upshot is something as nearly as possible the reverse of what was originally intended ... the Roman Church is primarily a State, and political considerations over-ride spiritual considerations habitually and universally'.[1]

1. Lord Halifax, *Leo XIII and Anglican Orders*, p. 390.

3

Renewed attempt at reunion – the 'Conversations' at Malines.

(i) Publication of the *'Lambeth Appeal'* of 1920. Church of England's openness to accepting a commissioning from other Churches as a way to reunion.

At the sixth Conference of Lambeth, held at the Archbishop of Canterbury's Palace in London from the 5th July to the 7th August 1920, the 252 bishops assembled there announced that they would be willing, in the cause of reunion of the Christian Churches, to accept a form of commissioning from the authorities of other Churches in order that the ministry of the Anglican clergy might be recognized by others.[1] The premise of the Appeal was that the divisions among Christians were a counter-witness to the Christian claim of being one body in Christ, and the assembled Anglican bishops humbly acknowledged 'this condition of broken fellowship to be contrary to God's will, and we desire frankly to confess our share in the guilt of thus crippling the Body of Christ and hindering the activity of His Spirit'.[2] In fact, this statement was intended principally for the non-episcopalian Churches, because the statement then went on to address those communions which did not possess episcopal structures and offered that 'terms of union having been satisfactorily adjusted, Bishops and clergy of our Communion would willingly accept from these authorities a form of commission or recognition which would commend our ministry to their congregations, as having its place in the one family life'.[3] The corollary was also offered, namely, that ministers of non-episcopal Churches should be offered episcopal ordination. The Anglican bishops acknowledged that it was not within

---

1. 'An Appeal to All Christian Peoples', *Conference of Bishops of the Anglican Communion, holden at Lambeth Palace July 5 to August 7, 1920*, (London: S.P.C.K., 1920), Section V, Report No. 8 of Committee on Reunion, pp. 132–161. Text also published in Lord Halifax, *The Conversations at Malines (1921–1925)*, (London: Philip Allan & Co., 1930), pp. 65–70.
2. *'Appeal to All Christian Peoples'*, p. 134.
3. *'Appeal to All Christian Peoples'*, p. 135.

their power to know how acceptable this offer would be to the other Churches, but nevertheless they made the Appeal in all sincerity as a token of their longing for Christian unity. The Appeal was generous and wide, so all-encompassing in fact that its formulation was capable of being applied also to the Church of Rome.[1]

This Appeal issued by the Church of England was the fruit of a whole impetus among the Christian Churches and denominational bodies of the early twentieth century, and in some ways the Anglicans were latecomers to the movement. The great Evangelical Revival was initiated primarily in Germany[2] as early as the late seventeenth century, but its influence and the passion of its adherents spread quickly throughout Europe and America during the following decades. In addition to its marked detachment from the Church as institution, one of the significant marks of this Evangelical Revival was its emphasis on missionary activity – of carrying the gospel to the ends of the earth as a primary task for all christians. This, in turn, gave birth to many of the voluntary Bible and Missionary Societies, and although not ecumenical by aim or in objective, their work in evangelism and particularly in collaboration in foreign missionary areas brought them into close contact with each other and developed a consciousness within the distinct groups concerning the value and importance of unity among christians.

A series of important international gatherings for the furtherance of missionary work were held, beginning in London in 1878 and 1888, continued in New York in 1900, which culminated in the World Missionary Conference in Edinburgh in 1910. At previous conferences, only those groups of the Church of England known as 'evangelical' had participated, and the organizers of the Edinburgh Conference worked hard to involve the Church of England as a whole. Two Anglican bishops who had been connected with the non-denominational Student Christian Movement, Bishop Edward S. Talbot and Bishop Charles Gore, were invited to join the preparatory commissions. The interven-

---

1. G.K.A. Bell, *Randall Davidson, Archbishop of Canterbury,* 2 Vols., (Oxford: Oxford University Press, 1935), Vol. 2, p. 1256.
2. The early roots of the Evangelical Revival can be found in the Pietist movement initiated by P.J. Spener in 17th century Germany, particularly with the six proposals for restoring religion proposed in his *Pia Desideria* (1675), F.L. Cross, *Oxford Dictionary of the Christian Church,* 1966, p. 1071.

tion of these two bishops was important in eventually persuading the Standing Committee of the Society for the Propagation of the Gospel to modify its decision not to attend the Edinburgh Conference, and consequently other Anglicans, including many Anglo-Catholics, were also represented at Edinburgh.[1] The Archbishop of Canterbury, Randall Davidson, despite a considerable body of objection from within the Anglican Church, accepted a personal invitation to deliver the opening address at Edinburgh, which he did on the 14th June 1910.[2]

Following the publication of the Lambeth Conference Appeal of 1920, and despite its possible application to the Roman Catholic Church, the Abbé Portal, who in the intervening years had continued to work actively in affairs of reunion through a new publication *Revue catholiques des Églises*,[3] was not struck immediately by this possibility, which seems also to have escaped notice in other Catholic circles. In fact it was Walter Frere, the superior of the Anglican Community of the Resurrection who pointed it out to Portal in a letter of 3rd December 1920. Frere had become intimately involved in matters of reunion, having been one of the instigators and founders of the Anglo-Catholic Congress (eventually to be united in 1933 with the English Church Union), and it was he who seems to have brought paragraph 8 of the Appeal to Portal's attention. The terms of the appeal and the offer of the Anglican bishops to accept some form of 'commissioning' from other Churches – although aimed at the non-episcopal Churches – provided the possibility of surmounting the great difficulty which had arisen because of the declaration of *Apostolicae Curae* on the invalidity of

---

1. Tissington Taylor, 'The World Conference on Faith and Order', in Rouse and Neill, *A History of the Ecumenical Movement*, pp. 405–407.
2. The organizers of the Conference had stated that, 'no resolution shall be allowed to be presented at all which involves questions of doctrine or church policy with regard to which the Churches or Societies taking part in the Conference differ among themselves'. This assurance encouraged Archbishop Davidson to give his support to the Edinburgh Conference, but the Standing Committee of the S.P.G. had declined to participate as late as December 1908, and this caused Davidson to hesitate in accepting his invitation till April 1910. Bell, *Randall Davidson*, Vol. 1, pp. 572–575.
3. Abbé Portal, in the years immediately following *Apostolicae Curae*, withdrew from an active presence in ecumenical affairs and occupied himself with setting up a new seminary in Nice. At the invitation of his religious superiors, he returned to Paris in 1899 to establish a house of studies at No. 88 rue du Cherche-Midi, just behind the mother-house of the Lazarists, which developed quickly into a centre for reunionists. He also began a little publication entitled *Petites Annales de Saint-Vincent-de-Paul* which, in 1904, then became *Revue catholiques des Églises*. It was during this period that Portal's interest in the Russian Orthodox Church grew, always within a perspective of reunion.

Anglican Orders. But did the Anglican Bishops in their statement really mean that they were ready to accept conditional 're-ordination' from the Church of Rome? It was in this context that Portal decided to write to Cardinal Mercier of Belgium, pointing out the importance of the Lambeth Appeal, and to try to re-launch some kind of dialogue between the Church of England and Rome.[1] The answer to Portal's niggling question of the application of the Lambeth Appeal to the Roman Church only came in a letter from his old friend Canon T.A. Lacey some two months later, in which Lacey revealed that he had been involved in the drafting of the Appeal for the Lambeth Conference, and he assured Portal that the mind of the Anglican bishops was that, if the cause of reunion required it, 'they would not shrink from "re-ordination" in the cause of union'.[2]

The question arises then of why Belgium and Mercier were chosen by Portal and Halifax for the re-launching their ecumenical initiative? Several places were suggested as possibilities, including the United States (a suggestion made by Frere) but both Portal and Halifax were reluctant to leave Europe. Since the Peace Treaty of Versailles after the 1914–18 war, and the vindictive treatment of Germany by France, political relations between France and England were not too friendly, and so Paris was not thought suitable. England itself was a possibility, although this would mean inviting the English Roman Catholic bishops, but Halifax liked the idea and began to plan for the 'conversations at Hickelton', Hickelton being his family home in Yorkshire. Geneva was another consideration, as Switzerland was a small neutral country, but it was also the base of the recent 'Faith and Order' and the 'Life and Work' meetings, and as the Holy See had forbidden Catholics from participating in these movements, too close a proximity might lead to suspicion of influence by these bodies. Geneva was also considered as something of a 'Protestant Rome' ever since the 17th century attempt to establish a union among the Reformation Churches on the basis of International Calvinism. The process of elimination led them to Belgium, that small country which had been established by the Treaty of London in 1830 as a buffer state between France and Germany, and whose destiny was to be a mediating one between the Great Powers.

1. Letter of Portal to Mercier, 24th January 1921, Archdiocese of Malines Archives (All references from *Archief Kardinaal Mercier (1851–1926)*.
2. Letter Lacey to Portal, 6th March 1921, Portal Papers, Paris.

Additionally, the fact that although Belgium had a mainly Roman Catholic population, its Constitution enjoined separation of Church and State. Brussels had also been one of the places mentioned by Pope Leo XIII as a suitable place for such discussions at the preliminary stage of the Anglican Orders debate, before that got bogged down in the diplomatic tussle with Westminster. Pope Leo XIII presumably thought Belgium a sort of theological half-way house between England and France, but more probably his favour was due to the fact that he had been Papal nuncio in Belgium before his elevation to the pontificate and he knew the country well. Another factor in Portal's mind would have been the international reputation of the Primate, Cardinal Désiré Joseph Mercier, both for his scholarship[1] and for his continued and outspoken defence of the Belgian people against the German forces of occupation under General Moritz von Bissing during the Great War of 1914-1918. Mercier's defence of the rights of the Belgian people through his numerous Pastoral Letters in particular, had accrued enormous respect for the Primate throughout the whole world.

For whatever reason, in Portal's long letter to Mercier on the 24th January 1921, he described at length the original project of discussions between the Anglicans and Catholics, how it had been side-tracked into a decision on the validity of Anglican Orders, and how the original intention, supported by Pope Leo XIII himself, had never been given the possibility of realization. Portal also pointed out to the Cardinal the latent import of the recent Lambeth Appeal and asked,

> 'if Your Eminence could judge whether there might be some practical conclusions to be drawn from these documents and considerations. I submit them to Your Eminence conscious that, more than any other person, you will be able to appreciate their value.'[2]

A subtle piece of diplomacy was included when Portal informed the Cardinal that Pope Leo XIII had considered Brussels the best centre for any such inter-Church discussions.

---

1. Cardinal Désiré Joseph Mercier (1851–1926), was the founder and first President of the neo-thomistic philosophy school *Institut Supérieur de Philosophie* at the University of Louvain, and the initiator in 1894 of the *Revue néo-scolastique de philosophie*: c.f. Édouard Beauduin, *Le Cardinal Mercier*, (Tournai: Casterman, 1966), pp. 45–54.
2. Roger Aubert, *Les Conversationes de Malines: Le Cardinal Mercier et le Saint-Siège*, Bulletins de l'Académie royale de Belgique, Classe des Lettres, (Bruxelles, 1967), p. 91.

(ii) Cardinal Mercier's own interest and involvement in ecumenism.

Unbeknown to Abbé Portal, Cardinal Mercier had his own interest in bringing together members of different Churches for discussions. Shortly after the end of the First World War, towards the end of 1919, the Cardinal had paid a visit to the United States, one of the purposes of which was to thank the American peoples who had generously donated funds for the rebuilding of many of the buildings and institutions in Belgium destroyed by fire during the war, including the University Library of Louvain. Whilst there he took the opportunity of visiting and addressing the Lower House of the General Convention of the American Episcopalian Church, then in session. During his speech of thanks, the Cardinal used an expression which immediately caused trouble for him, but one which obviously came from the heart and in response to the sense of fraternity which he had experienced. He told the American Episcopalian bishops,

> 'I salute you as brothers in the service of common ideals, brothers in the love of freedom – and let me add – brothers in the Christian Faith'.[1]

This particular phrase caused a sensation. Here was one of the most prestigious members of the Sacred College of the Roman Church addressing a group of Protestant bishops and calling them 'brothers!' Cardinal William O'Connell, Archbishop of Boston, was not at all pleased and he wrote immediately to Rome complaining about Mercier. Neither was Pope Benedict XV happy,[2] when it was brought to his attention. On the 9th February 1920, on the order of the Pope, Cardinal Merry

---

1. J. Dessain, *Les progrès de l'oecuménisme: l'incident Mercier 1919–1922*, in *Revue théologique de Louvain*, 5 ème année 1974, fasc. 4, pp. 469–470.
2. Pope Benedict XV (Giacomo della Chiesa), was previously secretary to Cardinal Rampolla. When Merry del Val was appointed Secretary of State to Pius X in 1903, one of his first steps was to sack della Chiesa from his post and have him sent to Milan as Archbishop. It was Merry del Val who kept della Chiesa's name off the list of nominations for Cardinal, until eventually Pius X personally inserted his nomination. Some three months later, when della Chiesa was elected as Pope Benedict XV in April 1914, one of his first acts was to sack Merry del Val from the post of Secretary of State and to request his immediate removal from the Vatican apartments, apparently murmuring that the stone which had been rejected by the builders had been made the headstone of the corner. c.f. J.J. Hughes, *Absolutely Null and Utterly Void*, p. 224, footnote 50.

del Val (then prefect of the Sacred Congregation), wrote to Cardinal Mercier expressing the astonishment of the Holy See about his statement to the American Episcopalians, and asking for an explanation. In March 1920, Mercier replied to the Pope with a *memoire* justifying his contacts with the American Episcopalians, and tried to explain that the dissident Churches were now being better organized in terms of the Faith and Order movement, and that it was time for Catholics to take more interest in the moves towards reunion. Pope Benedict was not happy with this reply and in a letter of the following month, he expressed his dissatisfaction to Mercier, saying that his explanations were unsatisfactory, and the Belgian Primate was duly reprimanded for his regrettable meeting with the 'pseudo-évêques épiscopaliens'.

In December 1920, Mercier went to Rome to meet with the Pope, and there he gave his explanations in person to Benedict, expressing his opinion that the time was ripe for some kind of initiative for reunion from the Catholic Church. The Pope asked him to write down his ideas, and the following day Mercier submitted a memorandum suggesting that he himself should invite one or two theologians from the non-catholic Anglicans and Americans, together with similar Russian and Greek representatives from the Orthodox Churches, to meet with him in Belgium to begin informal discussions on the differences separating their Churches. Mercier wrote:

> 'The painful heritage of divisions which the war has inflicted within the souls of men has given birth, at this particular moment in time, to a sincere desire for unity among peoples of different religious confessions. Already, during my voyage to the United States, I became aware of these sentiments, which I believe sincere, on the part of non-catholic theologians ... Your Holiness will perhaps judge that one day a call to the Anglicans, Americans, Russians, Greeks, etc. would be worthy of His apostolic zeal. However, in the meantime, would it not be useful to begin preparing the way for unity? I offer myself to begin such a preparation. After having requested prayers for a private intention of Your Holiness, I would like to invite to Malines, in succession, one or two theologians of the main dissident churches, especially the Anglicans and the Orthodox, where, during the space of a few days, I could put them in contact with a catholic theologian of sound doctrine and a loving heart ... My sole desire would be to prepare those loyal

souls for whatever solutions the Holy See might be disposed to offer at a time and manner of its own choice.'[1]

Cardinal Mercier ended his proposal by asking for permission to embark on this ecumenical enterprise by seeking '... a formal approval by Your Holiness ... for the tranquility of my own conscience and, if necessary, as a justification.' The memorandum is typical of Mercier's attitude and conception of his position as bishop, seeing himself as co-responsible with the Pope and other Roman Catholic bishops for the totality of the Church and its relationship to the world. This attitude was reinforced indubitably by the Faith and Work Conferences in Geneva during the summer of 1920, and the Appeal launched by the Lambeth Conference during the same year. The Archbishop of Canterbury had sent Mercier a copy of the Lambeth Appeal 'because of the interest which Your Eminence has taken in all that concerns the Christian well-being of Western Europe',[2] and Mercier replied thanking him and offering prayers for his efforts.

Mercier, however, not having received any response from the Pope to his request for such ecumenical meetings, wrote once more to Cardinal Cerretti at the Congregation for Church Affairs, but he soon actively dropped the matter when no reply was forthcoming.[3] It was in this context that the Abbé Portal's letter dated 24th January 1921 arrived on his desk. The Cardinal's reply to Portal was extremely cautious, as he

---

1. Memorandum of Mercier to Benedict XV, 21st December 1920, Archdiocese of Malines Archives, File 1.
2. Lambeth Palace Archives, Letter of Davidson to Mercier, 3rd May, 1921.
3. In Mercier's letter to Cerretti dated 25th January 1921, he calls the attention of the substitute Secretary of State to the fact that he had submitted his letter to the Pope just before he had returned to Belgium, but feared that it had somehow got lost: 'Just when I was leaving Rome, I gave Mgr Tedeschini a letter destined for the august hands of His Holiness. It concerned some special discussions, of a religious nature, which were to have taken place at Malines. I am now wondering whether, in the confusion surrounding my departure, this request has gone astray. Whatever the merits of my request, I would not want to rush a reply, either directly or indirectly, but His Holiness did say he intended to give me a written reply. I don't think I am being indiscreet in asking Your Grace to enquire from Mgr Tedeschini if a response can be given to my proposals.'
Letter of Mercier to Cerretti, 25th January 1921, Archdiocese of Malines Archives, File 1. In a post-script Mercier adds: 'Just today, whether by accident or by providence I don't know, a priest of the Mission, a Lazarist, sent me a copy of a letter which he had received from Cardinal Rampolla on the 19th September 1904. This letter is so much in harmony with the proposal which I have put to the Holy Father for approval, that I cannot restrain myself from telling you about it'.

was at this time still half-awaiting Rome's reaction to his own suggestion of ecumenical discussions. The next stage for Portal was to include a courtesy visit to the Cardinal during a planned visit of the 1914-1918 battle sites in Belgium which he had arranged in conjunction with Lord Halifax.

(iii) The Cardinal agrees to 'informal conversations' at his Palace in Malines.

On the other side of the Channel, Lord Halifax, now over 82 years old, found a new source of life and energy in this possibility of recommencing his efforts for reunion. After the death of his wife Agnes on 4th July 1919, he had virtually given up everything that had hitherto kept him occupied, including the presidency of the English Church Union, and had also made his farewell speech in the House of Lords. With the publication of the Lambeth Appeal, Halifax saw the possibility of picking up the threads of reunion again, and, as he wrote to Portal,

> 'There is every hope now that we might renew our efforts ... The idea would be to leave aside formulae and to proceed with conferences similar to those envisaged after your first meeting with Leo XIII.'[1]

Halifax would not move without Portal, however, and it is clear that he used Frere and Lacey to prompt the somewhat reluctant French Lazarist into action, although Halifax's biographer seems to think it was the other way about.[2]

Halifax had already planned to visit the Continent sometime during the

---

1. Letter of Halifax to Portal, 6th August 1920, Portal Papers, Paris.
2. Lockhart, *Charles Lindley Viscount Halifax*, Vo. 2, p. 267.
One other curious element concerning exactly whose initiative instigated this renewed effort for the cause of reunion is presented by Régis Ladous in his excellent book on Portal. He confirms that it was Lord Halifax who had to convince his friend Abbé Portal to take up the reins again, but then he adds that, Portal having been convinced, Halifax then confided to him that he (Halifax) had plotted with his friend Randall Davidson to initiate conferences in order to explore the possibilities of *rapprochement* opened up by the Lambeth Appeal. This suggestion that it was actually the Archbishop of Canterbury who was behind the initiative is not supported by any documentary evidence available, nor by the tone of Davidson's official letter of introduction to Cardinal Mercier.
Ladous, *Monsieur Portal*, p. 420.

autumn of 1921, principally to visit Portal whom he had not seen since the outbreak of war, and also to visit some of the major battle-sites of the Great War. Now, added to the itinerary was planned a courtesy visit to Cardinal Mercier in Malines. With this additional purpose in mind, Halifax asked Archbishop Randall Davidson, the Archbishop of Canterbury, if he would consider giving him a letter of presentation to the Belgian Primate. Dr Davidson replied, however, that he could not give Halifax a letter of presentation as this might possibly be regarded as an official letter of delegation, but he did consent to send a letter of introduction to Cardinal Mercier on behalf of Halifax. Dr Davidson's letter of 19th October 1921 is very cordial but quite precise in that he makes very clear that Halifax was going to Malines in a private capacity and in no way as a representative of the Church of England, albeit a highly respected member:

'I learn from Lord Halifax that he is about to pay a visit to France where he will meet his old friend the Abbé Portal, well-known I believe to your Eminence, and I gather that it is possible they may have occasion to go also to Belgium and may meet Your Eminence there. Lord Halifax is, as Your Eminence doubtless knows, a faithful son of the Church of England, who has, during a long life, interested himself in all that concerns the reunion of Christendom and specially perhaps the possibilities of a happier relationship between the Church of Rome and the Church of England. Lord Halifax does not go in any sense as ambassador or formal representative of the Church of England, nor have I endeavoured to put before him any suggestions with regard to the possibility of such conversations as might take place between Your Eminence and himself. Anything that he says therefore would be an expression of his personal opinion rather than an authoritative statement of the position or the endeavours of the Church of England in its corporate capacity. I cannot but think however that you would find a conversation with him consonant with the thought expressed in Your Eminence's letter to me of May 21st[1] and of the visions set forth in the Lambeth Conference Appeal. Lord Halifax's lifelong interest in the whole question must necessarily give

---

1. This is a reference to Mercier's letter of acknowledgement to Archbishop Davidson for sending him a copy of the Lambeth Appeal.

weight and importance to the opinion he expresses. I feel sure that Your Eminence will pardon me for thus writing to you about my old and valued friend Lord Halifax, who has devoted his life largely to the service of the Church he loves.'[1]

A similar reserve was shown by the Archbishop of York, Dr Lang, who expressed his opinion that official conferences between Anglicans and Catholics would be practically useless, unless the way had been paved by private discussion. He offered Lord Halifax his best wishes for the success of his coming visit to Malines.[2]

On Monday, the 17th October 1921, Halifax met up with Portal at Calais, and they spent that day and the following visiting some of the scenes of the great battles of the First World War – Poperinghe, Ypres, Mount Kemmel and the Messines Ridge. On Wednesday they called on Cardinal Mercier at Malines, where they were received graciously and invited to stay for lunch. It was during the course of this visit that Lord Halifax asked the Cardinal if he would be willing to host a meeting between Anglicans and Catholics. Mercier then asked the obvious question, namely, that for such a meeting between members of the Church of England and members of the Roman Catholic Church, surely the persons to approach would be the authorities of the Catholic Church in England? Halifax and Portal, doubtless recalling the opposition which they had encountered from England in their first attempt at an Anglo-Catholic *rapprochement*, replied that the attitude of mind was not yet favourable in England (*l'états des esprits s'y oppose*). In Halifax's opinion, 'the English Catholics are anxious only for individual conversions and reject any attempt at reunion. Any such attempt is impossible except outside England'.[3] The Cardinal therefore agreed to participate in such a meeting as Halifax and Portal had suggested, making clear that it would be simply private conversations. The Cardinal's motives were summed up later in a pastoral letter to his diocese in which he used the poignant phrase: 'Nothing in the world would permit me to allow one of

---

1. Letter of Davidson to Mercier, 19th October, 1921, Archdiocese of Malines Archives.
2. Letter of Archbishop of York to Lord Halifax, 17th October, 1921, Malines Papers of Lord Halifax, File A4 271 Box 1.
3. Anselm Bolton, *A Catholic Memorial of Lord Halifax and Cardinal Mercier*, (London: Williams & Norgate, 1935), p. 116.

our separated brothers to say that he had knocked on the door of a Roman Catholic Bishop and that that Bishop had refused to open the door for him.'[1]

This, then, was the immediate background to the actual beginning of the Conversations at Malines. From the outset the meetings were regarded as simple 'conversations', private meetings between individuals, and in no way as 'negotiations'. In order to negotiate one must have received a mandate, and neither Cardinal Mercier nor Lord Halifax had mandates to negotiate on behalf of their respective Churches. The goal of the Conversations was described sometime later by Mercier as a work of *rapprochement* which consisted of 'clarifying the atmosphere', of trying to rid themselves of misunderstandings and prejudices and to re-establish the historical truth. The immediate goal of the Conversations, therefore, was not reunion, but to clear the path for reunion.

---

2. D.J. Mercier, *Oeuvres Pastorales*, 18th January 1924, t. VII, (Louvain: 1929), p. 297; reprinted in J. Bivort de la Saudée in *Anglicans et Catholiques: le Problème de l'Union Anglo-Romaine, 1833–1933*, 2 Vols., (Paris: Librairie Plon, 1949), Vol. 2, pp. 140–152.

4

The first 'Conversation' of Malines in December 1921, its participants, and the consequences of the election of a new Pope in February 1922.

(i) Lord Halifax chooses the Anglican members, and visits Cardinal Bourne to keep him informed.

On his return to England, Halifax immediately began to make preparation for the first meeting at Malines. Cardinal Mercier had asked him to invite two Anglican theologians, and also to prepare a Memorandum of points which could be discussed. As the discussions were intended to be purely 'private', the choice of the participants was left entirely to Halifax, as the Archbishop of Canterbury later pointed out: 'Lord Halifax....on his own responsibility, invited two distinguished theologians to go with him very quietly to Malines'.[1]

In the Lambeth Palace archives there is a note giving some details of a meeting between Halifax and Archbishop Davidson dated 1st November 1921, almost immediately after the first encounter with Cardinal Mercier. Davidson writes:

> 'Halifax says that Mercier suggested that if we could send from England two trusted men not as formal delegates but as competent thinkers and ecclesiastical statesmen who could discuss the situation with Mercier, he (Mercier) would be ready after such interviews ... to go to Rome and talk the thing over with the Pope ... Halifax quite sees that such discussions would be rather for the promoting of good feeling than for the actual accomplishment of any defined plan.'[2]

The note continues to relate that they discussed various figures who might be suitable as companions at the first conversation, and the Archbishop notes that 'Halifax was doubtful about Gore because of his

---

1. G.K.A. Bell, *Randall Davidson, Archbishop of Canterbury*, 2 Vols. (London: Oxford University Press, 1935), Vol. 2, p. 1255.
2. Memorandum of Archbishop Davidson, Lambeth Palace Archives, Box 186, File 1.

occasional vagaries and fancifulness ... I did not discuss with him Frere, who is I think another possible man, supposing it might be thought desirable to send anyone at all'. This note of extreme caution continues when, on the 1st December 1921, Davidson received a letter from J. Armitage Robinson, the Dean of Wells, telling him that he had been invited by Halifax to attend the first Conversation at Malines (scheduled for the 6th December of that year). Robinson says that he had some initial misgivings but these were dispelled by Halifax, who said they needed wider representation of views than just his own. Robinson says that he deliberately did not consult with the Archbishop of Canterbury before leaving (he had seen Halifax's letter of introduction to Mercier and did not want to draw Davidson into making him some kind of 'official delegate') although he did give Halifax's London address (55 Eaton Square) where he could be contacted before leaving for Belgium. Davidson noted that he had telephoned Robinson as soon as he received the letter (which had been sent to him at Canterbury, whilst Davidson was in Lambeth Palace). Davidson continued in his note that '... he (Robinson) had wisely not consulted me so as to keep me entirely outside the business'. He thought it good that Robinson should go to Malines, 'for he is an admirable exponent of the true Church of England in its historical and doctrinal life'.[1]

The choice of J. Armitage Robinson by Lord Halifax and Abbé Portal as one of the participants at the Conversations was a particularly apt one. Not only was Robinson a renowned scholar, particularly in second century Christian texts and patristic writings, but he was a friend of the Archbishop of Canterbury, who was in the habit of spending some days each year before Easter at Wells. Robinson's position at Wells also facilitated amiable relations with Downside Abbey, and particularly with the scholars Edmund Bishop and Hugh Connolly. Among Robinson's acquaintances was Walter Frere. Robinson's upbringing and background were Evangelical in tendency, but his studies had left him with a much more Catholic vision of Christianity, although he disagreed with the High Church group on some important issues such as Reservation of the Sacrament. He himself would not adhere to any particular church party, so much so that when he was initially appointed to the Deanship of Westminster Abbey in 1899, *The Times* writer did not

---

1. Lambeth Palace Archives, Box 186, File 1.

THE FIRST 'CONVERSATION' – THE ELECTION OF A NEW POPE

know whether to call him a high-churchman with broad sympathies or a broad-churchman with high sympathies.[1]

After further consultations with Portal, it was agreed that the second of the two members to be invited should be Dr Walter Frere, the superior of the Community of the Resurrection at Mirfield and a noted Anglo-Catholic. Whereas Dr Frere agreed immediately to participate at Malines, Halifax had to enlist the help of the Archbishop of York in order to overcome the hesitations of Dr Robinson. After a somewhat lengthy pause, Robinson finally agreed. In discussing the various possibilities for membership of the Anglican participants, both Portal and Halifax seemed to have agreed very quickly that the one person they did not want was Dr Charles Gore,[2] the former Bishop of Oxford. Halifax was not impressed by Gore's theological tendency to modernistic thought as evidenced in Gore's publication *Lux Mundi*. Interestingly enough, it was this same Dr Gore whom the Archbishop of Canterbury later insisted upon becoming a member of the Conversations' team for the third of the Conversations, when the whole affair began to take on a somewhat more official nature.

The membership of the Anglican group having been decided, Lord Halifax made an appointment to see Cardinal Francis Bourne, the Roman Catholic Archbishop of Westminster. On the 29th November 1921, the interview with the Cardinal took place, and Halifax explained to him what was proposed for the meetings with Cardinal Mercier in Malines. In a letter to Portal written the same day, Halifax reported that

'I told him that we had seen Cardinal Mercier and talked with him on the subject of reunion of the Churches, etc. etc. "Ah! Cardinal Mercier," he said. "I know him well and have a great regard for him; we were at Louvain together. He is a great man, a most distinguished personality with strong influence. I am very glad that you have seen him." My visit was a complete success. I was entirely satisfied on

---

1. T.F. Taylor, *J. Armitage Robinson: Eccentric, Scholar and Churchman 1858–1933*, (Cambridge: James Clarke & Co., 1991), p. 83.
2. In a letter to Portal dated 31st October 1921, Halifax wrote that according to his information, both Gore and Frere should be avoided, but on the 15th November 1921 he had so modified his view after meeting with Frere that he now thought Frere would be excellent. Letter of Halifax to Portal 31st October 1921, Portal Papers, Paris.
cf. also Lockhart, *Charles Lindley Viscount Halifax*, Vol. 2, p. 273.

departing and asked his permission to come and see him after my return from Malines to tell him everything that had been said, and also, as I hoped, to ask for his good services to help in every possible way to bring about such conferences as Leo XIII discussed in 1894. The Cardinal was altogether sympathetic ...'[1]

It seems clear from this letter that Halifax, bearing in mind the difficulties which had arisen with Cardinal Vaughan during the Anglican Orders affair, made a special point of informing the then Archbishop of Westminster about the proposed meeting at Malines. Cardinal Bourne's biographer however, Ernest Oldmeadow, strongly contends that Halifax had not informed the Cardinal of the real intent of the Malines meeting. While not denying that Halifax had indeed seen Cardinal Bourne, he strongly refutes the suggestion that Halifax had gone with the intention of informing the English Cardinal of the full import of the impending Conversations with his brother Cardinal at Malines. Oldmeadow says that he received Bourne's clear assurance that Halifax had spoken in a general way, not mentioning the various negotiations with the Archbishop of Canterbury and the imminent meeting with Cardinal Mercier at Malines.[2] Taking account of the documentary evidence available, it cannot be denied that Lord Halifax visited Cardinal Bourne twice to inform him of the meetings with Mercier, but how much of the detail of the meetings he communicated is not clear. It would seem, however, that Oldmeadow is mistaken and, in fact, pleading a special cause.

1. Letter of Halifax to Portal, 29th November 1921, Portal Papers, Paris. Cardinal Bourne also mentioned to Lord Halifax that he had heard that Rome was making approaches to the Russian Orthodox Church, and had appointed a Russian Uniate priest to the Nunciature at Paris.
2. Ernest Oldmeadow, *Francis Cardinal Bourne*, 2 Vols., (London: Burns & Oates, 1944), Vol. 2, pp. 362–363.
Oldmeadow's biography of Cardinal Bourne is an extremely polemical defence of the Cardinal. He contends that any discussions or conversations held in England would have been with people who would have a much better understanding of the Church of England, and who would be cognizant of the fact that Lord Halifax was representative of only one group within the Anglican communion, that is, the High Church group or Anglo-Catholics, and that they were not speaking in any sense for the whole body of the Church of England. Oldmeadow states categorically that: 'Malines was chosen because Malines was ready to accept the spokesmen from England as typical Anglicans rather than minority men whose reading of their Church's character, worship and teaching would have been warmly repudiated by most of their co-religionists at home. Cardinal Mercier's strong point was not Church History; but even he should have smelt a rat when members of the notoriously heterogeneous and Protestant Church of England approached him with airs of a homogeneous sacerdotalist body, agreeing with Catholics on the Sacrifice of the Mass and differing from Rome only in faltering tones even on the Primary of Peter'. Op. Cit., p. 362.

THE FIRST 'CONVERSATION' – THE ELECTION OF A NEW POPE

Cardinal Bourne himself in a letter of 6th February 1924 addressed to the editor of *The Tablet* (Oldmeadow), states quite clearly that the Conversations were 'known to me in confidence all along'.[1] Even though Oldmeadow postulates Halifax's 'advanced years' as a possible excuse for the purported forgetfulness, there is little likelihood that the Viscount, whose sole purpose in life at this time was to get the meetings underway, would be likely to have 'forgotten' to mention the Malines arrangements to Cardinal Bourne. Two additional factors should nevertheless be taken into account. Firstly, that Lord Halifax would naturally have been hesitant to reveal anything which might endanger or abort the proposed meetings at Malines, given his experiences with Bourne's predecessor Cardinal Vaughan: secondly, that Oldmeadow himself was categorically against any sort of attempt at corporate reunion, as is evidenced by his personal correspondence with Cardinals Merry del Val and Gasquet in Rome and with Canon Moyes in England.[2]

The question of the Agenda was the other important point for consideration. Halifax drew up a short Memorandum,[3] based on those elements which were common to both the Anglicans and Roman Catholics and which were considered essential by both the Thirty-Nine Articles and the Decrees of the Council of Trent. In this Memorandum, Halifax recalls that Pusey had postulated that these two sources were compatible, and, if he were indeed right, here was a promising point of departure.[4] The Memorandum could consequently be divided roughly into two distinct parts, the first dealing with the constitution of the Church

---

1. Letter of Cardinal Bourne to editor of *The Tablet*, 6th February 1924, Archives of Archdiocese of Westminster, Ref. 124/4/2.
2. Oldmeadow, *Francis Cardinal Bourne*, Vol. II, pp. 353–414.
3. For the full text of the report (*Compte Rendu*) of the Malines Convesations discussions and Halifax's Memorandum, reference should be made to two publications by Lord Halifax: (1) Lord Halifax, *The Conversations at Malines: 1921–1925,* (Oxford: Oxford University Press, 1927); (2) Lord Halifax, *The Malines Conversations: (1921–1925): Original Documents*, (London: Philip Allan & Co., 1930).
In the second of these publications, however, is contained the original, unamended draft of Halifax's Memorandum, and not the revised edition which was actually presented by Halifax at Malines. The draft version actually published by Halifax subsequently received a good deal of modification, and should be read in conjunction with the corrections found in: Walter H. Frere, *Recollections of Malines*, (London: Centenary Press, 1935), pp. 15–19.
4. 'Dr Pusey said long ago, before the Vatican Council, in his preface to the late Bishop of Brechin's (Bishop Forbes) book on the Articles that there was nothing in the Council of Trent which need constitute a difficulty for the Anglican Church and that even the Papal Supremacy was open to an interpretation which Anglicans could accept'.

and the nature of the sacraments – baptism, eucharist, and the necessity of episcopal ordination – and the second dealing with the Lambeth Appeal. In posing a topic such as the 'constitution' of the Church, Halifax was trying to avoid walking immediately into the thorny issue of the nature of the Church in which both sides had clear and often opposing views. In many ways this 'First Conversation' was to have an exploratory perspective and, as Bishop Bell noted, was 'to see whether there was a case for the holding of conferences between Romans and Anglicans, with some real, though at first informal, encouragement from the highest authorities on both sides.'[1]

The Anglican side having now been composed, the group set off from London on Monday 5th December 1921, under the safe and sure direction of James, Lord Halifax's manservant, who supervised the travel and luggage throughout. J.G. Lockhart reports that they arrived in Malines in the late evening of the same day where they were welcomed in perfect English by the Cardinal's Chaplain, Canon F. Dessain, who was an former member of Christ Church at Oxford. He also noted that 'on the platform a pious Belgian, overawed by the ecclesiastical trappings of the Dean of Wells, knelt down and asked for a blessing, which Dr Armitage Robinson, recovering from his surprise, hastened to give him'.[2] In a letter to his son Edward on the 7th December, Lord Halifax described the routine of their daily meetings:

'We get up soon after 7. The Abbé Portal says Mass in the Cardinal's chapel which is at the top of the great staircase opposite the large drawing-room where we have our discussions. At 9 we have our

(Footnote no. 4 continued from previous page.)
Memorandum of Lord Halifax, *The Conversations at Malines* (1930), p. 74. In fact, Halifax was mistaken about this preface. It was written by Forbes and dedicated to Dr. Pusey – cf. A.P. Forbes, *An Explanation of the Thirty-Nine Articles*, (Oxford & London: James Parker & Co., 1871), pp. i–xl.
It is worthwhile noting, however, that this was also the fundamental argument of Newman in Tract 90, in which he argued that the doctrine of the Church of England had not been changed fundamentally at the Reformation. D.L. Edwards notes that, 'Almost half a century later, Gladstone – who took more trouble than Newman did to investigate the history of the Elizabethan settlement of religion – remarked to Lord Acton that Tract Ninety had been basically correct'.
David L. Edwards, *Leaders of the Church of England 1928–1944*, (London: Oxford University Press, 1971), pp. 61–61.

1. Bell, *Randall Davidson*, Vol. 2, p. 1256.
2. Lockhart, *Charles Lindley Viscount Halifax*, Vol. 2, p. 275.

THE FIRST 'CONVERSATION' – THE ELECTION OF A NEW POPE

coffee and then at 10 we assemble in the big drawing-room. The Vicar General[1] makes his appearance, then the Cardinal comes in. We exchange a word or so, then sit down round a table – the Cardinal, then me, then the Abbé, then the Vicar General, then Walter Frere, then the Dean of Wells, the other side of the Cardinal opposite me. It is quite a small round table and it is quite easy to hear what is said. We talk and discuss till one or thereabouts, then dinner or luncheon – the food in the evening at 7.30 is the same meal as at 1 or 1.30, all very good and appetizing cooking ... Then after luncheon we have time to rearrange our thoughts or take a walk till 4, when we meet again, talk and converse and discuss till 7. Dinner or supper at 7.30. The Cardinal presides at luncheon and dinner, and then after dinner we retire to our rooms about 9, where we write and do what has to be done till bedtime.

I think I may say that I am quite satisfied. Nothing, as I have said, can be kinder or more helpful than the Cardinal or apparently more anxious to smooth the way and get round difficulties, and both Walter Frere and the Dean have been most helpful. We began with going through and discussing my Memorandum which was generally approved of, and since that we have been going through the Lambeth Appeal for Unity. That I think has also been most satisfactory and useful. The Abbé tells me that he thinks the Cardinal is pleased and that we shall succeed in our object.'[2]

J. Armitage Robinson, the Dean of Wells, wrote a personal journal of his experiences at Malines, and it is clear from the content that he began almost as soon as he arrived in Malines.[3] He began by writing, 'the delightful simplicity of the Cardinal's notepaper tempts me at once to begin an account of our doings'. There were two immediate concerns

---

1. The Vicar General was Mgr Joseph-Ernst van Roey, who assisted Cardinal Mercier as theologian during each of the Conversations. Van Roey later succeeded Mercier as Cardinal Archbishop of Malines on the latter's death in 1926.
2. Letter of Lord Halifax to his son Edward, 7th December 1921, Malines Papers of Lord Halifax, File A2 278, I.
3. Journal of J. Armitage Robinson, Westminster Abbey Archives, Box 9, 5th December 1921, page 1.
This journal is a typescript document of some twenty-one pages which the Dean wrote specifically concerning his experiences at the Conversations at Malines. This Journal, together with a small collection of letters – mostly addressed to Mrs Robinson – were gifted to Westminster Abbey by Bishop John A.T. Robinson, a nephew of Armitage, on the death of his aunt. Bishop Robinson was aware that the then Keeper of the Muniments, Mr Tanner, was contemplating a biography of the late Dean.

expressed by the Dean – firstly, his weakness in expressing himself in French and, secondly, his puzzlement as to why he had been chosen as a member of the Anglican group. Regarding this latter point, he recounts that he spoke to the Abbé Portal before the meetings had begun, and tried to express in his poor French that,

> '... I did not belong to the "school" of Lord Halifax; that I was more in the centre and had "liaison" (happy word! I hope it was the right one) with both extremes; that my father was a devout Evangelical, and so on. But all so slowly and so badly that I think I gave the impression of being a dreadful schismatic whose one redeeming point was that I had yielded to the saintliness of Lord Halifax and had been tempted on to this dangerous ground.'[1]

(ii) The first 'Conversation', and content of discussion.

The Conversations began on Tuesday 6th December 1921. The Roman Catholic group consisted of Cardinal Mercier himself, Abbé Portal, and Mgr Van Roey, a Master of Theology of the University of Louvain and Vicar General to Mercier. At 10.00 am. the Cardinal invoked the Holy Spirit for guidance, and the Conversations opened with Lord Halifax presenting his Memorandum as a proposed basis for discussion. The Memorandum was accepted as such a basis, and discussion followed on each of the topics contained therein. The whole of the first day was spent in the reading and discussion of Lord Halifax's Memorandum, and the morning session tackled such points as the necessity of baptism for membership of the Church, the relationship of the 39 Articles to the Council of Trent, and the conditions under which a truth becomes an article of faith in the Catholic Church.

The first point for discussion on the agenda was baptism. Lord Halifax's account of this discussion gives the impression that there was ready agreement. In the *Compte Rendu* of this first session, Lord Halifax wrote, 'We were agreed on the point that baptism gave entry to the Church, but we left to one side the question whether one could, without being formally baptized, be a member of the invisible Church. We accepted also that the initiation constituted by baptism must be developed within an organized social life'.[2] The Dean of Wells notes in his

---

1. Journal of J. Armitage Robinson, 5th December 1921, p. 2.
2. Halifax, *The Conversations at Malines 1921–1925, Original Documents*, p. 11.

THE FIRST 'CONVERSATION' – THE ELECTION OF A NEW POPE

journal, however, that 'Lord Halifax's way of treating this had seemed very striking and rather novel. Without repudiating it they began to go off the distinction between the "visible" and the "invisible" church. I had to intervene and say that this was not the distinction of the N.T. or of the early Christian centuries; that to me the "invisible" part of the Church meant primarily those who had passed out of this world; that I had been taught to believe that everyone who was baptized was made a member of Christ and a child of God, and therefore a member of Christ's body the Church; that as baptism was a visible act, this must mean membership in the visible Church. I said that some of our English theologians were now trying to deny this (meaning Messers Stone and Puller); and I wished to know what they would say. They seemed quite to agree ...'[1] The Dean continued his account by noting that '... you may think from this that I was doing a great deal of the talking. But this was by no means the case. I was generally silent unless I was appealed to on various points to say whether I agreed with Lord Halifax or Frere as the case may be.'[2]

On this particular point of the baptism discussion, it may well be that Robinson was especially sensitive to the content of Lord Halifax's presentation, especially in the light of his emphasis on not belonging to the same school of Anglican thought, and hence safeguarding that the discussion did not venture beyond accepted Anglican teaching on baptism. In the Memorandum which Halifax presented as the basis of discussion for this first Conversation, sacramental baptism was presented as the 'ordinary' means of membership of the Church, although Halifax did note, 'to state this is not to assert that God cannot, if He so wills, and in fact never does operate outside the sacraments ...'[3] According to Walter Frere, indeed, it was Cardinal Mercier who brought up the point of distinction between 'visible' and 'invisible' Church, asking that both aspects be borne in mind.[4]

On the Council of Trent and the 39 Articles, it was Mercier who took up the reading of the Memorandum, which invoked the writings of both Pusey and Bishop Forbes of Brechin as being of the opinion that the

---

1. Journal of J. Armitage Robinson, 6th December 1921, pp. 1–2.
2. Journal of J. Armitage Robinson, 6th December 1921, p. 3.
3. Halifax, *The Conversations at Malines 1921–1925, Original Documents*, p. 72.
4. Walter Frere, *Recollections of Malines*, p. 23.

doctrines contained in the 39 Articles of the Church of England were susceptible of an interpretation not inconsistent with the Decrees of the Council of Trent. The Dean of Wells pointed out that there were very few people in England who knew anything about the Decrees of the Council of Trent, but in any case he himself would not subscribe to the view that the 39 Articles were all compatible with Roman Catholic teaching. There were some parts which he thought were clearly not. The Dean continued by saying that there had been a modification in the civil law in England about fifty years previously which had, in fact, altered the degree of assent to the 39 Articles which was required from the Anglican clergy, and what was necessary now was a general assent to the doctrine of the Church of England, without having to accept all and every proposition and phrase found in the 39 Articles.[1] He added that if the 39 Articles had not been imposed on the Church of England by civil law, they would most probably have fallen into oblivion. For these reasons he thought that the 39 Articles did not present a real obstacle, but it remained to be seen how much they did in fact approach the doctrine of the Council of Trent.

From the Council of Trent they then passed to the Council of the Vatican, and the Anglicans asked how a 'truth' became a truth of faith for Roman Catholics? The reply given was in three parts:
(1) A truth is accepted as 'of faith' if it is professed explicitly as faith by the whole Church.
(2) If an ecumenical council defines it as 'of faith'. In order that a council be ecumenical, it is necessary that it be either convoked or presided over by the Pope and approved by him.
(3) If the Pope speaks '*ex cathedra*' as head of the universal Church in defining a truth.
The Anglicans remarked that they could recognize neither the Council of Trent nor the Council of the Vatican as ecumenical, and that the three points or propositions which had just been explained would require study in depth as they presented great difficulties for their own position. Continuing with this theme, the Anglicans then asked if it should not be always the case that a council is necessary in order to decide on 'truths of faith'? The Catholic reply to this was that a council was only one of

---

1. This was enshrined in the Clerical Subscription Act of 1865. For a brief history of the background, cf. Chadwick, *The Victorian Church*, vol. II, pp. 131–135.

THE FIRST 'CONVERSATION' – THE ELECTION OF A NEW POPE

the means for defining whether a truth is a revealed one or not. However, it had to be stressed that the privilege of infallibility did not separate the Pope from the Church. The Pope, as such, could not act apart from the Church, of which he was the head. Concerning this point, what was stated in Lord Halifax's Memorandum expressed well this aspect of Roman Catholic teaching: '... no power is claimed there by the [Vatican] Council for the Pope apart from the Church; and that what it claims for the Pope is simply the power, after having taken every means to ascertain what the teaching of the Church is, on any given point, to declare what that teaching is in an authoritative manner. In short the power of the Pope is not the power to declare or impose a new dogma, but only the power to declare explicitly and authoritatively what is the faith committed by our Lord Jesus Christ to the Church's guardianship.'[1] Cardinal Mercier added the clarification that a dogma is not an expression of a new truth, but an authentic formulation of a truth contained from the very beginning in the deposit of revelation. It is the bringing to light of that which was in seed in the words revealed by Christ and the Apostles.

In the course of the afternoon session the same day, the participants discussed the sacraments of the eucharist, extreme unction and penance, and also the role of dogma and the exercise of jurisdiction. Two outstanding points in this session concerned the eucharist and the role of dogma. Concerning the eucharist, the minutes of this session record: 'on the doctrine of transubstantiation, the Anglicans said they admitted the changing of the bread and wine into the body and blood of Christ by the consecration. To the eyes of the Catholics, the word "transubstantiation" did not mean anything other than this'.[2] On the point which was raised about communion under both species, the Catholics explained that this had been the standard practice of the universal Church, but that its restriction to only one species had been due to practical reasons and not dogmatic motives, and hence was merely a question of discipline which could easily be reversed.

Concerning dogmas, everyone recognized that there were truths of faith

---

1. This is one of the important corrections to Lord Halifax's Memorandum as published in his book, *The Conversations at Malines: 1921–1925: Original Documents*, on p. 74. For the authentic corrected version reference should be made to Walter Frere, *Recollections of Malines*, pp. 15–16.
2. Lord Halifax, *The Conversations at Malines (1921–1925): Original Documents*, p. 14.

which imposed themselves. The Anglicans, however, wished to know by what criterion the Catholics could discern *defined* truths of faith from those which were not. The Catholic participants replied that when authority wished to define a truth of faith, certain formulas were used, such as '*si quis dixerit ... anathema sit*', or, in the case of the definition of the Immaculate Conception, '*definimus auctoritate ...*'

On the question of jurisdiction, both Anglicans and Catholics agreed that episcopacy had been established by divine will, but the Anglicans remarked that they would wish for a good deal more freedom to be left to the local Churches than was actually the case in the Roman Church. The Dean stated that he felt that 'any National Church ought to have a measure of Home Rule; and, while bound by loyalty to the whole Church, should not be tied in lesser matters. Thus the Bishops should be free to govern their dioceses and not be subjected to a series of orders from outside'.[1] The Catholics replied that the scope for the rights of local bishops within the Catholic Church should not be underestimated, as was shown when German Catholics voted against Bismarck's laws despite the exhortation to the contrary by Pope Leo XIII, and when the Belgian bishops took the same attitude against the school laws in Belgium.[2]

The following day, the 7th December, the Conversations continued with a reading and discussion of the Appeal of the Anglican Bishops at the Lambeth Conference of 1920. Concerning Chapter IV of the Appeal, the Anglicans noted that a certain diversity in unity was necessary, especially concerning disciplinary matters, adding that the Church of England was very desirous of retaining its own usages. One point of considerable divergence appeared when the participants came to discuss Chapter VI of the Appeal. The Anglican bishops had proposed, 'that the visible unity of the Church will be found to involve the whole-hearted acceptance of the Holy Scriptures, as the record of God's revelation of Himself to man, and as being the rule and ultimate standard of faith ...'[3] The Catholics objected to the use of the term *ultimate standard*, because

---

1. Frere, *Recollections of Malines*, pp. 26–27.
2. Lord Halifax, *The Conversations at Malines (1921–1925): Original Documents*, p. 15.
3. Lord Halifax, *The Conversations at Malines (1921–1925): Original Documents*, p. 68. The complete text of the Lambeth Appeal is published in Lord Halifax's book as Annex 1, pp. 65–70.

THE FIRST 'CONVERSATION' – THE ELECTION OF A NEW POPE

Holy Scripture has to be interpreted, and it was the Church alone which had the right to interpret.

But the lengthiest discussion took place on Chapter VII of the Appeal, that concerning the episcopate. The bishops at Lambeth had been proposing the episcopate as a means of maintaining the unity and continuity of the Church (obviously directed towards non-episcopalian Churches). Cardinal Mercier, on being asked for a rigorous evaluation of this particular chapter, replied that the episcopate, in itself, could be an agent of unification, but even the bishops needed a visible head, a sign of their own unity among themselves. 'Imagine', said the Cardinal, 'that there were two station-masters at Victoria Station. What a number of accidents would be recorded on the following day!'[1] According to Lockhart, someone apparently retorted that Victoria was only one of many stations in London and that each had its separate chief.[2] Both the Dean of Wells and Dr Frere inserted here a point about the Orthodox Churches, which they saw as in the same position as the Anglicans, and thought that they should not proceed without them. Dr Frere stated that he had no difficulty in admitting a head or leader as a centre of unity, but he would only accept this as *jure ecclesiastico* and consequently as a development of the organization of the Church.

On this continuing topic, Lord Halifax felt that, important though a visible head might be, it was through the Holy Spirit that the unity of the Church was maintained. To insist too much on the necessity of a visible head seemed to resemble the conduct of the people of Israel when they demanded a king.[3] Another part of the discussion centered on that part of the Lambeth Appeal (Chapter VIII) which had brought about the very Conversations themselves, namely, the chapter dealing with ordinations. The actual wording of this section is important enough to be quoted in full.

'We believe that, for all, the truly equitable approach to union is by the way of mutual deference to one another's conscience. To this end, we who send forth this appeal would say that if the authorities of other Communions should so desire, we are persuaded that, terms of union

---

1. Lord Halifax, *The Conversations at Malines (1921–1925): Original Documents*, p. 19.
2. Lockhart, *Charles Lindley Viscount Halifax*, Vol. 2, p. 277.
3. Lord Halifax, *The Conversations at Malines (1921–1925): Original Documents*, p. 20.

having been otherwise satisfactorily adjusted, Bishops of our Communion would willingly accept from these authorities a form of commission or recognition which would commend our ministry to their congregations as having its place in the one family life. It is not in our power to know how far this suggestion may be acceptable to those to whom we offer it. We can only say that we offer it in all sincerity as a token of our longing that all ministries of grace, theirs and ours, shall be available for the service of our Lord in a united Church.'[1]

Concerning this section of the Appeal, the Dean of Wells and Dr Frere noted first that the formulation of this chapter had in mind principally the non-episcopal Protestant Churches, such as the Presbyterian Church of Scotland, who claimed a presbyterial ministry coming from the Apostles, and also the Methodists who claimed that their ministry of the Word and Sacrament was blessed by the Holy Spirit. In his journal, the Dean explained, 'We asked them without denying the value of their own ministry, to have it regularised by Episcopal ordination, and offered on our part to have our ministry supplemented by such authorization as would render it acceptable to them and their people. This general offer included our regularization by the Roman or the Orthodox church, provided in all cases that other points of controversy were satisfactorily dealt with.'[2] This, of course, would have been an admirable answer to the difficulties posed by Leo XIII's Bull, *Apostolicae Curae*, concerning the question of Anglican Orders, but, surprisingly enough, Cardinal Mercier showed himself to be somewhat reticent on this question, saying that 'ordination *sub conditione* might be required and might be found satisfactory, but some sort of supplement also might be a conceivable plan of regularization'.[3] Armitage Robinson noted in his journal, however, that the Abbé Portal expressed the opinion that the Appeal had been an act of great humility on the part of the bishops of the Church of England.

The morning of Thursday 8th December was spent principally in polishing up the minutes of the discussions, which charge had been assigned to Frere and Portal. In response to a question from Armitage Robinson concerning the degree of discretion which the participants should observe, the Cardinal expressed the following opinions:

1. '*An Appeal to All Christian Peoples*', Section V, Report No. 8, p. 135.
2. Journal of J. Armitage Robinson, 7th December 1921, p. 2.
3. Frere, *Recollections of Malines*, p. 29.

THE FIRST 'CONVERSATION' – THE ELECTION OF A NEW POPE

1. Absolute discretion as regards the Press.
2. To minimize the number of persons with whom one spoke about Malines, and then only in a confidential manner.
3. It would be legitimate and useful to keep the respective competent authorities informed, but again in a confidential manner.
4. Not to announce the names of the participants unless it was absolutely necessary.
5. The *Compte Rendu* of the Conversations should be confidential.

Finally the Cardinal expressed the joy and edification which these meetings had been for him, and Halifax responded by thanking the Cardinal for his generous hospitality and his constant kindness which they had all experienced. Both Halifax and Robinson offered to host any further meetings, should they be proceeded with. The conclusion of this first of the Malines Conversations ends on a humorous note as far as the Dean of Wells was concerned. His gentle but sharp sense of humour comes out clearly in his journal's description of the final day, 'The Cardinal is most insistent on sending us to Brussels in his motor ... The Pontifical Mass this morning was very striking. The Cathedral seemed quite full to the end of the nave, and the number of men seemed as great as of the women. The singing was beautiful – a large quire of boys and men in the organ-gallery at the west end. The modulation of voices from softness to a great rolling sound was splendid. The Creed was sung alternately by boys at the west end and by the whole congregation – the simple tune that we have in Merbecke. I lost my place in it, because there was no kneeling at the words "And was incarnate". I was told afterwards that the practice is hardly known in Belgium apart from the monasteries – What would some of our High Church friends say?'[1]

(iii) Changes which affected the progress of the Conversations.

There is no doubt concerning the positive and enthusiastic impression that all the participants experienced at this first Conversation. The charity and breadth of vision of the Cardinal impressed all the Anglicans, and the piety and sincerity of the latter deeply touched the Cardinal and the other Roman Catholic members. Dr Robinson had an interview with the Archbishop of Canterbury on his return to England, and he reported to Lord Halifax in a letter of 12th December that 'I gave

---

1. Journal of J. Armitage Robinson, 8th December 1921.

your message to the Archbishop, who went through with the keenest interest so much of the English summary of the proceedings as Dr Frere had got ready in time. He was much impressed and confident that our gathering was both of importance and true service'[1]. Dr Frere's assessment was similar, expressing the view that there were great hopes for peace if this modest beginning was kept discreetly quiet and not widely discussed. Dr Robinson also wrote directly to Cardinal Mercier on the 17th December, thanking him and explaining why he had acted as a brake on Halifax's enthusiasm:

'I count it a high honour to have been received by Your Eminence and to have been allowed to speak in confidential freedom as to the doctrinal position of the Church of England and the possibility of some understanding between it and the Church of Rome. If I seemed to be a drag on the enthusiasm of our generous and saintly friend Lord Halifax, it was because I am convinced that no good can come from any presentation of our position which would not be accepted by the central body of our Churchmen with which I am more particularly in sympathy. Thus I have learned since my return that an English clergyman named Boudier, representing the very extreme "High Church" party, has had an interview with the Holy Father and spoken as if the English Church were quite ready to make a general submission to the Papacy. Such action is only mischievous: for even Lord Halifax, I am convinced, would strenuously repudiate it. Our conversations with Your Eminence, on the other hand, will I believe have done much to inform you as to the true position of those who seek an approach and an understanding on the basis of the Lambeth Appeal. I do not myself look for immediate results. But I venture to regard our meeting as a token of hope; and I trust that Your Eminence having begun so good a work will be guided by Providence to forward it in ways that may open before you. There is no one whose name goes so directly to the hearts of Englishmen; and in this fact a great power may lie in the future, if it please God to draw us closer together. I reported the proceedings to our Archbishop, who was more than contented with what I told him, though his position demands a discreet silence at the present stage...'[2]

1. Letter of Dr Armitage Robinson to Lord Halifax, 12th December 1921, Malines Papers of Lord Halifax, File A4 271, Box 1.
2. Letter of Dr Armitage Robinson to Cardinal Mercier, 17th December 1921, Archdiocese of Malines Archives, Box 1, No. 12.

THE FIRST 'CONVERSATION' – THE ELECTION OF A NEW POPE

Both Portal and Halifax were more ebullient about their reactions, and in their correspondence to one another gave thanks to God for the mutual support of their friendship which had brought them to this day: 'Can we really be at the dawn of a new epoch?', wrote Portal, 'Everything encourages such a belief. We can only thank God for His goodness in using us to join up afresh threads which had been so brutally broken. Our old friendship surely had no need of reward, but that it pleases God to add to it this joy is indeed good and makes it even sweeter and more precious.'[1]

On Cardinal Mercier's side, although satisfied with the results of this first meeting, there was still the question not only of keeping Rome informed of what was happening, but of obtaining some kind of authorization. We have already seen how the Cardinal's request to Pope Benedict XV to initiate such a series of meetings with separated brethren had gone unanswered, but the Cardinal obviously felt no need for authorization for this first 'Conversation', on the grounds that it was not he who had initiated it but the Anglicans. Indeed it was this point that the Cardinal insisted upon later in his correspondence with Archbishop Davidson (letter of 15th December 1923), when Davidson was preparing his own public letter of explanation about the Conversations. Mercier stated quite clearly that 'I had no relation with Lord Halifax, either direct or indirect, at the time he and Abbé Portal presented themselves at my home ... It would therefore be incorrect to say that I had taken the initiative to invite some Anglicans to a debate'.[2]

Events now began to overtake any plans that Mercier may have considered, for on 22nd January 1921, some six weeks after the meeting in Malines, Pope Benedict XV died. Cardinal Mercier, together with his fellow Cardinals in the Roman Catholic Church, headed for Rome in order to participate in the conclave to elect a new Pope. Archbishop Davidson mused in another letter to Frere on the 4th February, 'what a strange thing it would be if your Cardinal host were to remain in the Vatican. I do not imagine that it is probable; but I have heard it suggested as not quite improbable'.[3] On the 6th February 1921, Achille

---

1. Letter of Abbé Portal to Lord Halifax, 21st December 1921, Portal Papers, Paris.
2. Letter of Cardinal Mercier to Archbishop Davidson, 15th December 1923, Archdiocese of Malines Archives, Box 2.
3. Letter of Archbishop Davidson to Walter Frere, 4th February 1922, Lambeth Palace Archives, Box 186, File 1.

Ratti was elected Pope and assumed the name Pius XI.[1] Ratti, who had been Archbishop of Milan, was a personal friend of Cardinal Mercier, and the day after the election, Mercier met with him in private. Among hand-written notes in the Malines archives, Mercier kept a little paper noting the things he had mentioned to the new pontiff, including the point about the meetings with the Anglicans which he had already broached with Benedict XV. Beside this particular point, Mercier had written Pope Pius XI's reaction, 'I see nothing but good from these meetings'.[2]

There now comes a rather confusing episode in which the desire and efforts towards ecumenical discussions between Rome and Canterbury ends up with crossed-wires and misunderstanding. The key to this move was the election of that same Pope Pius XI. With a new regime being established in Rome, a Jesuit professor at the Gregorian University, Fr Michel d'Herbigny,[3] whom Mercier had originally approached in September 1920 regarding the feasibility of ecumenical meetings, had the opportunity to discuss Anglican-Roman Catholic relations with Cardinal Gasparri, the Vatican Secretary of State, and mentioned in the course of their discussion the meetings which Mercier had originally proposed to him. Gasparri had evidently heard nothing of these proposed meetings, but he said that he was convinced that such meetings could be both useful and profitable.[1] D'Herbigny apparently added the

---

1. J.A. Dick records that this was the conclave wherein Cardinal Merry del Val came within a few votes of being himself elected Pope. He did, however, apparently break the conclave rules by mounting a campaign for his election, and Cardinal Gasparri was reported as saying that, 'during the conclave Merry del Val's ambitions knew no bounds so much so that he incurred excommunication'. cf. J.A. Dick, *The Malines Conversations Revisited,* (Leuven: University Press, 1989), pp. 77–78.
2. Aide-Memoire of Cardinal Mercier, on the occasion of an audience on the 7 February 1922.
   '5. The idea of the Holy Father Pope Benedict XV: private meetings with the Anglicans: Halifax, Dean of Wells, Frere: Resurrection
   6. The idea of private meetings with the Anglicans approved by Benedict XV. A first meetings was held on 8–10 December 1921: I describe the character and the results of this to reassure myself that I have the approval of my superiors.'
   R. 'I can see nothing but good from these meetings.'
Archdiocese of Malines Archives – Voyage à Rome.
3. Fr. Michel d'Herbigny SJ (1880–1957), had been a professor of Scripture at the Jesuit Scholasticate in Enghien (Belgium) from 1912–1921, before being transferred to Rome as Professor of Ecclesiology at the Gregorian University (1921–1923). He was later deeply involved in secret missions to Russia in trying to help the bishops of that country in the aftermath of the Bolshevik Revolution.

THE FIRST 'CONVERSATION' – THE ELECTION OF A NEW POPE

comment that if such meetings ever took place, it would probably be better to have them in Belgium, as there were some among the Church of England who would more readily accept an invitation to Malines than to Rome. The Secretary of State asked d'Herbigny to see if Cardinal Mercier would draw up a memorandum on the subject, and he would himself present it to the Pope. Consequently, d'Herbigny wrote to Cardinal Mercier on the 11th March 1922, communicating Cardinal Gasparri's request for a memorandum.[2]

At this point the complications begin to multiply, because in the same archive there is a letter from the same Cardinal Gasparri, dated the same day (11th April 1922), in which the Cardinal Secretary of State thanks Mercier for a letter of the 3rd April 1922, 'concerning a discreet encounter with the Anglicans', which letter Gasparri said he had placed before the eyes of the Pope.[3] The letter continues,

> 'The Holy Father fully approves of what Your Eminence has done up to now. Try to enlighten our brothers as to their error, he said, and thence to lead them to the truth and unity ... Continue your work therefore, most eminent Lord, with the same tact and the same prudence, and may the good God bless your zeal.'

Mercier replied to Gasparri on the 24th April 1922 saying that the response of the Pope 'affirmed his conscience and gave him great pleasure'. He concludes by saying that he would continue his modest efforts for reunion by counting on the prayers of fervent souls and the blessing of His Holiness.[4] So, at last, Cardinal Mercier had received the blessing of the Holy See for his initiative in arranging meetings with the Anglicans, and the way was now open in arranging such talks, but the problem now was – with which group?

Fr Michel d'Herbigny, having launched his proposal towards Mercier, was already trying to gather a group of interested Catholic theologians to make up one side of the proposed conference, and he seemed intent in making it an all-Jesuit affair. He entered immediately into correspon-

---

1. R.J. Lahey, *The Origins and Approval of the Malines Conversations*, Church History, Chicago, t. XLIII, September 1974, p. 371.
2. Letter of D'Herbigny to Mercier, 11th April 1922, Archdiocese of Malines Archives, B 1.
3. Letter of Gasparri to Mercier, 11th April 1922, Archdiocese of Malines Archives, B 1.
4. Handwritten copy of letter from Mercier to Gasparri, 24th April 1922, Archdiocese of Malines Archives, B 1.

dence with Fr Leslie Walker SJ of Oxford, who had recently published some articles on the subject of reunion, informing him that there was the possibility of either official or semi-official talks between the Roman and Anglican Churches.[1]

The initiative for this second series of talks, on a more official level than those of the 'Conversations', seems to have come from Revd G.K.A. Bell, Chaplain to the Archbishop of Canterbury, who had already written to d'Herbigny on the 30th March 1922 asking if anything could be suggested to realize unity between the Anglicans and the Church of Rome. D'Herbigny consulted with Cardinal Gasparri, and there is no doubt that Rome treated this as an official communication from the Church of England. D'Herbigny replied to Bell on the 11th April 1922 and, although he stated that he spoke 'with no authority', he also said 'with certitude' that on the part of the Holy See, such suggestions would find only 'sincere affection and goodwill'.[2] The Jesuit concluded by asking if a representative of the signatories of the Lambeth Appeal or a delegate of the Archbishop of Canterbury ('Lord Président')[3] could be sent, either to Rome or to Cardinal Mercier at Malines, to begin to confer with competence and authority on questions raised by the Appeal.[4]

Dr Bell replied to d'Herbigny almost immediately (1st May 1922), and this letter was significant because it took up with seriousness the suggestion of either official or at least semi-official talks between the two Churches. Bell wrote,

---

1. Letter of Walker to Mercier, 6th June 1922, Archdiocese of Malines Archives, B 1.
2. Letter marked 'Confidential – Not for publication in any form', from Fr d'Herbigny to Dr Bell, 11th April 1922, Malines Papers of Lord Halifax, File A4 271, Box 1.
Dr Bell also drew up a memorandum, a copy of which he sent to Halifax, of a meeting which he had on the 26th april 1922 with Fr Leslie Walker SJ. Bell sums him up as interested in reunion, knowledgeable, but unaware that meetings had already begun in Malines.
3. It is interesting to compare the difference of approach of Fr Michel d'Herbigny and Cardinal Mercier in addressing the Anglicans. Mercier, under the influence of Abbé Portal, always addressed Randall Davidson by his title of Archbishop of Canterbury and referred to the Anglicans as 'separated brothers'; Fr d'Herbigny, in accord with Roman thinking, went through all sorts of contortions to avoid using any title which might give some inkling of recognition of Anglican Orders, and hence his letter is addressed to the 'Lord President of the Lambeth Conference'. In Roman eyes, the Anglican authorities were pseudo-bishops.
4. Letter of d'Herbigny to Bell, 11th April 1922, Archdiocese of Malines Archives, B 1.
D'Herbigny drew up a summary of the request from Bell entitled *'Une demande venue de Cantorbéry'* for presentation to Cardinal Gasparri, together with his proposed reply to Bell. So even though he said he spoke with 'no authority', it is clear that his reply was approved by the Secretary of State.

THE FIRST 'CONVERSATION' – THE ELECTION OF A NEW POPE

'I greatly appreciate your courtesy in writing to me as you have done in your letter of April 11th. The words which you use with regards to the Appeal issued by the Lambeth Conference in August, 1920, are of great importance. I note your information as to the cordiality of the feelings for the advancement of the work of Reunion which are entertained by those who hold high office in the great Church which you serve. I cannot doubt that the manifestation of such feelings would be welcome to many of those who gave their signatures to the Appeal, and to many others to whom the cause of Christian Unity is dear. Great interest attaches to the opinion which you express as to the possibility of Conferences, whether in Rome or at Malines, Conferences moreover of an authoritative and competent character. I have had the opportunity of a full conversation with Father Walker with regard to this possibility, and indeed on the whole subject of your important letter, and since that conversation further communications have passed.'[1]

On the same day, 1st May 1922, Bell wrote to Fr Walker at Oxford, informing him that

'I have told the Archbishop of Canterbury of our talk last Wednesday, and I need not say that he was deeply interested in all he heard with regard to the important matter from Father d'Herbigny. I find that I was right in my impression that it would make a great difference to His Grace's view of the whole matter if he were to receive a communication from the Vatican itself, suggesting a Conference on Reunion, whether such Conference were to place (sic) in Rome or at Malines. I have only to add the assurance that such a suggestion would be most sympathetically received by the Archbishop. I know that there are difficulties. But in view of the fact that the Archbishop took the initial step in formally sending the Lambeth Appeal to the Cardinal Secretary of State for submission to the Pope, it would not seem unreasonable that the next step should lie with the Vatican authorities. I am sending a brief letter of thanks to Father d'Herbigny,[2] and you are of course quite at liberty to show him this letter if you think well.'[3]

1. Typed copy of a letter of Bell to d'Herbigny, 1st May 1922, Archives of Archdiocese of Malines, Box 1, Allegato IV, No. 7.
2. D'Herbigny had sent Bell a 2-page paper entitled '*Outline of provisional scheme for a conference between representatives of the Church of England and of the Churches in communion with Rome.*' Archdiocese of Malines Archives, Box 1, Allegato VI, No. 12.
3. Letter of Bell to Walker, 1st May 1922, Archdiocese of Malines Archives, Box 1, Allegato V, No. 9

The fact that Father Walker did use Bell's letter in his communications with d'Herbigny is evident from the fact that d'Herbigny sent some copies of correspondence to Cardinal Mercier on the 15th May 1922, and so they found their way into the Malines archives. In his reply dated the 19th May, Cardinal Mercier informed d'Herbigny for the first time that meetings of the kind he was proposing had, in fact, already begun the previous year. He explained that on the 6–7–8th of the previous December, they had held initial meetings in confidence with three Anglican theologians, who were very highly considered in their own Church, and who were very desirous of Catholic unity. He explained that the meeting had been kept secret, both in Belgium and in England, as he thought this to be an indispensable condition for their success. Mercier then added the curious phrase, 'I believe, nevertheless, that the Archbishop of Canterbury learned later about it, whereas Cardinal Bourne was unaware of it and, without doubt, is still unaware.'[1] Did Mercier really mean that neither the Archbishop of Canterbury nor Cardinal Bourne had known about the first Conversation? Or was he referring to the content of the discussions, as these had not been published or made public? The correspondence and reports which we have examined would surely tend to eliminate the first hypothesis, so the probability is that Mercier was emphasizing to d'Herbigny the 'private' nature of the Malines meeting and the cautious but limited nature of any official authorization by the authorities of either Church. This new proposal of d'Herbigny (and supposedly given support by Rome) outlined meetings which would have either official or semi-official backing from the respective competent authorities, and this is why Mercier begins his letter by saying, 'I will therefore await confidently an invitation from the Holy See'. Mercier also states in his letter his presumption that the two Catholic theologians mentioned in the documents he had received, Father Leslie Walker SJ and d'Herbigny himself, had not met with those in England who had already met with the Cardinal in Malines. For this reason, he continued, he thought it imprudent to instigate two parallel series of meetings with representatives of the same bodies, and so he would prefer to continue with the Conversations already begun, unless instructed to the contrary by the Roman authorities.[2]

1. Typed copy of letter from Mercier to d'Herbigny, 19th May 1922, Archdiocese of Malines Archives, B 1, No. 4.
2. Letter of Mercier to d'Herbigny, 19th May 1922, Archdiocese of Malines Archives, B.1, No. 4.

THE FIRST 'CONVERSATION' – THE ELECTION OF A NEW POPE

On the 31st May 1922, the Cardinal Secretary of State, Gasparri, wrote to Mercier detailing the history of the Bell-d'Herbingy correspondence, and inviting the Belgian Cardinal to request the Archbishop of Canterbury to send 'some representatives' to Malines for a first exchange of ideas on reunion between the two Churches. Gasparri stressed that this initiative should come from Mercier himself, should remain strictly personal and confidential, and, he insisted, should not be connected with the Anglican initiative to promote an inter-denominational movement for peace.[1] The exchanges should remain strictly within the field of religious questions.[2]

Finally, Father Leslie Walker SJ entered into the long list of correspondents to Cardinal Mercier. His letter of the 13th June 1922 is extremely illuminating, coming as it does from an English Roman Catholic priest, and reflecting something of the attitudes prevailing in the English Catholic Church of the period. After describing the history of his own involvement (and, incidentally, staking a claim for his own possible participation), he wrote that from his discussions with Dr Bell, he knew that the Archbishop of Canterbury, should a Conference be called, thought that the members should consist of accredited representatives of both Churches, and that the suggestion of a Conference should come from the Pope through the Secretary of State. 'Nothing has been done so far', he continued, 'beyond unofficial pourparlers, so that no harm will arise, if the scheme falls through. On the other hand, if a Conference is

---

1. This was probably a reference to the preparations under way for an ecumenical conference in Stockholm organized by the Life and Work movement, and reflects to some degree the Vatican's fears of any political tinge to its new and tentative involvement in ecumenical matters. cf. Roger Aubert, *Bulletin de l'Académie royale de Belgique*, t. LIII, p. 138, footnote (1).

2. Letter of Gasparri to Mercier, 31st May 1922 (Prot. No. 3856), Archdiocese of Malines Archives, B. 1.

In this same file (B. 1, No. 15) in the Malines Archives, there is a mysterious typed copy of a letter written in French, which purports to be from the Pope to Archbishop Davidson. This letter, which has no date and no signature, is, in effect, a direct invitation from the Pope to the Primate of England to send official representatives to Malines to discuss with Cardinal Mercier and 'our proper representatives' those doctrinal and practical problems which need to be resolved in order to establish the enlarged unity of all communions with the Apostolic See: ('... *devraient encore être résolue pour établir et manifester publiquement l'unité élargie de tous dans la communion de cette Chaire Apostolique* ...')

This may have been Mercier's attempt to help the Pope to draft a letter which would put the Malines discussions on an official footing in a satisfactory manner, and also giving Mercier the official support which he was seeking. There is no way of confirming whether this letter was actually sent to Rome or simply remained in Mercier's files.

possible in the opinion of our authorities, I think Anglicans would welcome it, and that good might ensue'.[1]

Walker expressed his personal opinion about the outcome of such proposed conferences in the following terms:

'With respect to the possible result I should like to say quite frankly that I am not over hopeful. The Anglicans understand quite clearly that the faith-basis of reunion must be our basis, not theirs; and it is on the understanding that we are not prepared to go back on past definitions of faith that they would meet us. The question here is whether they can be persuaded to accept our faith-basis, and <u>on other matters</u>[2] whether an accommodation can be reached which would meet their demands. The strength of the Protestant party within the Anglican Church is still sufficiently great to make the issue very doubtful.'[3]

Father Walker had by this stage obviously heard of the first Conversation at Malines from d'Herbigny, because he then began to undermine the basis of such meetings:

'I understand ... that Your Eminence has also been approached privately by a small group of Anglicans with a view to an unofficial conference. If I may be allowed to say so, I doubt whether a private Conference – and I have had some experience of them – can lead anywhere. It is not with private individuals, however estimable and however highly placed, that we must deal if we would expect results, but with official bodies, either with the Anglican Church as a whole or with, say, the English Church Union; and I doubt whether the English Church Union would as yet be prepared to enter into negotiations with us independently of the bishops of their Church, much as they despise them. Mr Bell agrees with me here, and assures me of what is evident to anyone living in this country, namely that private individuals do not represent the Church for which they claim to speak, but are almost invariably eccentric in one direction or another. If therefore your Eminence is prepared to go on with this matter I would urge that it be an official Conference of duly appointed representatives that be called together.'[4]

1. Confidential letter of Leslie Walker to Cardinal Mercier, 13th June 1922, Archdiocese of Malines Archives, B. 1, No. 6.
2. Underlining by Fr Walker.
3. Confidential letter of Leslie Walker to Cardinal Mercier, 13th June 1922, Archdiocese of Malines Archives, B. 1, No. 6.
4. Letter of Walker to Mercier, 13th June 1922, B 1., No. 6.

THE FIRST 'CONVERSATION' – THE ELECTION OF A NEW POPE

It is difficult to make sense of this second initiative from the Anglican side, for there is no doubt that Bell was not simply acting on his own authority, but that the Archbishop of Canterbury knew and approved of what he was doing,[1] and may even have been himself the initiator. Bell, in his biography of Archbishop Davidson, makes no reference at all to this correspondence or of the Archbishop's possible involvement in it. It is likely however, that Davidson was attempting to prod the Vatican into making some kind of official recognition or, at the very least, to acknowledge its involvement in private discussions with the Church of England at Malines, and was perhaps even using Walker and d'Herbigny to this end. That he remained suspicious of Rome is certain, noting in a letter to the Archbishop of York with reference to the proposed second series of talks that,

> 'It does not seem to me that we ought to turn it down abruptly, and on the other hand we must take care not to rush effusively into intercourse in which we have to deal with very clever – I do not want to say crafty – people'.[2]

This question of whether there should be a second parallel series of talks at Malines which would include d'Herbigny and Walker under the auspices of Cardinal Mercier, was, as we have seen, rejected by the Cardinal in his letter of the 19th May 1922 to d'Herbigny, but the other possibility of expanding the number of participants at the Conversations was a subject which remained under consideration virtually till the eve of the second Conversation in March 1923. Mercier was very open to this possibility, and it was only the reluctance of Archbishop Davidson (who felt himself being pushed to nominate 'representatives' and consequently to make it official from the Anglican side) which convinced Mercier not to pursue the idea.

It is clear also that Lord Halifax was seriously considering Fr Walker SJ as a possible participant in the second Conversation. In recounting to Portal the results of his visit to Cardinal Bourne, he noted in passing that he was writing the letter on his way to Oxford to visit the Jesuits, among whom was Father Walker 'of whom we have spoken'. After an initial enthusiastic reaction to Fr Walker, Halifax then began to read some of

---

1. Bell and Walker had a private meeting at Lambeth Palace on the 26th April 1922, following which meeting Bell drew up a memorandum for the Archbishops of York and Canterbury. He also sent a copy to Lord Halifax.
Dick, *The Malines Conversations Revisited*, pp. 82–83.
2. Letter of Davidson to Lang, 24th April 1922, Lambeth Palace Archives, Box 189.

Walker's published articles, and his ideas about Walker's suitability as a participant began to change.[1]

(iv) Publication of Cardinal Mercier's Pastoral Letter to his Diocese, and his request to Halifax to translate and publish it in English.

Throughout the whole first half of 1922, in the midst of the flurry of correspondence and the efforts of Mercier to obtain for the Roman Catholic side of the Conversations some form of recognition from Rome, it seems odd that when the Cardinal received the first official messages of support from Rome (in Gasparri's letters of the 3rd April and 31st May 1922), Mercier did not immediately inform Halifax or Portal. Undoubtedly, the unexpected appearance of Fr d'Herbigny and Fr Walker on the scene at exactly this point, with their proposal (supported by Gasparri, moreover) for Conferences with official or semi-official representatives, caused the Cardinal to hold back his information in case Rome should support this new cause rather than the Conversations already initiated. If this were to be so, then fresh encouragement to Halifax and Portal at this particular moment might have caused even greater hurt and disillusionment at a later stage if a new series of Conferences were insisted upon by Rome. This would be very much in keeping with Mercier's charity and regard for his friends, and so the Cardinal maintained silence on the matter. Hence, neither Halifax, Portal, the Archbishop of Canterbury nor, presumably, Cardinal Bourne of Westminster, were given any inkling that Rome was now in favour of the principle of Anglican-Catholic talks.

In September 1922, however, the whole affair was brought to the notice of the general public by the publication by Lord Halifax of a pamphlet entitled *A Call to Reunion, by Viscount Halifax, arising out of Discussions with Cardinal Mercier, to which is appended a translation of the Cardinal's Pastoral Letter to his Diocese.*[2] Originally this was intended as a response to a request from Cardinal Mercier for the publication of an English translation of his February 1922 Pastoral Letter to his Diocese. Mercier's Pastoral concerned the papacy (highlighted by the

---

1. 'The reunion of the Church of England with Rome on the basis proposed by Fr Walker will *never* succeed' (emphasis by Halifax). Letter of Halifax to Portal, 30th November 1922, Portal Papers, Paris.
2. Published in London by Mowbrays, 1922.

THE FIRST 'CONVERSATION' – THE ELECTION OF A NEW POPE

recent election of Pius XI) and the rights of the successors of St Peter. But Halifax was not at all keen to publish it unadorned as he considered some phrases and expressions would fall harshly on English ears. However, once started on the project, the Viscount warmed to his subject and, together with a foreword, included also an account of the first Conversation and the text of the Memorandum which had been discussed. Because of the agreement to keep the Conversations private, Halifax had to obtain the consent of the other participants, and although not all agreed on the wisdom of his project, Halifax went ahead with publication.

Archbishop Davidson did his best to distance himself from any involvement with the publication. He told Halifax in a letter from Venice on 18th September that, 'he had no objection to the pamphlet', provided that it stood as Halifax's work alone.[1] Still from Venice, he addressed another letter to the Archbishop of York stating that neither archbishop should be involved in the publication as this would seem to make them a party to the Conversations – especially as they were negotiating with the Non-conformists at the same time, and had not said anything to them about dialogue with Rome.[2]

With the publication of his pamphlet, Lord Halifax lost no time in following it up. In a series of letters with the Archbishops of Canterbury and York, and with Armitage Robinson, it seemed that all were convinced that some kind of recognition should come from Rome. The problem was, how that response was to be elicited. In a letter to Robinson on 6th October 1922, Halifax suggested that one way might be to ask Archbishop Davidson to write to him (Halifax) mentioning that

> 'if Cardinal Mercier writes to him to ask for the appointment of representatives of the Church of England to confer about reunion, he and the Archbishop of York will at once consider how to comply with his wishes and who to send.'[3]

---

1. Letter of Davidson to Halifax, 18th September 1922, Lambeth Palace Archives, Box 186, File 1.
Halifax had actually asked both Archbishop Davidson and Cardinal Bourne for a note in support of the idea of the Conferences which he could publish. Letter of Halifax to Portal, 16th September 1922, Portal Papers, Paris.
2. Letter of Davidson to Lang, September 1922, Lambeth Palace Archives, Box 186, File 1.
3. Letter of Halifax to Robinson, 6th October 1922, Lambeth Palace Archives, Box 186, File 2.

In a similar vein he had already written to Cardinal Mercier urging him to put before the Pope all that had transpired and had been written, and to urge the Holy Father to authorize the necessary conferences with a view to facilitating such steps as might lead to the reconciliation of Rome and Canterbury.[1] Mercier now gave the first definite indication that he had already sought and obtained through a confidential channel such authorization from Rome, and he assured Halifax that the continuation of the meetings at Malines was thought to be a good thing by the Vatican:

> 'It is already several months since I received, through an authoritative but confidential channel, the assurance that our exchange of views was approved at the Vatican and that their continuation was seen there to be a good thing ... I had represented our three friendly visitors to Malines on December 6–8 1921, as private individuals, however high their status in England and in the Anglican Church. Now I infer from your letter that the Anglicans with whom we shall engage in conversation the next time will be "Anglicans named by the Archbishop of Canterbury in order to consider, etc ...".'[2]

Despite this personal assurance of the Belgian Primate that he had backing from Rome, this was still not sufficient for the English Anglican bishops. Archbishop Davidson, in a very considered letter to Lord Halifax, spelt out clearly his point of view and his reticence. The letter, dated 30th October 1922, is in two parts, the first marked *Private* and

---

1. Letter of Halifax to Mercier, 22nd September 1922, Archdiocese of Malines Archives, A.1.
Halifax ends his letter by saying 'This ... seems to be the one step necessary at the present time'.
2. Letter of Mercier to Halifax, 29th September 1922, Malines Papers of Lord Halifax, File A4 271, Box 1.
It is interesting to observe that at this delicate stage of negotiations for authorization that Lord Halifax himself began to question whether this would change the nature of the Conversations:
'But, and this is the big question – are we really prepared for such formal meetings? It would be a terrible thing if such formal conferences should fail – that would be the end of all negotiations, at least for the present.
The choice of participants to take part in such conferences would be extremely difficult, and I ask myself if it would not be better, as a first step, that there should be conferences which are not formally authorized but rather with the understanding that they were being held with the good will and approbation of Rome on the one hand and our Archbishops on the other.' Letter of Halifax to Portal, 8th November 1922, Portal Papers, Paris.

THE FIRST 'CONVERSATION' – THE ELECTION OF A NEW POPE

addressed to Halifax alone, and the second, quite separate, intended for forwarding to Cardinal Mercier. The text of the first reads;

'My dear Halifax, I have treated you very badly. I ought many days ago to have written to you on the very important matter of the intercourse with Cardinal Mercier, but the pressure on me has been beyond almost anything in my experience. The confusion of public affairs at home and abroad has had its bearing upon my own daily work and everything has suffered. I enclose a letter of a rather less personal character which I shall be glad that you should transmit, if you desire to do so, to the Cardinal. I am afraid that you may think me a little backward in eagerness of response or readiness to accept whatever in the way of conferences may be offered us. But I do not feel that I can in honesty go further. The conference will I think do good whether it be official or unofficial, but if it is to have even a semi-official character the Vatican must go *'pari passu'* with ourselves in giving authorization thereto. Their mode of giving it may be their own affair, but it must be given in such a way as to make it clear that it is incapable of subsequent repudiation. This seems to me really essential. Your pamphlet will awaken, no doubt is already awakening, wide interest. I note the generous allowance you make for the manner of the Cardinal's expression of his view about the claims of the Pope on the allegiance of Christendom. What you say on p. 21 is undoubtedly true. None the less it is well I think that English readers should have before them what those claims really include and phrases like those which the Cardinal uses (say in the middle of p. 28 of your translation, and again near the foot of the page) cannot possibly be ignored when we are promoting the kind of conference which may be useful. As I have said, I believe in its usefulness whether it be official or unofficial, but my own action in the matter has to be very carefully guarded if I am to be faithful to what I believe to be a trust laid upon us by God as well as men. To me there is immense interest and pathos in your appeal to us. During these many years you have been in the forefront of our endeavours to promote such reunion as may be wise as well as practicable. If all the difficulties are still insuperable – and indeed it is not easy to exaggerate their formidableness – you at least have faced them bravely.'[1]

---

1. Letter of Davidson to Halifax, 30th October 1922, Lambeth Palace Archives, Box 186, File 2.

The second of the letters, which was enclosed, and which was intended for Cardinal Mercier, stated very clearly Davidson's conditions. The text reads as follows:

'My dear Lord Halifax,
I have been considering carefully what you have told me as to your desire that such conferences as you have already held with Cardinal Mercier may be continued or resumed and that others may take part in it who should along with yourself be nominated by the English Archbishops, not of course as plenipotentiaries but as accredited spokesmen carrying behind them the weight of such formal authority as we can give them by being ourselves responsible for entrusting them with the task. The matter is so important to the world's life and so immense in its possibilities and in its bearing on the Faith of Christendom that I cannot doubt that we should be right, if the necessary conditions are satisfied, in furthering the proposal. But these necessary conditions are of very great importance. I could not lend myself to giving authoritative 'mission' to spokesmen of the Anglican Church for conferring with spokesmen of the Church of Rome unless there be an authorization on the part of the Vatican corresponding to that which is given from Lambeth. It is not for me to prescribe the exact manner in which that authorization should be conveyed – whether by a letter from His Holiness the Pope, or the Cardinal Secretary of State on his behalf, or otherwise. But it must emanate from the centre and not from any ecclesiastical leader however distinguished he be in person or in office. If anyone goes from England as sent by me or the Archbishop of York and myself to take part in such a conference those with whom he confers must hold credentials not less authoritative. I repeat that it does not follow from this that what such emissaries might agree to say would be binding upon those who send them or upon the Church at large. They would go to confer and to make suggestions – nothing more. The suggestions would have to be considered by those whose responsibility is of a central kind. I feel it necessary to make this clear at the outset of any new discussions or arrangements which may be in contemplation.
Having said this by way of caution I want to add the assurance, which in truth you do not need, of the deep earnestness of my desire and prayer on behalf of that unity in the Church of God whereof Our Master himself spoke. In our *Appeal to all Christian Peoples*, put forth by the Lambeth Conference, the Bishops made it abundantly

THE FIRST 'CONVERSATION' – THE ELECTION OF A NEW POPE

clear what is our united feeling, our united aim, and our united prayer. We may surely rely upon the highest blessing from Our Lord himself upon those who can in any way set forward so great a thing.'[1]

The Archbishop's chaplain and biographer, G.K. Bell, reports that in a private conversation on the following day (31st October 1922), the Archbishop remarked that, 'an authoritative request from the Vatican, or at least an authoritative endorsement of Cardinal Mercier by the Vatican, was indispensable. If Mercier died, it would be perfectly possible for the Vatican to disclaim all responsibility for Mercier's action with the observation that he was certainly "a very good man, but a little weak in his old age". If, however, the Vatican were committed, it would be a very different matter.'[2]

(v) Mercier's request to Pius XI for support for the Conversations, and his receipt of the letter of authorization.

When Cardinal Mercier received Halifax's next letter dated 9th November 1922, together with the enclosure of the Archbishop's text, he was left with little choice other than to approach Rome again if he wished the Conversations to continue. What authorization he had already received had been a personal one addressed only to himself. What was now needed was a more specific approval which he could show to the Anglicans as proof that Rome really was supporting the meetings. On 14th November 1922, Mercier decided to write directly to the Pope. After two short paragraphs referring to the Russian Orthodox, he launched into his request by stating that the Pope had doubtless seen Lord Halifax's pamphlet on Reunion (which indeed the Pope had not), and then recalled the informal meeting which had already been held at Malines in 1921. He stated that the Anglicans wished these 'Conversations' to continue, but that the Archbishop of Canterbury was desirous of some sign of goodwill from the Roman authorities. Hence, requested Mercier, would the Holy Father authorize him to say that the Holy See approved and encouraged these Conversations? Lest there be any hesitation in the Pope's mind, Mercier reminded him that Rome had little to lose if the talks were not successful – the blame and humiliation could be

---

1. Letter of Davidson to Halifax (intended for Cardinal Mercier), 30th October 1922, Lambeth Palace Archives, Box 186, File 2.
2. Bell, *Randall Davidson, Archbishop of Canterbury*, Vol. 2, p. 1257.

left at Mercier's door. If they were successful, then Mercier was totally ready to transfer them to Rome or elsewhere at the Holy See's request.[1]

The Belgian Cardinal did not have long to wait before a reply arrived. In a letter dated 25th November, Cardinal Gasparri informed him that, although the Pope had not yet received a copy of Halifax's pamphlet – which he would very much like to read – he authorized Mercier to tell the Anglicans that the Holy See approved and encouraged the Conversations and prayed with all his heart that God would bless them.[2]

Having now obtained the type of explicit authorization from Rome that both he and the Archbishop of Canterbury had been seeking, the Cardinal wrote immediately to Halifax with the news, and Halifax informed Archbishop Davidson. The Archbishop asked if the Cardinal could now write directly to him as 'a three-cornered correspondence, though in some cases useful, is never quite satisfactory; it always has an element of possible misconception and mistake'.[3] Cardinal Mercier responded to this request on the 10th January 1923, explaining to the Archbishop the approval he had received from Rome, and also raising the possibility of increasing the number of persons at the next Conversation:

> 'If you are able to name as your delegates the three persons with whom we have had a first exchange of views, and possibly to add to them others selected by yourself, we should, on our side, be ready to name an equal number of friends to collaborate in our effort for reunion ... So arranged, the fresh conversations, without being authoritative, would be invested with more importance and weight'.[4]

The Archbishop's reply expressed his satisfaction with the recognition

---

1. Typed copy of letter of Mercier to Pope Pius XI, 14th November 1922, Archdiocese of Malines Archives, B.1.
R.H. Lahey points out that, paradoxically, in this same letter Mercier requests Pius XI to proclaim as a dogma of faith the universal mediation of Mary, probably not realizing that this would add further complications for the Church of England. Lahey, *The Origins and Approval of the Malines Conversations*, t. XLIII, p. 380, footnote 69.
2. Letter of Gasparri to Mercier (Prot. No.10726), 25th November 1922, original in Archdiocese of Malines Archives, B1.
The all-important phrase of this letter in the original is: '*He [the Holy Father] authorizes Your Eminence to say to the Anglicans that the Holy See approves and encourages your Conversations and prays with all his heart that the Good God will bless them*'.
3. Bell, *Randall Davidson, Archbishop of Canterbury*, Vol. 2, p. 1258.
4. Letter of Mercier to Davidson, 10th January 1923, reproduced in full in Bell, *Randall Davidson, Archbishop of Canterbury*, Vol. 2, p. 1258.

THE FIRST 'CONVERSATION' – THE ELECTION OF A NEW POPE

from Rome, but he resisted Mercier's suggestion for adding other members to the informal conversations, saying that he thought this was what Mercier would prefer.[1] In fact, this was not at all what Mercier preferred, as he was hoping that the Archbishop would nominate his own spokesman and even suggest the programme for discussion which, after study together in the Malines group, would then be taken by each side for study and examination by their own experts and theologians.[2]

Mercier obviously envisaged an ever-growing involvement of both sides.[3] However, because of 'the great reserve of the two Archbishops of Canterbury and York',[4] the Cardinal agreed to welcome the same participants as before at his palace at Malines in March 1923.

(vi) The beginnings of adverse reaction, both from Cardinal Bourne and from the Anglican side.

When Cardinal Mercier had received the Gasparri letter of authorization

---

1. Letter of Davidson to Mercier, 2nd February 1923, Bell, *Randall Davidson, Archbishop of Canterbury,* Vol. 2, p. 1259.
2. Some of Mercier's ideas are similar to (and may even be based on) the programme for the Conversations as outlined by Walter Frere in a letter from his community at Mirfield to Archbishop Davidson on 4th December 1922. Frere wrote down the results of his reflections, covering some nine points, but which included the following proposals:
   1. to bring the Conversations more under the shelter of the Lambeth Conference Appeal, and given the same (or similar) status as the talks with the Nonconformists:
   2. to keep the Church of England side confined only to the two Archbishops of Canterbury and York, and to avoid for the present the Scottish and Irish bishops;
   3. a two-level group, having those appointed as envoys to the Conversations, and also a larger and more representative group which would include the Evangelicals and the Broad Church. (Some names were even suggested such as 'Headlam and Kidd, perhaps others from Oxford; Nairn as Regius Professor and Whitney from Cambridge; Goudge and Gore from London; Moulsdale from Durham; some representing theological colleges, etc.) This would have the advantage of carrying a larger weight of opinion (both Church and public), and also put the whole of the next move upon a much more solid and broad basis';
   4. the larger Conference would have the responsibility of amending and adding to whatever draft of instruction or memorandum was drawn up by the groups of envoys.
   Letter of Frere to Davidson, 4th December 1922, Lambeth Palace Archives, Box 186, File 3.
3. 'I fear that the Archbishop has misunderstood me in this matter. My intention was not at all to chase away new members from the forthcoming conference, especially his delegate or delegates. I wanted, on the contrary, that if he felt that he could not attend the conference himself, to assist at least with his delegate'.
Letter of Mercier to Halifax, 4th February 1923, Malines Papers of Lord Halifax, File A4 271, Box 2.
4. Letter of Mercier to Halifax, 12th February 1923, Malines Papers of Lord Halifax, File A4 271, Box 2.

in November 1922, one of the first things he did was to write to Cardinal Bourne of Westminster informing his colleague of what had taken place at Malines the previous December, and of the approval of the Holy See for these Conversations to continue. Mercier explained that he wished to keep Bourne 'in touch with what had happened since then', and asked for prayers and any advice that the English Cardinal could offer.[1]

Cardinal Bourne replied on the 4th December 1922, acknowledging Mercier's letter and enclosing some newspaper clippings from *The Tablet* and *The Universe*, both of which were critical of the Anglican efforts for reunion. Bourne's letter reflected his own reservations about the affair.[2] The letter states in full:

'My dear Lord Cardinal,
I am most grateful for your letter and for the information that you give me as to the attitude of the Holy See regarding the informal conferences with Lord Halifax and his friends. Lord Halifax came to see me before his visit to Malines, and called again the other day to place me '*au courant*' of the situation. While I have the highest respect for his entire good faith and excellent intentions, I am convinced that he is far from clear as to his own viewpoint. He has always been very vague and inconsequent. Moreover he represents only an infinitesimal group of Anglicans who, while they admit the need of a central authority, are by no means convinced that the actual existence of such an authority is *an essential part of the Divine Constitution of the Church*. The enclosed article in the '*Tablet*' states, I think, quite fairly the present position of Anglicanism which has never been more divided and confused than it is now. Still I think that these informal conferences may well be encouraged, though in my opinion it will be a *very long time* before anything definite can emerge from them.
I was very sorry to hear that Your Eminence has been unwell, and I trust that you are now quite well again,

Yours always affectionately in J.C.,
F. Card. Bourne, Abp. of Westminster.'

---

1. Typed copy of letter of Mercier to Bourne, 30th November 1922, Archdiocese of Malines Archives, B.1.
2. Original hand-written letter of Bourne to Mercier, 4th December 1922, Archdiocese of Malines Archives, B.1.

THE FIRST 'CONVERSATION' – THE ELECTION OF A NEW POPE

The importance of this letter, together with Mercier's of the 30th November 1922, is that it disproves the allegation of Ernest Oldmeadow, Cardinal Bourne's biographer (and also editor of *The Tablet* from April 1923), that Bourne knew nothing about the Conversations till they all became public knowledge at the end of 1923. Cardinal Bourne's attitude at this time might be described as neutral but pessimistic, but his attitude gradually changed in the course of time as events unfolded and he was indubitably influenced by the growing negative Press campaign in Britain.[1] There was a growing apprehensiveness among English Catholics about these meetings between Anglicans and Continental Catholics, and resentment in England that they themselves, the obvious channels of communication, were being avoided or ignored.

Abbé Portal was also growing uneasy at the obstacles and negative portents which seemed to be re-appearing from the Anglican Orders affair. The appearance of the Jesuits on the scene (Walker and d'Herbigny) aroused an almost English mistrust, and, as he expressed in a letter to Halifax, 'the conflict of rival influences will soon begin at Rome, and the Cardinal must be careful not to furnish our adversaries with any weapons they can make use of. I hope your Archbishops realize the Cardinal's position and will do what they can to assist him. That he should have already written as he has to the Archbishop of Canterbury is a fact of importance'.[2] 'You know as well as I do', he wrote on the 16th of January 1923, 'that the day Merry del Val thinks he can put a spoke in the wheel he will not fail to do so'.[3]

The Archbishop of Canterbury, in the meantime, was having his own problems. He had confided to the other Anglican bishops, then assembled in London, what had taken place at Malines, and had encoun-

---

1. The two articles contained in this file in the Malines Archives are one from the Rev O.R. Vassall-Phillips, CSSR, in *The Universe* (27th October 1922) and a two-page leader (unsigned) in *The Tablet* (2nd December 1922). Both of these are highly critical of Lord Halifax's pamphlet 'A Call to Reunion', and also the Viscount's speech to the English Church Union in Sheffield, using as principal argument the fact that Halifax represented only one small faction of a very divided Church.
2. Letter of Portal to Halifax, 10th January 1923, Malines Papers of Lord Halifax, File A4 271, Box 2.
3. Letter of Portal to Halifax, 16th January 1923, Malines Papers of Lord Halifax, File A4 271, Box 2.
'You know as well as I do that the day Merry del Val thinks he can put a spoke in the wheel he will not fail to do so, both for the event in itself and for personal motives with regards to the Cardinal'.

tered from them expressions of considerable doubt and misgivings.[1] The problem of the revision of the Prayer Book was another element which caused him anxiety, as he had to ensure that it passed through the Church's Convocation, General Assembly and the British Parliament. One success on the horizon was the recognition of the validity of Anglican Orders by the Patriarch of Constantinople on behalf of the Orthodox Church,[2] so much so that Portal thought he was paying too much attention to the Orthodox and not enough to the Roman Catholics, but in truth the Archbishop felt much uneasiness about the forthcoming Roman encounter.

The situation on the eve of the second Conversation at Malines was consequently a rather tense one, with many tender and even sore points skirted round but not resolved. The enthusiasm of Mercier, Halifax and Portal for the continuation and even development of these meetings was undoubtedly the force that carried them through to the next stage, where the participants went to Malines with at least a degree of official backing and authorization from their respective authorities. Once again their sincerity, integrity and obvious deep-rooted desire to advance the cause of reunion sustained them, but this would be the last Conversation at which their participation as simple 'friends' would predominate. After this second Conversation, the 'experts', whether historians or theologians, would increasingly take over the agenda and discussions in an attempt to allay the fears of the leaders of their respective Churches.

---

1. One outspoken critic was Herbert Hensley Henson (1863–1947), Bishop of Durham. He objected to Davidson giving any official cognizance to something which he considered a personal initiative of Halifax: 'The representatives of the Church of England are still to be Lord Halifax, Father Frere, and Dean Armitage Robinson. I objected that these gentlemen were not properly competent to speak for Anglicanism, since the first had declared himself in substantial agreement with the Roman Church, the second was one of the new Anglo-Catholics, and the third was a very cryptic type of Anglican'.
Herbert Hensley Henson, *Retrospect of an Unimportant Life*, 3 vols., (London: 1942–1950), vol. 2, p. 139.
2. G.K.A. Bell, *Documents on Christian Unity*, (London: Oxford Univ. Press, 1930), pp. 93–99.

5

The second and third 'Conversations' – (13th/14th March – 7th/8th November 1923); some intermediary problems.

(i) Preparation of the Agenda for the second meeting.

As preparation for the next meeting at Malines, the members of the Anglican side decided that it was important to prepare the agenda together. Despite the wishes of Cardinal Mercier for an increased membership of the Conversations, he accepted Archbishop Davidson's reluctance on the matter and the representatives remained the same six persons who had met in December 1921, three Anglicans and three Roman Catholics. It was again the Anglicans who prepared the Memorandum for discussion, although a suggestion that the Catholics prepare a similar document never seems to have been followed through.[1] Consequently, towards the end of February 1923, J. Armitage Robinson (the Dean), Dr Frere and Halifax spent two days drawing up a Memorandum for discussion at Malines, the Dean having already consulted with the Archbishop on the 21st of that same month. This memorandum turned out to be restricted principally to practical issues concerning the Church of England which would have to be solved were doctrinal agreements ever reached between the two Churches. A copy of the proposed Memorandum was sent to Cardinal Mercier prior to the meeting, and the preface read, 'Following the precedent of the previous conversations, we desire to send beforehand to your Eminence a short memorandum specifying some points with which we suggest that the approaching conference should deal. Though only the same representatives will come as before, they will come with a certain measure of authority and recognition from the Archbishops of Canterbury and York. And if the extent of the recognition which their Graces have felt able to give seems disappointing, we would point out that the conferences deal with matters affecting the Anglican communion as a whole, and that the Archbishops of the two Provinces only are naturally

---

1. Lockhart, *Charles Lindley Viscount Halifax*, Vol. 2, p. 287.

restricted in the amount of countenance which they on their own account can give in matters which properly concern the larger body. At our former conference we considered at some length the question of the Papal Supremacy in the light of the Decree of Infallibility. We desire now to leave aside dogmatic controversy in order to consider possible methods of a practical kind by which, supposing a reasonable measure of agreement on doctrinal matters were reached, the Anglican communion as a whole might be brought into union, more or less complete in the first instance, with the Holy See.'[1] The practical nature of the contents of this Memorandum were a surprise to Cardinal Mercier, who was expecting a more doctrinal-centred discussion, but he nevertheless accepted the proposed agenda.[2]

Two particular aspects of this agenda can be noted immediately. First that the *fact* of reunion as objective of the Conversations is taken almost for granted. This is in sharp contrast to the gradual *growth* of unity coming from sharing of differences which the commission preparing for the Faith and Order conference was proposing as a methodology for their 1925 meeting in Lausanne, and which will be considered later in full. The second aspect to note is that the practical nature of the agenda for this second Conversation evidently reflects more the membership and experiences of the individual Anglican participants than it would of the wider Anglican communion. As J.G. Lockhart points out in his biography of Lord Halifax, this emphasis on practical issues seems out of place at this particular point in the Conversations, as there were many much more serious points of dogma and doctrine to be settled before even the smallest practical issue could be dealt with, but, on the other hand, by taking some of the practical issues now and seeing if there were indeed possible solutions to them, then the real implications of reunion would be made clearer and it would be possible to revert once again to the doctrinal differences. If, however, it were obvious that there were no

---

1. Lord Halifax, *The Conversations at Malines (1921–1925), Original Documents*, pp. 79–80.
2. The memorandum did conclude with the following phrase, indicating the purpose of a 'practical' agenda: 'The topics of a practical nature which we have outlined appear to us to call for preliminary consideration. If an understanding could be reached as to the solution of the questions thus raised, it would pave the way to further conferences of a yet more authoritative kind'. Lord Halifax, *The Conversations at Malines (1921–1925), Original Documents*, Annex III, p. 82.

practical solutions to the question of reunion, then to have held detailed doctrinal discussions would have been a waste of time.[1]

Nevertheless, the lack of doctrinal content at this second Conversation is still more surprising from the instructions that the Archbishop of Canterbury had written out for inclusion by the Anglicans in the discussion; 'Don't detract from the importance of the XXXIX Articles. Don't budge an inch as to the necessity of carrying the East with us in ultimate Reunion steps. Bear constantly in mind that in any admission made as to what Roman leadership or "primacy" may mean, we have to make it quite clear too that which it must not mean – i.e. some of the very things which the Cardinal's Pastoral claims for it'.[2] What the Anglican Memorandum did in fact present in general terms was:

1. The historical development of the Anglican communion, from twenty-one bishops at the time of the Reformation, to a world-wide communion of three hundred and sixty eight bishops, with its own particular rites and customs. What account, therefore, was to be taken of this historical development and expansion of the Church of England?
2. The jurisdiction of the Pope in the eventuality of reunion. What effect would this have on the principle of non-interference in local affairs?
3. The possibility of the granting of the pallium by the Pope to the Archbishop of Canterbury; this was in connection with the regularization of Anglican Orders.
4. The position of the existing Roman Catholic hierarchy in England.

The Anglican party left for Belgium on Tuesday the 13th March 1923, and again were guests of Cardinal Mercier at his palace in Malines. The meetings were scheduled for the 14th and 15th of March. The membership of both groups was exactly the same as at the first Conversation:

---

1. Lockhart, *Charles Lindley Viscount Halifax*, Vol. 2, pp. 287–288.
In a letter from Halifax to Portal, the Viscount wrote: 'There would be a real advantage in discussing the question of those rights recognised by the Holy See vis-à-vis Canterbury rather than the theological question of the extension of the Pope's power. It is the practical questions which will interest the English more than the theological questions.' Letter of March 1923 (no precise date on letter, but referring to preparations for the second Conversation), Portal Papers Paris.
2. Bell, *Randall Davidson, Archbishop of Canterbury*, Vol. 2, pp. 1260–1261. The reference here to the 'Cardinal's Pastoral' is to Cardinal Mercier's 1922 Pastoral Letter to his clergy on the occasion of the election of Pope Pius XI, which Halifax had translated and published in English in his pamphlet '*A Call to Reunion*', (London: Mowbrays, 1922).

Mercier, Portal and Van Roey on the Roman Catholic side; Robinson, Frere and Halifax as the Anglican group.

(ii) The discussions of the second Conversation.

On the morning of the 14th March 1923, the Cardinal opened the session by welcoming the participants, and expressing his satisfaction that all the members of the previous meeting had once again been able to come. Straight away, however, he asked the question which was on the minds of all the Roman Catholic members – namely, what degree of authorization had the Anglican members received from the authorities of their Church? The Anglicans replied by stating that the two archbishops had authorized the present participants. Although they had not chosen the participants, the Archbishop of Canterbury had stated in a private letter that 'they were a wise choice',[1] and the Archbishop of York was of the same opinion. In addition, the Archbishop of Canterbury had also informed the other Anglican bishops about the Conversations, and they had also given their approval to the authorization which he had extended. The Roman Catholics responded by stating their surprise that the approbation given by the archbishops had not been more formal, and Abbé Portal pointed out that such a mandate to authorize discussions with other Churches had already been given by the Lambeth Conference. To this it was replied that it was not due to a lack of good will on the part of the archbishops, but simply a desire not to involve all the bishops of the Anglican communion at this particular time for, as Frere pointed out, they felt that they could not go any further without making public what was already in process.

Mgr Van Roey enquired if the Memorandum as presented was a fair reflection of the views of the body of Anglicans in general, to which Robinson replied that although it had been composed by the three Anglicans present, they themselves represented different aspects of the Church of England; in any case, the Memorandum did not offer solutions but simply questions, and these questions were ones which would interest almost every member of the Church of England sympathetic to reunion. Lord Halifax confirmed the Dean's statement, adding that the general public would accept very well the idea that such practical

---

1. Lord Halifax, *The Conversations at Malines (1921–1925), Original Documents*, p. 28.

matters as dealt with in the Memorandum were important in discussions of reunion. Portal noted that he thought it important to educate public opinion on these matters.

On the points of the Memorandum itself, the Cardinal began by stating that, although such answers as they might come up with at these conversations were purely conjectural, they would perhaps serve a useful purpose in preparing the ground for later. He then asked what the position of the Archbishop of Canterbury was with regard to his jurisdiction over the other bishops. The reply was that, as with the other archbishops, he exercised metropolitan authority over his own province. Additionally, as Archbishop of Canterbury, he was regarded as the nominal centre and head of the Anglican communion, without having any practical jurisdiction over those dioceses in communion with Canterbury. As such, he convoked any world-wide conferences such as the Lambeth gatherings, and he presided at them. His advice was sought, but he could not impose his will on the bishops of other provinces. Dr Robinson explained further that this was the reason for emphasizing the development of the Anglican Church in the Memorandum. Not only had the Church grown and developed, but also its system of organization which gave a certain unity to the Church. If union came about, it would be with the whole of the Anglican communion, and it was hence necessary to ask if the powers claimed by the Pope could be harmonized with the present organization of the Anglican communion? Would it be possible, for instance, to accept papal supremacy in a way which did not impinge on the powers of each local bishop,[1] reserving to the Pope only those questions which concerned the general interests of the universal Church?

Abbé Portal explained that there were two schools of Catholic thought on this matter. The first saw the derivation of all matters of jurisdiction directly from the Pope. The second school of thought argued that the jurisdiction of the local bishops came directly from Our Lord as to the Apostles, but it was clearly understood that the exercise of this jurisdiction had to be authorized by the Pope. Portal added that the granting or authorization of such jurisdiction had a varied background according to

---

1. The difficulty which the Dean of Wells was trying to overcome in this point was the accepted axiom of the Church of England that '*no foreign authority has jurisdiction in England*'.
cf. Lord Halifax, *The Conversations at Malines (1921–1925), Original Documents*, p. 39.

the period of history and countries concerned, and he cited the example of jurisdiction having been granted to heads or patriarchs simply on the grounds of being in communion with the Church of Rome. Mgr Van Roey noted that it was important in discussing this matter to distinguish between the Pope's 'rights' and the 'exercise of those rights'. The Pope could never renounce his 'right' to ordinary and immediate jurisdiction, but he could, in practice, restrain his exercise of those rights and only intervene in exceptional and important matters. The Cardinal noted that sometimes what began as a purely local affair had repercussions throughout the universal Church.

A short discussion was held on the future position of the Roman Catholic Church in England should reunion take place. The Anglicans did not wish to take the initiative in suggesting changes, but the Roman Catholic participants did not consider a duality of rite co-existing in England a great problem. This type of situation had occurred elsewhere, especially in the East.

The tender issue of Anglican Orders was next on the agenda. Dean Robinson noted in his journal the intervention which he had made. He told the meeting that the Roman Church had done them a 'cruel wrong' in rejecting their Orders, and one which would never be forgiven.

> 'They would have to repent of it, and at the least say they were only somewhat doubtful, not null and void. We for the sake of charity would be willing in practice, if all other matters were arranged, to allow the doubt to be removed by a ceremony arranged between the Archbishop and the Pope alone. Then the Archbishop by a like ceremony would set the other Metropolitans right, and they their own bishops.'[1]

Robinson argued also for only a nominal acknowledgement of the Pope's jurisdiction over the Church in England, suggesting that although he thought that the Archbishop ought to receive the pallium from the Pope, nevertheless the Pope should not exercise any jurisdiction within England. The Dean would only admit papal jurisdiction in a very limited sense because, as he stated in his journal, '... we Englishmen always had been and would be inconsistent'.[2]

---

1. Journal of J. Armitage Robinson, 14th March 1923, p. 1.
2. Journal of J. Armitage Robinson, 14th March 1923, p. 2.

SECOND AND THIRD 'CONVERSATIONS' – INTERMEDIARY PROBLEMS

The discussions ranged over the kind of 'rectification' that would be required. Mgr Van Roey gave as his opinion that the Archbishop of Canterbury could be conditionally re-ordained by the imposition of hands by the Pope or the Pope's delegate, and that the Archbishop himself would then do likewise for his suffragans. Lord Halifax, on the contrary, thought that perhaps the 'rectification' could be confined to the 'porrection',[1] accompanied by some suitable formula which would clarify totally the 'Intention' of the Church of England. Van Roey did not think this would be sufficient as Anglican Orders were considered by the Roman Church as at least doubtful, objectively speaking, and hence the imposition of hands, even if it was *sub conditione*, would probably be judged necessary. On being asked by the Cardinal whether the Archbishop of Canterbury would accept such a 'rectification', the Dean replied that, if the dogmatic issues had been resolved, then he thought that the Archbishop 'would resign himself to such conditions'.[2]

Abbé Portal's next intervention was an obvious attempt to pour soothing oil on this very sensitive issue. He pointed out that there appeared to be two aspects to the problem: the Catholics could not ask the Anglicans to deny over three centuries of their history; on the other hand, the Anglicans could not ask the Catholics to reverse the nullity judgement on their Orders which had been in force for the same three centuries. This was now a matter for theologians. They should try to find an acceptable means of arriving at the desired goal, always keeping in mind the sensitivities of both parties, just as diplomats do analogously in civil and political matters. The Lambeth Conference seemed to have opened the door on one possibility. Dean Robinson added to this his wish that the question of Orders be re-opened, because, he continued, it was felt in England that a great injustice had been done by the mother Church to her daughter, and it would be important to find a means of making reparation for this hurt in order to smooth the path for any eventual 'rectification'.

The afternoon session of that day was occupied in discussing that point of the Memorandum which dealt with the nomination and consecration

---

1. The *'Porrection'* (or handing on of instruments) is that moment in the ordination ceremony of a priest when the chalice and paten are handed to him, symbols of the sacrifice of the body and blood of Christ.
2. Lord Halifax, *The Conversations at Malines (1921–1925), Original Documents*, p. 33.

of bishops in the Church of England, once the position of the Archbishop of Canterbury had been regularized. The Anglicans pressed the point that the Pope should not intervene in the choice and consecration of suffragan bishops in England. Abbé Portal expressed the view that the Anglican system of elections then in use in the British colonies might well be acceptable, but in England itself – where the right of nomination lay with the Crown – it was impossible to exclude the right of the Pope to present and nominate bishops. The Cardinal further asked what guarantee would the Pope have under the present system that the choices made would be good? The Anglicans replied that the Metropolitan would be responsible, and that he would represent the authority of the Pope, from whom he would have received the pallium.

The Cardinal, without expressing his own opinion on this question, stated that the matter deserved serious consideration and should be submitted to the competent authorities. Dean Robinson concluded this particular part of the discussion by expressing the hope that a general council would recognize the Archbishop of Canterbury as patriarch.

The final point of the Memorandum for discussion was that pertaining to certain rites and customs which the Church of England would wish to see retained as part of historical and organizational development, namely, the retention of the vernacular in the English Rite liturgies, Holy Communion under both species, and the right of the clergy to marry. On these three issues, Cardinal Mercier stated that he thought there would be little difficulty in conceding the first two elements, but on the third, the marriage of the clergy, he thought that those clergy presently married would probably be allowed to continue their ministry in their married state, but he saw great difficulty in conceding that newly ordained clergy would be allowed to marry. His Eminence believed that the Roman Church would ask that new candidates for the priesthood be required to accept the state of celibacy. Abbé Portal added that it would be wrong to base this particular matter on the example of the Catholic Uniates, because Rome would certainly fear that the discipline of celibacy, which was so strongly maintained in the West, would be compromised in certain countries if married clergy were admitted in England. It also had to be recognized that the marriage of bishops was contrary to the long-established traditions of the Orthodox Church as well as the Roman Catholic Church.

SECOND AND THIRD 'CONVERSATIONS' – INTERMEDIARY PROBLEMS

The Anglicans countered this argument by justifying their usage for reasons of practical order and, although recognizing theoretically the advantages of celibacy, they would not want to see it as an obligation imposed on the clergy in England.

When the discussions were concluded on this first day, the participants agreed that each side should draw up a summary of the discussions for presentation to their respective authorities, and the Dean of Wells and Cardinal Mercier accepted to do so for their respective groups.

The following day, the 15th March 1923, was mostly spent reading and adjusting various points of the two different summaries which had been prepared, and the participants signed each of the documents as having been participants at the discussions. This was meant to be simply an acknowledgement of each side's summary of the discussions, but it caused much difficulty later when the Archbishop of Canterbury misunderstood the implications of the signatories and thought that they were agreed statements. Both these summaries are included as Appendix 2.

The remainder of the day included a decision to delay for some weeks making any more public pronouncements on the Conversations, as the Cardinal requested he be given time to communicate with Rome.[1] The Dean expressed the hope that Archbishop Davidson would write to the Cardinal to express his appreciation for the meetings, and he hoped that the Conversations would continue with expanded representation. Once again Lord Halifax expressed the gratitude of all the members for the gracious hospitality of the Cardinal, and the second Conversation ended in the early evening.

It is important to underline the amicable nature of these first two meetings between the Anglicans and Roman Catholics which, while discussing important topics of divergence, nevertheless maintained throughout

---

1. Cardinal Mercier did his utmost to keep Rome fully informed on all the developments concerning the Conversations. When he had originally received the Memorandum for the second Conversations, he sent a copy immediately to Rome together with a letter informing the Pope of the date of the next meeting, He was no doubt anxious due to the increasing antagonism towards the idea of himself being engaged in meetings with the Anglicans, because he also noted in his letters that the English Catholic Press, viz. *The Tablet* and *The Universe* were not in favour of the meetings.
Letters of Mercier to Pius XI, 1st and 2nd March 1923, Archdiocese of Malines Archives, B. 1.

a cordiality and generosity of spirit which had not been allowed to manifest itself before simply because there had been no precedent to meetings of such a kind. We shall see in due course how the tone of the third Conversation adopted a more formal and academic theme, both because of the increasing importance which new delegated members gave to it, and also because of the personalities of the 'experts' who were added to the two sides. It is also interesting to note the impression each side gave to the other, particularly evident perhaps in the Cardinal's surprise at how importantly the Anglicans felt about recognition of their history and possible means of 'authentication', that is, the whole issue of the pallium.[1] It is undoubtedly because of this that the Cardinal decided to ask Dom Lambert Beauduin to prepare the famous Memorandum *'L'Église Anglicane, Unie non Absorbée'*, which Mercier personally presented at the fourth Conversation.

(iii) Concerns of Archbishop Davidson after the second Conversation, and his suggestions for future discussion.

The Anglicans returned home to England apparently well satisfied with the results of their meeting, and Dr Frere and the Dean of Wells reported to the Archbishop of Canterbury on 16th March 1923, bringing copies of the two signed summaries. Here began a misunderstanding which had a not insignificant impact on the attitude of the Archbishop to subsequent meetings. Dean Robinson was evidently not a well-organized person, as is evidenced by his losing his passport on the outward journey to Malines, and now he had mislaid some parts of his own papers. Neither did he make clear to Archbishop Davidson at this time the significance of the signed summaries, namely, that each group had countersigned the other paper not as a mark of approval but to simply to signify the correctness of the text.[2]

---

1. Aubert, *Les Conversations de Malines*, in *Bulletins*, p. 119.
2. Lockhart, *Charles Lindley Viscount Halifax*, Vol. 2, p. 289.
In a letter from Frere to Halifax of the 19th March 1923, Dr. Frere explains the mix-up over the signing of the documents: 'You know what a muddle there was about the signed papers. What the Dean did with his I don't know; anyway I had to give him the residue which was all that was left for me, for him to give to the Abp. (Archbishop), but that is defective for the Dean had signed it in the wrong place; consequently the R.C.'s signed it wrong too and you and I not at all'.
Mirfield Deposit of W.H. Frere, File 1.6/2 Malines.

SECOND AND THIRD 'CONVERSATIONS' – INTERMEDIARY PROBLEMS

Of particular worry to Davidson was the whole matter of the 'pallium' which had been discussed. In his position as Archbishop of Canterbury, charged with the delicate political balancing act of maintaining an equilibrium between the diverse groups which composed the Church of England, he knew what use could be made of this issue by opponents of reunion and indeed opponents of the Church of England. The pallium, a symbolic scarf embroidered with four crosses, traditionally made of wool from lambs bred at the Church of St. Agnes in Rome, was customarily placed on the tomb of St. Peter in Rome the night before being invested on Metropolitan Archbishops. From the 11th century onward, the pallium had to be received in person by each Metropolitan, who was required to take an oath of obedience to the Pope. In the course of time the pallium had come to symbolize the granting of jurisdiction by the Pope to his Metropolitan.

For Archbishop Davidson it was a serious error of judgement to begin talking about means of recognition of the jurisdictional rights of the Archbishop of Canterbury before having come to an agreement on the claims of Papal supremacy and the other great doctrinal differences between Canterbury and Rome. On the 19th March 1923, Davidson wrote a long letter to the Dean of Wells expressing his reservations:

> 'I take no exception whatever to your plan of discussing first some of the administrative questions you have dwelt upon, provided it is kept always in mind that there are great outstanding questions of a doctrinal sort which would require deliberate discussions and some measure of settlement before administrative problems could even arise. I should personally place among the foremost of these the doctrine of the Roman Catholic Church as to the position, the jurisdiction, and the powers of the Papal See. The deep significance of that matter may very easily be slurred over in common talk by admitting as an historical and practical matter of so-called general knowledge the "primacy" of the Bishop of Rome. In certain senses this is an indisputable historical fact. But as used by Roman Catholics his primacy means a great deal more. Though the Vatican Council emphasized and increased what we deem the false doctrine of the Pope's independent and autocratic status as sole Vicar of Christ, the claim had of course been made for many centuries. Its recognition is virtually, and is now even technically, *de fide*. It therefore affects in the widest way, both doctrinally and administratively, the whole

question of the relation of the Church of Rome to the rest of Christendom. It bears upon almost every problem that can come up for discussion. If we are bound – as I certainly believe we are – to discard as untrue the theory that the Bishop of Rome holds *jure divino* in the Church of Christ a position of distinct and unique authority, operative everywhere, and perhaps even – though here I speak with reserve – that, directly or indirectly, it is through that channel alone (at all events in the West) that the Ministerial Commission can be rightly or validly exercised, there is an obvious inappropriateness in discussing other Church questions until that fundamental question has been brought to a clear issue ... There are also, as your Conversations have shown, large differences between us, with which the question of Papal status is only indirectly concerned, and these would call of course for full and far-reaching discussion ... But the point I have referred to lies so clearly *in limine* that I would urge you, when you next meet (and I hope your conversations will be resumed ere long) to let it be placed in the arena of your deliberations with a view to some sort of definite statement on either side. Such statements may of course in the first instance be provisional only. But the question is so vital a one that it is really essential to the whole.'[1]

The intention of the Archbishop in writing this letter to the Dean of Wells was not only to make clear his own position, but he hoped that the Dean would forward a copy of it to Cardinal Mercier. Davidson instructed the Dean to retain a copy of his letter together with all the other documentation referring to the Conversations which, as the Dean afterwards wryly remarked, was the Archbishop's method of 'insurance by memoranda against posthumous misunderstanding'.[2]

Bishop Gore was another who disliked the contents of the summaries which had been brought back from Malines. In a letter to the Archbishop on the 19th March 1923, Gore wrote that,

---

1. Letter of Archbishop Davidson to the Dean of Wells, 19th March 1923, as cited by Bell, *Randall Davidson, Archbishop of Canterbury*, Vol. 2, pp. 1265–1266.
2. Bell, *Randall Davidson, Archbishop of Canterbury*, Vol. 2, p. 1265.
Davidson later changed his mind and told the Dean not to send his letter to Cardinal Mercier. This was after he had read Halifax's letter of the 22nd March addressed to the Dean and the various criticisms contained therein.
Letter of Robinson to Halifax, 26th March 1923, Malines Papers of Lord Halifax, File A4 271, Box 2.

'... the concessiveness of our delegation to Malines, apparently at the first Conversation and certainly at the second, seems to me more disastrous and perilous the more I think of it. It astonished me to hear from the Dean what he was prepared to admit as to Roman supremacy, and that he is prepared to contemplate the (conditional) reordination of the Anglican clergy from top to bottom.'[1]

More pertinent still was the comment which the Archbishop's secretary, Dr Bell, noted in his diary: 'after Gore's strong reaction to the memoranda.... the Archbishop says he might have to throw the Dean, Frere and Halifax to the wolves'.[2]

Archbishop Davidson's increasing reticence, bolstered by Bishop Gore, was the cause of great disappointment to Lord Halifax. He saw looming a repetition of Archbishop Benson's failure to take a courageous initiative in 1894 during the Anglican Orders debate, and in a letter of the 22nd March 1923 to the Dean, he expressed his great sorrow,

'I cannot write to the Archbishop. I might say what I should regret. It may be that I exaggerate, but when the letter came last night I felt as if all were ending, all that I most cared about, all I had most hoped for, and that for the rest of my life there was nothing more to do but try to forget what might have been, and to look forward to the time when, if it were to be denied to us on earth, we might hope to be one with one another in Heaven.'[3]

In addition to sending Halifax a copy of his letter to the Dean, Archbishop Davidson also wrote asking the Viscount for absolute secrecy, to which Halifax acceded. At the same time Halifax asked the Dean not to send the Archbishop's letter to Cardinal Mercier.

The Archbishop now wrote directly to Cardinal Mercier. On the 24th March 1923, he addressed the Cardinal in the following terms:

'I have now seen the Archbishop of York, and I am in a position to

---

1. Letter of Gore to Davidson, 19th March 1923, as cited in G.L. Prestige, *The Life of Charles Gore*, (London: William Heinemann, 1935) p. 480
2. *Bell Papers*, 18th March 1923, Diary 1921–1923, No. 256, p. 8.
3. Letter of Halifax to the Dean of Wells, 22nd March 1923, Malines Papers of Lord Halifax, File A4 271, Box 2.

write further to Your Eminence with regard to the recent conversations at Malines.

The Archbishop of York unites with me in thanking Your Eminence for the kindly care you are taking in this whole matter, and for the clearness with which you have set forth the position taken by yourself, and by those with whom you act, as regards certain fundamental questions, doctrinal and administrative.

We clearly understand the wish which those who represented the Anglican Church expressed, that attention should be given at this early stage to the administrative questions relating to the course of practical action which might conceivably be followed if an agreement had, after discussion, been provisionally reached on the large doctrinal matters which underlie the whole. It was right that these practical matters should not, even at this early stage, be left wholly in the air. They must be reduced to more or less definite form.

I do not want at this stage to say of any proposal of a merely administrative sort whether it is or is not out of the question. For it would be necessary first to know what the administrative act implies. The obtaining of that knowledge will, I hope, be the task of the further conferences.

I do not doubt that Your Eminence will agree with me in thinking that, after all, the really fundamental question of the position of the Sovereign Pontiff of the Roman Catholic Church must be candidly faced before further progress can be made. The ambiguity of the term "primacy" is well known to us all. It has an historic meaning which can be accepted without difficulty. If, however, it is understood as implying that the Pope holds *jure divino* the unique and solemn position of sole Vicar of Christ on earth, from whom as Vicar of Christ must come directly or indirectly the right to minister validly within the Church, there ought to be no delay in discussing that implication and expounding its essential bearings. For it would not, in my judgement, be fair to Your Eminence or to others that I should encourage further discussion upon subordinate administrative possibilities without expressing my conviction that such a doctrine of papal authority is not one to which the adherence of the Church of England could be obtained. I say this simply for clearness' sake, and not as meaning that I desire these conversations to end. There may be explanations forthcoming on Your Eminence's part of which I have no knowledge. If such there be, it would certainly be well that the discussions should go on.

I have explained to my three Anglican friends what I feel upon this anxious and difficult matter, and have encouraged them to look forward to a resumption of the conferences. So great is the importance of this matter and its issues, that no effort on the part of any of us should be spared which may contribute towards the ultimate attainment of Unity within the Church of Christ.

It might be possible to augment to a small degree the numbers of those who take part in further deliberations. Such addition would have obvious difficulties of its own. But on this, and on any other points, I should of course be most anxious to hear further from Your Eminence to whose courtesy we owe so much.'[1]

The Archbishop's reserve about the course that the Conversations seemed to be taking is quite clear in this polite but firm letter. Halifax was disappointed by the tone of the letter, but Davidson wondered whether he had not been firm enough.[2]

Cardinal Mercier replied to the Archbishop's letter at considerable length on the 11th April 1923. In his reply he stated that he was gratified to learn that both Archbishops had taken note of the Memoranda which had been produced at the second Conversation, and had given them a sympathetic reception. Mercier then explained that he was fully in agreement with Davidson about the need to tackle the doctrinal question of the Papal supremacy, and explained that it was the Anglican group who had suggested dealing in a preliminary way with the practical and administrative problems of reunion. This was a surprise to him, he continued, but as it was their wish to comply with the appeal from these 'loyal and generous souls who had of their own accord come to meet us, we felt that we ought, without making any objections, to agree to the proposition which was put before us'.[3]

Cardinal Mercier continued by asking the Archbishop if he and the

---

1. Letter of Davidson to Mercier, 24th March 1923, Archdiocese of Malines Archives, A II, No. 8.
2. Davidson wrote to Halifax on the 12th April and stated; 'I confess to feeling pricks of conscience as to whether in writing to the Cardinal, and even to yourself, I have been firm enough in what I have said about the difficulties which lie ahead'.
Letter of Davidson to Halifax, 11th April 1923, Malines Papers of Lord Halifax, File A4 271, Box 2.
3. Letter of Mercier to Davidson, 11th April 1923, Malines Papers of Lord Halifax, File A4 271, Box 2.

Archbishop of York would let him know their opinions on the questions which had been discussed at the second Conversation (i.e the 'practical' questions) in the interests of clarity, for which they had already, in Davidson's letter, thanked the Cardinal of Malines. This would help the two groups to take up their task again with more assurance and on firmer ground. Mercier continued,

> 'having said that, in all frankness and in the interests of the cause in which we are collaborating, I come readily to the "fundamental" question of the position accorded to the Sovereign Pontiff in the Roman Catholic Church. The logical train of our conferences, as well as the mutual duties of loyalty on the part of members who meet there, oblige us to take up again this examination of the primacy of the Bishop of Rome, successor of Peter, defined as a dogma of the catholic faith by the Vatican Council. Our third conference, which like you I hope may be soon and, to a certain extent, enlarged, will assume then the task of studying this doctrine more thoroughly, and will apply itself, in accordance with your decision, to making more precise its significance .'[1]

The remainder of this long letter consists of a detailed explanation by the Cardinal of the doctrine of the Petrine primacy, the meaning of the term 'Vicar of Christ', and concludes with an exposition of the theology of the direct and divine origins of the ordinary jurisdiction of the individual bishops.

This letter from Cardinal Mercier, polite, straightforward, stating clearly where he stood on the doctrinal question of the Petrine claims, in some ways underlines the difference in conception of their personal teaching authority between the two Archbishops of Canterbury and Malines. Mercier obviously felt secure in expounding the various aspects of Papal claims, knowing it was the accepted dogma of the Roman Catholic Church, as decided upon by the bishops in Council and confirmed by the Pope as supreme authority. Archbishop Davidson (and Archbishop Lang of York) did not want to venture their opinions (as requested by the Cardinal) on the two Memoranda from the second Conversation, reflecting in another way the synodical and collegial nature of the

---

1. Bell, *Randall Davidson, Archbishop of Canterbury*, Vol. 2, pp. 1269–1270.

Church of England's decision-making process. This is made clear in another of Davidson's letters to Mercier on the 15th May 1923, 'My point to-day is simply to make clear to Your Eminence why it is that I cannot at present meet the desire which you express when you say "Would you not feel yourself able to let us know your evaluation ... of the conclusions", etc'.[1] Clearly Mercier did not grasp how delicate a situation the Archbishop of Canterbury felt himself to be in with three important but diverse initiatives coming at him from different and largely opposing angles – the Revised Prayer Book, the discussions with the Nonconformists, and the Malines Conversations. Neither did Mercier understand the lack of power actually invested in the position and person of the Archbishop of Canterbury in terms of teaching authority within the Church of England. This is clear from a previous letter to Lord Halifax dated 24th April 1923, where Mercier confided,

'Speaking quite confidentially I may and ought to tell you that in my opinion the danger at the present moment is lest the Archbishops should be unwilling to take in hand the fundamental question at issue and the question of opportunity and of its application. They are the guides of their flocks, and they ought to form clear ideas and personal convictions as to the line of their spiritual government. That done, there will be time to ascertain how to induce others to accept what their conscience will have told them is the truth and the end to be pursued.'[2]

The reluctance of the archbishop to make any further pronouncements on the proceedings at Malines was actually quite understandable to Lord Halifax. In a letter to Portal on 28th May 1923, the Viscount wrote:

'Certain things are developing in our ecclesiastical world of the moment which could have important results for reunion, and I think that the Archbishop is right to maintain silence about what we are doing. However, after the forthcoming conference, or a little later, that will be neither possible nor advantageous.'[3]

---

1. Letter of Davidson to Mercier, 15th May 1923, Malines Papers of Lord Halifax, File A4 271, Box 2.
2. Letter of Mercier to Halifax, 24th April 1923, cited in Bell, *Randall Davidson, Archbishop of Canterbury*, Vol. 2, p. 1273.
3. Letter of Halifax to Portal, 28th May 1923, Portal Papers, Paris.

In the midst of this growing feeling of pessimism, Lord Halifax determined to counter it with two personal initiatives of his own; firstly he wanted to publish another pamphlet defending the primacy of St Peter *jure divino*, and secondly he proposed to speak at a public meeting of English Churchmen to be held at Church House on the 7th July under the presidency of Bishop Burge, then Bishop of Oxford. The first project resulted in the publication of Halifax's pamphlet *Further Considerations on Behalf of Reunion* in the autumn of 1923, but the second project had to be aborted due to totally unexpected circumstances. Archbishop Davidson, on hearing of Halifax's intention to speak on the subject of reunion at the Church House meeting, tried to dissuade him but to no avail. Then, on 10th July, the Anglican Bishop of Zanzibar, Bishop Frank Weston, during a meeting of the Anglo-Catholic Congress at the Albert Hall, sent a telegram on behalf of the Congress to the Pope which read, 'Sixteen thousand Anglo-Catholics in Congress assembled offer respectful greetings to the Holy Father, humbly praying that the day of peace may quickly break'.[1] The telegram was sent to Cardinal Bourne of Westminster and then forwarded to Rome.

Additionally, in the same month of July, Miss Maude Petre, the biographer and friend of Fr George Tyrrell, wrote to *The Guardian* in favour of the movement towards reunion.[2] As a consequence of these events, and in the light of the declared opposition of the Archbishop of Canterbury, the Bishop of Oxford withdrew his acceptance of chairing the Church House meeting, and it was cancelled.

(iv) The choice of additional members for the third Conversation.

When it came to choosing additional members to go to the third Conversation at Malines, the Archbishop of Canterbury had little difficulty in choosing at least the first, Bishop Charles Gore. It had been Bishop Gore who had been, since the beginning of the conferences, one of the main proponents of the need for caution on the part of the Archbishop of

---

1. James Good, *The Church of England and the Ecumenical Movement*, (London: Burns & Oates, 1961), p. 110.
2. Halifax recounted the incident thus: 'Miss P. is connected with our English aristocracy and is also, as you know, involved with Fr Tyrrell ... she is a woman of much intelligence ... I have known her for a long time. Her letter is interesting, the article in The Guardian is good, and I hope that my reply will not displease you'.
Letter of Halifax to Portal, 29th June 1923, Portal Papers, Paris.

SECOND AND THIRD 'CONVERSATIONS' – INTERMEDIARY PROBLEMS

Canterbury. Gore himself was an Anglo-Catholic, but had never been identified with the main-stream body of Anglo-Catholics, indeed, was held as suspect by many of them because of his introduction of a scientific approach to theological exegesis as exemplified in his publication *Lux Mundi*. He was a well-known and distinguished scholar, an outspoken critic of the Roman Church, and in 1923 was conducting a public controversy in print with the French Roman Catholic historian Mgr Pierre Batiffol. In response to Archbishop Davidson's invitation to join the Malines groups, Gore replied that, 'I think it is of such immense importance – with a view to your retaining your present position in real mental vigour as long as possible – that you should be relieved of any anxiety in whole or in part, that if you seriously believe my joining the party for Malines would relieve you, I cannot doubt that I ought to agree to go'.[1] As a second additional member, Davidson invited Dr Beresford James Kidd, Warden of Keble College in Oxford and a noted church historian, to complete the Anglican group. There had been some talk of seeking a representative from the Liberal or Evangelical wings of the Church of England, but the difficulty of finding someone suitable was too great, and so Dr Kidd was invited.[2]

With Gore's nomination to the Anglican group, it was almost a foregone conclusion that one of the new Roman Catholic members would be Mgr Pierre Batiffol,[3] with whom Bishop Gore had been in dispute. Batiffol was acknowledged as perhaps the leading French church historian of the times, a disciple of Mgr Louis Duchesne of the Institut Catholique of Paris. The choice of a second member was more difficult. Abbé Portal was very much in favour of widening the net and, because of his contacts and work with the Russian Orthodox, he favoured nominating Père Pierre Iswolski, chaplain to the Russian Orthodox refugees in Brussels, whom he introduced to Cardinal Mercier. Portal even went so far as to ask Iswolski how the Eastern bishops would react to an invitation to participate in an ecumenical council, and the Russian bishops in

---

1. Letter of Bishop Gore to Archbishop Davidson, 31st July 1923, published in Bell, *Randall Davidson, Archbishop of Canterbury*, Vol. 2, p. 1277.
2. Lockhart, *Charles Lindley Viscount Halifax*, Vol. 2, p. 295.
3. Mgr Pierre Batiffol (1861–1929). French historian and Rector of the Institut Catholique de Toulouse. His writings on the Eucharist and his friendship with some Modernist scholars caused him to be unjustly suspected of Modernism, and his books were placed on the *Index of Forbidden Books* in 1907. His later very learned studies on Church history were in part an attempt to reassure the Church authorities of his soundness.

exile replied (through Iswolski who sounded them out) that they would not like to be drowned in the great sea of Catholic bishops, but if they were invited to conferences dealing with reunion then they would willingly come. The Cardinal, however, was not in favour of enlarging the Conversations to a tripartite basis (Anglican-Orthodox-Roman Catholic), preferring for the moment to confine himself to charitable assistance for the Russian refugees.[1] Portal even considered, after consulting Mercier, the possibility of a German Catholic bishop as a participant, given the interest shown by the Catholic press in Germany.

From the English side of the Channel, the favoured candidates came from the Order of Preachers (Dominicans). In France as well as in England the Dominicans were regarded as sympathetic to reunion. In England, Fr Vincent McNabb OP and Fr Bede Jarrett OP had been both encouraging Halifax's efforts for reunion through private correspondence and in various publications, and were initially considered possible participants for Malines. Apart from being sympathetic to the cause of reunion, to have at least one English Roman Catholic participant would have given a new orientation to the Conversations, which, till now, consisted exclusively of Continental Catholics. Fr Vincent McNabb, however, was increasingly concerned about the effects of Modernism on the Church of England and the High Church group in particular, and was in correspondence with Halifax about this particular matter.[2] Fr Bede Jarrett thought that the Church of England was hopelessly compromised, and he advised Halifax to convert to Roman Catholicism as

---

1. Abbé Portal's vision of ecumenism was very wide. He had contact with the secretariate of the Faith and Order movement, which kept him constantly supplied with information, most of it marked 'not for publication'. In a letter to Ralph W. Brown on 11th April 1926, shortly before Portal's death, the Abbé explained that his idea all along was to try to instigate conferences with the Protestants parallel to those of Malines. Knowing the difficulties which Rome would put in the way of joining any Faith and Order meetings, he wrote: 'I do not believe that the Roman Catholics will join your meeting at Lausanne. But why do you not profit from the occasion by asking the bishop of Fribourg to receive you together with two or three of your colleagues when your general assembly is finished? You will thus establish conversations analogous with those of Malines and that can be a beginning. If you accept, you can write a letter to the bishop and send it to me. I will send it on to his address, supporting it as best I can. It is probable that before then we shall be publishing a sort of resume of the conferences at Malines from the catholic point of view, and these can serve as a basis for the conversations of Lausanne or Fribourg'.
Letter of Portal to Brown, 11th April 1926, Portal Papers, Paris, Box H.
2. Letter of Vincent McNabb to Lord Halifax, 5th June 1923, Malines Papers of Lord Halifax, File A4 271, Box 2.

SECOND AND THIRD 'CONVERSATIONS' – INTERMEDIARY PROBLEMS

quickly as possible. Although both Portal and Mercier were favourable to Fr Jarrett joining the group at Malines, Halifax was not happy with Jarrett's attitude concerning Anglican Orders,[1] an issue which the Viscount would like to have seen re-opened, and eventually Halifax decided against the Dominican. Another possibility as participant was the Jesuit priest, Fr Francis Woodlock SJ, who was also in correspondence with Halifax, but he was strongly against the idea of 'corporate reunion', and, although considered at this time as 'friendly',[2] he wrote polemically against such ideas as Halifax propounded. In the end however, the French historian at the Institut Catholique of Paris, Père Hippolyte Hemmer, was the one to be invited, matching the areas of competence of his opposite number Dr Kidd. The opportunity of involving a notable personage from among English Roman Catholics slipped away, giving added force to the later accusation that the meetings were held at Malines because the continental Catholics did not understand the English mentality and could be more easily misled.

The date for the third Conversation was set for 7–8th November 1923, but before that happened, Archbishop Davidson called all the members of the Anglican group together for a meeting at Lambeth on 2nd October 1923. In addition to the participants who would be going to Malines, Davidson invited some trusted advisors, including Dr Thomas Drury (Bishop of Ripon), Canon Vernon Storr, Canon Oliver Quick and Dr Jenkins. The Archbishop, conscious of his increasing personal involvement because of his nomination of the two additional members for Malines, sought to make clear that he was not trying to dictate the agenda for the forthcoming Conversation, but he urged that questions of an administrative kind should be put aside for the present until the essential doctrinal problems had been tackled. He then quoted from a private memorandum which he had drawn up some two months previously (19th August 1923), outlining the type of questions he hoped would be dealt with: 'The position and authority of Holy Scripture, the meaning and authority of Tradition, the existence or non-existence of a Supreme Authority upon earth, a Vicariate of Christ, and what it means as regards both doctrine and administration: then further, the introduction of such dogmas as that of the Immaculate Conception, or again, and in another field, the definite teaching of the Church of Rome as to

---

1. Dick, *The Malines Converations Revisted*, pp. 111–112.
2. Lockhart, *Charles Lindley Viscount Halifax*, Vol 2, p. 298.

Transubstantiation and the attendant or consequent doctrines and usages ... For it ought to be made clear on the Anglican side, beyond possibility of doubt, that the great principles upon which the Reformation turned are our principles still, whatever faults or failures there may have been on either side in the controversies of the sixteenth century. It would be unfair to our Roman Catholic friends to leave them in any doubt as to our adherence, on large questions of controversy, to the main principles for which men like Hooker or Andrewes or Cosin contended, though the actual wording would no doubt be somewhat different today. What those men stood for, we stand for still, and I think that in some form or other that ought to be made immediately clear.'[1]

Both Lord Halifax and Abbé Portal were keenly aware of the increasing reserve of Archbishop Davidson and of the growing anxiety of Cardinal Mercier. The Cardinal was fearful that the next Conversation would dissolve into a controversial exchange between Bishop Gore and Mgr Batiffol, and he did not see his place, a Cardinal of the Church, charged with the office of peace-maker, as being a party to such an exchange. He suggested that there be a preliminary discussion between these two without him being present, but Archbishop Davidson would not hear of this.[2] The key to the solution as seen by Halifax and Portal was that Bishop Gore should be exposed to the Cardinal's personality, to be able to witness at close hand the holiness and charity of the Cardinal; 'It is important that Gore should get to know the Cardinal properly. The conversion of Gore to our ideas is the chief point at the moment. That accomplished, half the battle would be won'.[3] Portal saw that they must succeed in convincing Gore that an understanding in regard to the primacy of the Pope was not impossible.

---

1. Memorandum of Archbishop Davidson, 19th August 1923, Malines Papers of Lord Halifax, File A4 271, Box 3.
Although the part of the Archbishop's memorandum quoted in the text above seems solely to be a hard-line re-statement of the principles of the Reformation, this is not true of the whole of the memorandum. The large introductory section deals with his acknowledgement that anything discussed at Malines could be made the centre of controversy between red-hot Protestants and intractable Papists! It would be easier to leave the whole thing alone. But, he continued, that would be turning a deliberate deaf ear to the little whisper of tentative enquiry which came from the Roman side, and he saw it as his duty to Christianity and to the Lambeth Conference not to refuse to participate in any genuine endeavour to reach the goal of Jesus' prayer for unity.
2. Dick, *The Malines Conversations Revisited*, p. 113.
3. Letter of Halifax to Portal, 3rd October 1923, Portal Papers, Paris.

SECOND AND THIRD 'CONVERSATIONS' – INTERMEDIARY PROBLEMS

(v) The third Conversation at Malines – 7/8th November 1923.

In preparation for this third Conversation, a series of discussion papers had been prepared and distributed in advance to the participants. Dr Robinson prepared a paper entitled *The Position of Saint Peter in the Primitive Church: A Summary of the New Testament Evidence*,[1] and Dr Kidd prepared two papers, the first entitled *The Petrine Texts, as employed to A.D. 461*,[2] and the second entitled *To What Extent was the Papal Authority Repudiated at the Reformation in England?*[3] A further two papers were composed by Mgr Batiffol in reply to the first two Anglican papers.[4]

The third of the Malines Conversations took place on the 7th and 8th November 1923. As the very titles of the papers would suggest, this encounter was predominantly a scholarly one and the discussions were all of a historico-doctrinal nature. There was a new formality about this meeting because of the increased number of participants and because of the nature of the subjects being discussed. Armitage Robinson had known Pierre Batiffol for many years, and he commented that, although in good form, he was looking much older as to be practically unrecognisable. However, the Dean was not too happy with the Archbishop's choice of Dr Kidd as a member of the Anglican group, a choice he thought was really unsuitable due to the latter's overbearing manner and his suspected closeness to the Roman position. J.G. Lockhart, in his biography of Lord Halifax, described this meeting in the following terms: 'The Third Conversation, though as friendly in its temper as its predecessors, marked a new stage. The representatives met with a deepened sense of their responsibility to their respective authorities. The privacy and some of the informality of the early meetings had disappeared; it was no secret that certain persons were conferring at Malines and why; and if the representatives had no power to commit their principals, they were uncomfortably conscious of a capacity to compromise them. While on the Roman side the invitations to Batiffol and Hemmer in no wise differed from those to Van Roey and Portal, on the Anglican

---

1. Lord Halifax, *The Conversations at Malines (1921–1925), Original Documents*, pp. 80–133.
2. Lord Halifax, *Original Documents*, pp. 123–133.
3. Lord Halifax, *Original Documents*, pp. 151–158.
4. Lord Halifax, *Original Documents*, pp. 103–122 and pp. 135–149.

side the selection of Gore and Kidd by the Archbishop gave a semi-official complexion to the delegation. The gathering was larger, the discussion were more formal and theological. The agenda was prepared more thoroughly and the Minutes were recorded more fully.[1] The newcomers on either side were throughout in the forefront of the debate, while Mercier, Halifax, and Portal gave the impression of retiring a little into the background. The Cardinal ... was unwilling to appear as a controversialist, while the enlargement of the conference, and consequently of the conference table, made it difficult for Halifax, with his growing deafness, to follow the conversations as closely as he would have liked.'[2]

The *Compte Rendu* for this third Conversation is fairly brief.[3] Only the chief points of the topics touched upon during that first day (8th November) are mentioned, and the largest part is taken up with the text of two Summaries which the groups produced at the end of the first day's discussions. Robinson's journal notes that he was very pleased by the participants' reception of his paper, noting that 'they took it very kindly but thought I was "trés rigoreux" and "radical". I said at the end that I was delighted to be called radical, because I was generally thought so conservative'.[4] The second day (9th November) began with the presentation of these summaries, the Anglican Summary reading as follows:

A Summary of the New Testament Evidence as to the position of St Peter:
1. The point with which we are concerned in this brief Statement is solely the position of St Peter among the other apostles, as evidenced by the New Testament.

---

1. Abbé Portal was replaced by Hippolyte Hemmer as one of the two Secretaries. Walter Frere remained as the other.
2. Lockhart, *Charles Lindley Viscount Halifax*, Vol. 2, p. 301.
3. Neither Halifax nor Portal seemed very pleased with the '*Compte Rendu*' of this third Conversation: 'Like you I regret a little what is found in the '*Compte Rendu*' but I suppose that we ought to be content all things considered'.
Letter of Halifax to Portal 29th November 1923, Portal Papers, Paris.
4. Journal of J. Armitage robinson, 7th November 1923, p. 1.
The *Papers of J.A. Robinson* preserved at Lambeth Palace Library (Mss. 2222, 2223, and 2224) present little originality in connection with the Dean's participation in the Malines Conversations, being confined mostly to his own collection of documentation concerning the meetings, together with some letters from the other participants, copies of which can be found in other archives. Some of the documents are incomplete, as, for example, the memorandum presented by the Dean which is preserved only in part (Mss. 2222, pp. 27–31).

SECOND AND THIRD 'CONVERSATIONS' – INTERMEDIARY PROBLEMS

2. We recognise that St Peter was the accepted chief or leader of the apostles, and was so accepted because he was treated so by the Lord.
3. In the passage of St Matthew XVI, we recognise that it was to St Peter as the chief or leader of the apostolic company that Our Lord made the threefold promise: but we find in the New Testament reason to believe that the promises there made to one, were fulfilled to all the twelve, – so that all constitute the foundation of the church, all have the keys of the kingdom, and all have the authority to bind and loose. St Peter's special position therefore we hold to have lain, not in any jurisdiction which he alone held, but in a leadership among the other apostles.
4. What is here said from Biblical Evidence is not intended to exclude the consideration of the hearing of the later tradition of the church upon the whole subject.[1]

Following Dr Frere's reading of the Anglican Summary, Dr Robinson added that he had not included his personal conclusions in the paper which he had presented. He thought that the Summary of his group did not exhaust the sense of the promises made to Peter, particularly if account were taken of the interpretations of the ancient Fathers of the Church and of the providential events of history.

The Catholic Summary was presented by M. Hemmer:
I. There are abundant indications in the Synoptic Gospels and in the Gospel of St John that Peter fulfilled a special role with regard to Jesus and among the disciples.
   This service was not tied to the fact that he was the first to be called by Jesus, nor to the spontaneity of his character, but rather to the will of Jesus.
   The Saviour manifested this will more explicitly by the 'You are Peter' of St Matthew, by the 'strengthen your brothers' of St Luke, by the 'Simon, son of John, feed my sheep' of the fourth Gospel.

II. This Will manifests itself in the Acts by the fact that Peter appears and acts as the chief of the primitive community (*leader of the Church*).
    Saint Paul, who claimed the apostolate to the gentiles, recognises

---

1. Lord Halifax, *Original Documents*, pp. 44–45.

Peter as the apostle of the circumcised, and has no word which challenges Peter's right to a more extended mission.

III. We profess that the Gospel texts, notably those of 'You are Peter' and the 'Feed my sheep', express a prerogative of Peter, foundation of the Church and her principle of unity.
We concede that the events of history have shed light on these texts which have made more clear their real meaning.

IV. The Vatican Council has defined as part of the catholic faith the universal primacy of jurisdiction conferred on Peter by the authority of these two texts of 'You are Peter' and 'Feed my sheep'. It declares that the denial of this primacy is contrary to the sense manifested by Holy Scripture, such as the Catholic Church has always understood them.
The Council did not indicate the numerous witnesses which attest to this tradition of interpreting the texts, but which can be found in patrology and in ancient Christian writings.[1]

Following this presentation of the two Summaries of the previous day, Dr Kidd then read his paper on the texts relative to St Peter up to the year 461, and Mgr Batiffol replied with a paragraph by paragraph approach. There was a reasonable agreement on quite a number of points. Bishop Gore, however, wanted to clarify his own position on Greek and Latin approaches to unity in the Church, stating that he was not in agreement with the interpretation given to St Cyprian or St Irenaeus. With the consent of Dr Kidd and the other Anglicans present, the conclusions of Dr Kidd were then modified to read:

1. That the Roman Church was founded and built up by St Peter and St Paul, according to St Irenaeus (*Adv. Haer*. III, 3, 2).
2. That the Roman See is the only historically-known Apostolic See of the West.
3. That the Bishop of Rome is, as Augustine said of Pope Innocent I, president of the Western Church (*Contra Julianum Pelagianum*, I, 13).
4. That he has a primacy among all the bishops of Christendom; so

---

1. Lord Halifax, *Original Documents*, pp. 45–46.

that, without communion with him, there is in fact no prospect of a reunited Christendom.

5. That to the Roman See the churches of the English owe their Christianity through 'Gregory our father' (Council of Clovesho, A.D. 747) 'who sent us baptism' (Anglo-Saxon Chronicle, Anno 565).[1]

During the afternoon session of the 9th November, Dr Kidd read the second of his prepared papers, this one dealing with the measures which were taken at the time of the Reformation to reject the Pope's authority. At the conclusion of the lecture, M. Hemmer said that it was no great advantage discussing official parliamentary or synodal documents as they spoke for themselves. What was interesting was the total lack of declarations on the part of Anglicans of the time on the mission and teaching authority of the Pope, at least in the texts quoted.

In an exchange on the meaning of the term 'jurisdiction', Dr Robinson stated that the Anglican Church could not accept the term 'universal jurisdiction', either as claimed for St Peter or for the Roman Church. A more acceptable expression would be 'spiritual leadership' or 'a general superintendence' understood as the duty to 'care for the well-being of the Church as a whole'. Dr Robinson thought that this interpretation would be easier to accept, and was better than a primacy of honour. Dr Gore, however, disagreed, stating that he would find it difficult to accept 'general superintendence' and would prefer 'spiritual leadership'. This difference of opinion even among the Anglicans is indicative of the tenor of the whole discussion. Walter Frere noted that the biblical arguments that Robinson had proposed were not really faced by the Romans, and that the two sides gradually slid into an impasse.[2]

At the end of the second day's exchanges, the Roman Catholic participants asked whether they should sign a document of those points which they all seemed to agree upon (a summary of which the Abbé Hemmer had already drafted), but the Anglicans, conscious no doubt of the furore

---

1. Lord Halifax, *Original Documents*, p. 47.
2. 'My own impression at the time was that our biblical argument had not been really faced; apparently one or two texts concerning St. Peter had hypnotised the Roman Catholics in their outlook, to the exclusion of the scriptural description of the Church itself.'
W. Frere, *Recollection of Malines*, pp. 42–44.

caused by the signing of the second Conversations statements, preferred to leave the *Compte Rendu* to speak for itself. The Conference thus ended in a spirit of hope and renewed friendliness.

In terms of achievement, probably the greatest result was the extremely positive impression that Dr Gore had of Cardinal Mercier, just as Halifax and Portal had hoped. In a letter of the 10th November 1923, Dr Gore thanked the Cardinal for his gracious hospitality and also his openness in receiving 'us heretics' and allowing them to speak their mind freely. He concluded his letter by expressing, 'I felt to the bottom of my heart your "tolerantia perseverantissima", and I ask pardon if I spoke a single word more than was necessary to explain my position. Whatever eventually results from these conferences, I hope that we can all feel that it is a good thing to meet and to understand each other'.[1]

---

1. Letter of Dr Gore to Cardinal Mercier, 10th November 1923, Archdiocese of Malines Archives, A III, No. 7.

6
Controversy grows as Conversations are made public.

(i) The Conversations are made public – Archbishop Davidson's Letter.

The Anglicans who were present at the third Conversation returned to England quite contented with the results of the meeting. Bivort de la Saudée quotes two letters, one from Dr Gore and the other from Dr Kidd, both of whom expressed their satisfaction to Cardinal Mercier.[1] Cardinal Mercier was particularly pleased with the letter from Gore,[2] as it had seemed during the Conversations that Gore was being the most resistant to the attempts at conciliation, so much so that at one stage during the third Conversation the Cardinal had rounded on him and accused him of obstinacy.[3]

Although no official papers had been published concerning the meetings at Malines (indeed it had not yet been made public that such a series of meetings were being held), nevertheless, unofficial news of the Conversations had spread around in Catholic circles and in Anglican and Methodist circles. The extent of this unofficial news was such that they were being compared to the ill-fated attempts at Anglo-Catholic rapprochement which had taken place at the end of the 19th century.[4] That this was so was well illustrated in a letter of Abbé Edouard Beauduin to Lord Halifax on the 29th December, 1923, written from Strasbourg, thanking Halifax for sending him a copy of his book *Leo XIII and Anglican Orders*, and wishing him more success with the Conversations than he had had with the question of Anglican Orders. In this same letter, Beauduin drew a rather pessimistic parallel between certain of the participants and conditions surrounding the two attempts at reunion: 'I note that the scenario remains the same: Pius XI takes up

---
1. Bivort de la Saudée, *Anglicans et Catholiques*, p. 100.
2. Prestige, *The Life of Charles Gore*, p. 483.
3. Lockhart, *Charles Lindley Viscount Halifax*, Vol. 2, p. 305.
4. A discussion of this will be found in Lord Halifax's book *Leo XIII and Anglican Orders*, (London, Longmans Green, 1912).

the role of Leo XIII and Cardinal Gasparri that of Cardinal Rampolla, Canterbury that of York, and also, alas, *The Universe* that of *The Tablet*, and indubitably Cardinal Bourne that of Cardinal Vaughan; finally, both Cardinal Merry Del Val and Cardinal Gasquet are still there'.[1] Beauduin concluded, however, by expressing the hope that the end result might be happier.

This situation of unofficial discussions regarding something which did not 'officially' exist was especially disturbing to the Archbishop of Canterbury, Randall Davidson, who was by nature a very prudent man. He resolved, therefore, to publish some kind of letter regarding the Conversations at Malines. Lord Halifax, when contacted, wished to publish the actual reports of the Conversations themselves, but Davidson and the other Anglican participants preferred the idea of a letter from the Archbishop of Canterbury to the other bishops of the Anglican communion, in which the Conversations would be presented as emanating from the general movement towards reunion with the various Churches as an effect of the Lambeth Appeal.

Davidson sent a copy of his proposed letter to Cardinal Mercier, who disagreed rather strongly with several points of the content. The main points of disagreement were (i) that the Conversations were not directly resulting from the Lambeth Appeal,[2] (ii) that the Archbishop was making the whole thing appear too official, (iii) that he [Mercier] was opposed to Davidson publishing the letter of approbation from Rome, a copy of which Mercier had passed on to the Archbishop for his personal information.[3] In this last point Cardinal Mercier was emphasising that

---

1. Bivort de la Saudée, *Anglicans et Catholiques*, p. 111.
2. Mercier insisted that he had had nothing to do with the Lambeth Appeal, and that he could not admit that the Malines Conversations followed as a consequence of that Appeal. He had, said Mercier, received Lord Halifax as a friend, and, in fact, the Archbishop''s name had not even been mentioned during the whole of the first meeting.
Lockhart, *Charles Lindley Viscount Halifax,* Vol. 2, pp. 303/304.
3. This was a letter from Cardinal Mercier to Archbishop Davidson, dated the 10th January 1923. It was in reply to Davidson's request that the Catholic participants in the Conversations should have approbation from the Roman authorities. The crux of this letter was the following phrase:-
'... on our part we have the pleasure of informing you that his Eminence the Cardinal Secretary of State has been authorized to let me know that the Holy See encourages the Conversations and prays ... that the Good Lord will bless them'.
This mention of authorization is a reference to a letter received by Mercier from the Secrtary of State, Cardinal Gasparri, dated 25th November 1922.
Text in Bell, *Randall Davidson, Archbishop of Canterbury*, p. 1258.

CONTROVERSY GROWS AS CONVERSATIONS ARE MADE PUBLIC

his letter was a private communication and that Archbishop Davidson, in proposing to publish this letter, was using it as a prop to make the Conversations look more official than they in fact were. Lastly, he asked the Archbishop to place more emphasis in the conclusion on the power and charity of Christ.[1]

Lord Halifax was not very pleased with the text of the proposed letter either, and he told the Archbishop so. In particular he was annoyed with the difference in tone used in the letter when talking of considerations of reunion with the various Protestant groups, and on the other hand when it talked about reunion with Rome. The Archbishop changed the text of the letter in accordance with the various criticisms he had received, but even the final text – which was issued on 25th December 1923 – was still not completely to Halifax's liking.[2] However, it seems that the other Anglican participants of the Conversations were perfectly content with it.

The immediate effect of Davidson's Christmas Letter addressed to 'The Archbishops and Metropolitans of the Anglican Communion' was not only the storm of protest which he had been fearing, but also an animated discussion of the principles involved. Frere remarks on two points which can be taken as indications that the reactions were not so violent as might have been expected. First, the delegates of the Methodist Churches, who were at this time having occasional meetings with Anglican representatives, naturally enough raised the question of the discussions going on between Anglicans and Romans. The explanations which were given were accepted without any protest. Secondly, the matter came up in the Convocations[3] in the form of a statement made

---

1. Bivort de la Saudée, *Anglicans et Catholiques*, p. 111.
2. Once again Halifax makes comparison with the hesitations and fears of Archbishop Benson during the Anglican Orders affair and the hesitations of Archbishop Davidson concerning the Conversations: 'The whole of the Archbishop's letter to the Metropolitans betrays the uneasiness which the Malines Conversations arouse in him ... it's a little like the hesitations of Archbishop Benson who, at the time of Cardinal Rampolla's letter, had all the cards in his hand.'
Letter of Halifax to Portal, 4th January 1924, Portal Papers, Paris.
3. *Convocations* are meetings of the bishops of the provinces of Canterbury and York. In the Church of England this consists of two Houses, an Upper House of bishops, and a Lower House of representatives of the ordinary clergy.
For a fuller explanation and short history of Convocations, cf. *New Catholic Encyclopaedia*, Washington 1967, Vol. 4, p. 294/295.

by the Archbishop of Canterbury in a speech which he delivered in the Upper House on 6th February 1924.[1] Although in his Christmas letter Davidson had emphasised to a large degree his communications with the Orthodox Church and their recognition of the validity of Anglican Orders, all within the context of responses to the Lambeth Appeal, in his address to Convocation he dealt principally with the Malines Conversations. The reception of his statement by the assembled bishops was muted, but no great exceptions were taken apart from one single bishop who protested.[2]

(ii) Initial reaction of English Catholics to the news of Malines.

The Roman Catholics in England, however, seemed to take the matter more seriously, and many were greatly upset to find out what had been going on. But even considering this, the final effect was not as outraged as one might have expected from a situation such as then existed in England, where the Catholics were still very much in a 'ghetto' situation in the sense that the majority regarded 'reunion' very much (if not entirely) in terms of the complete submission of the other Churches to Rome. This concentration of the Catholic Church in England on 'individual conversions' rather than a vision of 'corporate reunion'[3] was one of the reasons which Portal had put forward in favour of approaching Continental Catholics rather than the English Catholic hierarchy. It was

---

1. The text of the speech by the Archbishop of Canterbury in the Upper House of Convocation on February 6th, 1924, is published in the Report issued by the Anglican members at Malines in 1927 entitled *The Conversations at Malines 1921–1925*, Oxford University Press, pp. 50/59.
The full text of this important speech can be found at the end of this volume as Appendix 3.
2. Davidson had already informally met with the English bishops on the 25th January to brief them on what was happening at Malines. One particular bishop, Herbert Hensley Henson, recounts that he objected to the continuation of the Malines meetings, particularly on the grounds that the Anglican 'representatives' were not truly representative. Henson further noted that "a good number of the bishops felt rather uncomfortable".
Herbert Hensley Henson, *Retrospect of an Unimportant Life*, 3 vols. (London: 1942–1950), vol. 2, p. 139.
3. 'Corporate reunion' is the term used to refer to the union of the Church of England *as a body* to the R.C. Church, rather than the union of individuals or small groups. This topic of corporate union was brought up by a letter of Lord Halifax to *The Times* on 22nd February 1924, in which, commenting on Cardinal Mercier's recent Pastoral Letter, he said that '... it emphasies the duty of English Roman Catholics to consider how they can assist in bringing about the corporate reunion of the Church of England with the Holy See, rather than merely considering how best to secure individual conversions'.

also the first question that Cardinal Mercier asked during the initial meeting with Halifax and Portal in October 1921 when they paid their first tentative visit to Malines. 'Why don't you address yourselves to the English Catholics and their authorities?' he asked. 'Because', he was told, 'their disposition is opposed to it. The English Catholics only want individual conversions, and they exclude all attempts at union. It is therefore necessary to renounce all efforts at reunion unless they are undertaken outside England.'[1] The fact also that the Anglicans were meeting with 'Continental' bishops rather than with their own English hierarchy (who had a much more limited outlook as regards ecumenism), might have given the impression that they were being sold-out in some manner. This mentality is reflected in an article from the Rome correspondent of *The Times*, published in the edition of 30th December 1923, who remarked rather scathingly on the French and Belgians mixing in English affairs, and suggesting that the Pope should not allow himself to be influenced by such goings-on.[2] Lord Halifax remarked to Portal in a letter of 5th January 1924, that the instigators of this dispatch from Rome were surely the Cardinals Merry Del Val and Gasquet.[3]

(iii) Cardinal Bourne's reactions.

The reactions of the leader of the Roman Catholic Church in England,

---

(Footnote no. 3 continued from previous page.)
Note: The reply to Halifax's appeal by Revd P. Keating S.J. contained in an article in *The Month*, gives a good example of the mentality of English Catholics at that time. The analogy of fishing with a rod and line or with a net, is used to explain the difference between individual conversions and 'corporate reunion', but the point is made very strongly that even in the event of the conversion of the Anglicans **as a body**, each individual would, after reception and individual (if conditional) baptism, have to guarantee their understanding and acceptance of the Roman Catholic claims.
To English Catholics there was practically no question of accepting a reunion with Anglicanism as a whole, except under these conditions.
The Month, March 1924, pp. 260/262.

1. Edouard Beauduin, *Le Cardinal Mercier*, (Tournai: Casterman, 1966), p. 116.
2. Bivort de la Saudée, *Anglicans et Catholiques*, p. 113.
Roger Aubert mentions that Portal wished that Mercier would protest to *The Times*, but the Cardinal was under pressure from Rome not to blow up the matter so that it looked official. In a letter of 30th December 1923, Cardinal Gasparri, after having learned of Davidson's letter, wrote to Mercier telling him to ensure that the newspapers did not get the idea that these meetings were taking any sort of official character.
Aubert, *Bulletins de l'Academie Royal de Belgique*, p. 109.
3. Letter of Halifax to Portal, 5th January 1924, Portal Papers, Paris.

Cardinal Francis Bourne, are pivotal to this part of the history of the Conversations, and yet are difficult to ascertain from his few public statements. His official biographer, Ernest Oldmeadow, who was also at the time editor of *The Tablet*, casts Cardinal Bourne in the role of opponent to the Conversations on two particular points: (a) that the Cardinal did not know that the Conversations were taking place till they were made public in December 1923 by Archbishop Davidson, and, (b) that these 'conversations' were being conducted by a Belgian Cardinal and Continental Catholics rather than with the English Cardinal and English theologians.

(a) This first point has already been touched upon in Chapter 4, but because of its importance we will now examine it more thoroughly. It has been noted that Dr Frere, in his book, *Recollections of Malines*, stated that before the opening of the Conversations, i.e. November 1921, 'Lord Halifax, very prudently, had a satisfactory interview with Cardinal Bourne'. This was a bone of contention with Oldmeadow, who, though not denying that Halifax had indeed seen Cardinal Bourne, strongly refutes the implication that Halifax had gone with the intention of informing the English Cardinal of the impending Conversations with his brother Cardinal at Malines. Oldmeadow says that he received Bourne's clear assurance that Halifax had spoken in a general way, not mentioning the various negotiations with the Archbishop of Canterbury and the imminent meeting with Cardinal Mercier at Malines. Oldmeadow was obviously suggesting some kind of subterfuge on the part of Halifax to make it seem that Cardinal Bourne was aware of the meetings at Malines, although later he did try to give some leeway or excuse to Halifax on account of the latter's advanced years and forgetfulness. However, this would seem to be at odds with the fact that Halifax's main objective at his advanced state of life was successfully to initiate these meetings, and it would be most unlikely that he would have 'forgotten' to mention the arrangements for Malines by accident. Oldmeadow further declared that when Dr Frere had been put right on this matter of the Halifax-Bourne meeting of November 1921, 'Dr Frere, who himself had had to complain of inaccuracies on the part of Lord Halifax, immediately accepted the correction and declared his willingness to concur in a public disclaimer.'[1]

---

1. Oldmeadow, *Francis Cardinal Bourne*, Vol. 2, pp. 362/363.

Additionally, when Cardinal Mercier received the letter of approval from Cardinal Gasparri on the 25th November 1922, he evidently sent a copy of it together with his own letter to Cardinal Bourne. Cardinal Bourne's reply to Cardinal Mercier mentioned that Halifax had been to see him *twice*, once before the Conversations had begun, and again in late November 1922. Bourne was not very hopeful of any serious outcome from the meetings, because, principally, the Church of England was so divided and that Lord Halifax represented only a small minority within that Church. Nevertheless, he thought that the Conversations should be encouraged.[1] Cardinal Bourne's biographer, Oldmeadow, categorically denies that Bourne was informed of the Conversations before the end of 1923, when news of the Conversations were made public.[2] This is manifestly inaccurate, as there is documentary evidence that Mercier personally wrote to Bourne on the 30th November 1922, enclosing a copy of his letter to Lord Halifax and which, he tells Bourne, 'is to keep you informed of what has happened since then.'[3] Cardinal Mercier concluded his letter by asking his fellow Cardinal to keep him and his ecumenical efforts in his prayers, and stated that he would be profoundly grateful for any advice that Bourne could offer, especially as the latter lived in daily company with the Church of England and could offer insights from which Mercier could readily profit.

Cardinal Bourne's reply to Mercier was prompt (4th December 1922), and he thanked Mercier particularly for the information on the Holy See's attitude to these Conversations. Regarding Lord Halifax, Bourne mentioned that he had been to see him twice, but that, although he had the highest respect for Halifax's good faith and excellent intentions, he found that he was far from clear as to his own standpoint.

> 'He has always been very vague and inconsequent. Moreover he represents only an infinitesimal group of Anglicans who, while they

---

1. Lahey, *The Origins and Approval of the Malines Conversations*, Church History, Chicago, XLIII, p. 370.
2. Oldmeadow, *Francis Cardinal Bourne*, Vol. 2, p. 365.
3. Letter of Mercier to Bourne, 30th November 1922, Archdiocese of Malines Archives, File 3, No. 1.
'I commend this humble effort of charity to the prayers of Your Eminence. It is superfluous to tell you that I would be profoundly grateful for any advice or suggestions which you may be able to give me. You who live in daily contact with the Anglican church can provide me with points of enlightenment which I would be most happy to profit from.'

admit the need of a central authority, are by no means convinced that the actual existence of such an authority is *an essential part of the Divine constitution of the Church*' (Bourne's emphasis).[1]

In the Westminster archives there is a letter addressed to Mr Oldmeadow, then editor of *The Tablet*, sent to him from Rome by Cardinal Bourne. Dated 6th February 1924, it referred to Mercier's Pastoral Letter to his clergy in which he had informed them of the meetings at Malines. Cardinal Bourne instructed the editor of *The Tablet* to

'give it the most sympathetic and cordial treatment, and quote largely from it. In a sense the most important words are ... "it is sufficient for us to know that we proceed with the agreement of the supreme authority, blessed and encouraged by It": *which reveals the fact, known to me in confidence all along, that the conversations were held with the knowledge, approbation and encouragement of the Holy See.*[2]

It is difficult to see how Oldmeadow, as Bourne's biographer and having access to the Cardinal's personal files, should have taken such a contrary stance. In addition, the Cardinal's letter from Rome had been addressed to him personally as editor of the Catholic periodical. It is clear from the tone of his writing that Oldmeadow was against the idea of the Conversations with the Anglicans, and of the view that Halifax and his companions were trying to pull the wool over the eyes of Mercier and the Continental theologians in presenting the Church of England as a homogeneous body with a single view of doctrine and belief. He was scarcely less scathing of the Abbé Portal and others on the continent whom he accused of being naive with regards to Anglicans.

The Abbé Portal, who had been in Malines with Mercier, wrote to Halifax on the 10th January 1923. In his letter, Portal hoped that Halifax

'will be pleased with the copy of the enclosed letter which the Cardinal has written to the Archbishop of Canterbury. He wrote it

---

1. Letter of Bourne to Mercier, 4th December 1922, Archdiocese of Malines Archives, File 3, No. 2.
2. Letter of Bourne to Oldmeadow, 6th February 1923, Archdiocese of Westminster Archives, 124/4/1.

with his own hand, and as his writing is somewhat difficult to read, it would perhaps be as well that you should send him the typed copy of the letter. It seems to me that the letter contains all that you wished and that it complies with all the wishes expressed by the Archbishop. The letter had to be prudent for the Cardinal is aware that there are rocks ahead on our side as well as yours. Cardinal Bourne, in acknowledging the receipt of the communication made to him by the Cardinal [Mercier] of Cardinal Gasparri's letter approving of the continuation of our conversations, sent him an article from *The Tablet* which indicated very clearly his attitude, and one may be sure that Merry Del Val and Gasquet, etc. will adopt the same position, if indeed they have not already done so. The conflict of rival influences will therefore soon begin at Rome, and the Cardinal must be careful not to furnish our adversaries with any weapon they can make use of. I hope your Archbishops realise the Cardinal's position and will do what they can to assist him. That he should already have written as he had to the Archbishop of Canterbury is a fact of importance.'[1]

(b) On the second point of criticism, namely that the meetings were being held with Continental Catholics rather than with their English counterparts, Oldmeadow proposed very strongly that it was because meetings or discussions held in England would have been with people who would have had a much better understanding of the Church of England, and who would be cognizant of the fact that Lord Halifax was not representative of the whole of the Church of England, but only of one section, namely, the High Church group or Anglo-Catholics. Oldmeadow stated categorically that

'Malines was chosen because Malines was ready to accept the spokesmen from England as typical Anglicans rather than minority men whose reading of their Church's character, worship and teaching would have been warmly repudiated by most of their co-religionists at home.'[2]

Oldmeadow's case is that Cardinal Mercier should not have undertaken such a series of talks without consulting his English Catholic colleagues,

---

1. Letter of Portal to Halifax, 10th January 1923, Malines Papers of Lord Halifax, File A4 271, Box 2.
2. Oldmeadow, *Francis Cardinal Bourne*, Vol. 2, pp. 362/363.

particularly his fellow Cardinals, Bourne, the Archbishop of Westminster, and Gasquet, the other English Cardinal who was serving in Rome itself, and who had also served on the enquiry into Anglican Orders.

Another point of umbrage was the way that the Abbé Portal had been introduced to the Church of England during his visit in the 1890s. Oldmeadow noted that the Abbé was shown little of the established Church save for its Anglo-Catholic side. 'He attended ritualistic Churches, was introduced to "high" Bishops, saw anglican convents and stayed for some days with the Cowley Fathers in Oxford.' He appeared to avoid contact with English Catholics who might have been able to give a more balanced opinion of the Church of England, continues Oldmeadow, and 'when Cardinal Vaughan courteously arranged a luncheon party at which the Abbé was to meet two experts in his own line (Abbot [afterwards Cardinal] Gasquet and Mr Edmund Bishop), the Frenchman did not turn up.'[1] Oldmeadow suggests that all of this was a key to the English Catholic dislike of the 'machinations' which reached a climax at Malines.

In January 1924, Cardinal Bourne made reunion the subject of his Lenten Pastoral Letter, which was to be read in all Churches and Chapels of the Diocese on Quinquagesima Sunday. The text of the Lenten Pastoral was also published in full in *The Tablet* of 8th March 1924. The Cardinal took a prudent and balanced view of the subject, and tried to fit the Malines Conversations into the overall quest for Church unity. He began by saying that he and others 'have noted with thanksgiving to God that on all sides there is a renewed and intensified longing for such union; and a keen realisation that disunion is evidently contrary to the declared will of our Lord and Saviour, and the cause of untold harm to men. At the same time', he continued, 'it is clear that on the part of our fellow-countrymen who do not accept the authority of the Holy See, there is almost complete misapprehension of the sole basis of union

---

1. Oldmeadow, *Francis Cardinal Bourne*, Vol. 2, p. 360.
Oldmeadow's accusation should be compared with the much simpler explanation in Lord Halifax's biography where, explaining the details of Abbé Portal's visit to England, J.G. Lockhart reconts that whilst they were in Yorkshire, "Business in the House of Lords recalled Halifax to London, Portal remaining in Yorkshire; and – apparently by the temporary miscarriage of a letter – an invitation to the Abbé to have luncheon with Cardinal Vaughan on Tuesday, August 14th, was not received in time to be accepted'.
cf. Lockhart, *Charles Lindley Viscount Halifax*, Vol. 2, p. 49.

CONTROVERSY GROWS AS CONVERSATIONS ARE MADE PUBLIC

which is in conformity with the will of Christ – namely, the frank and complete acceptance of divinely revealed truth.'[1] Bourne explained what the attitude of Catholics should be towards the quest for reunion; it must be an attitude 'of intense sympathy manifested both in constant and more fervent prayer for the restoration of England to that unity of Christendom which it once enjoyed and so greatly honoured; and in a readiness to explain and elucidate in every way those teachings of the Catholic Church which are still so often misunderstood and misrepresented by our fellow-countrymen.'[2]

Two further important points were developed by the Cardinal in his Lenten Pastoral: first, that the English Catholic bishops were prepared to make any sacrifice for the cause of reunion of the Churches, even to the extent of resigning their Sees if it would help unity between Catholics and Anglicans. This is a reference to the French hierarchy who, just over a century previously, were all asked by the Pope to resign from their dioceses so that religious peace and proper Church order could be re-established in republican France; and, secondly, that 'it is to us a matter of rejoicing that members of the Establishment, to whatever school of thought they may belong, should seek from representative Catholics, whether they be in France, or in Belgium, or here at home, or in any other country, a more complete understanding of what the Catholic Church really teaches. Such contact, with the help of the Holy Spirit, must be productive of good, even though no actual result may be immediately attained.'[3]

The latter part of this last sentence indicates somewhat the Cardinal's pessimism that any concrete or practical good would come from the meetings in Belgium, but, on the whole, his Letter was positive and constructive. At the very least, he was not adopting an obstructionist position.

In the Mercier archives at the Grande Seminaire, Malines, there is a series of press cuttings[4] included with a copy of Cardinal Bourne's Lenten Pastoral which are quite illuminating. One of these, from the French publication *La Semaine Religieuse de Paris*, dated 12th April

---

1. Francis Cardinal Bourne, *Pastoral Letter for Lent 1924*, London, 1924, pp. 3/4.
2. Bourne, *Pastoral Letter for Lent* 1924, p. 5.
3. Bourne, *Pastoral Letter for Lent 1924*, p. 7.
4. Archdiocese of Malines Archives, File 30, B.9.

1924, after giving a summary of Bourne's Pastoral, includes reactions from various English personages.[1]

The secretary of the Church Association,[2] M. Barron, commented to those who considered reunion an ideal to be attained that the Church of Rome condemned to eternal damnation those who reject their teachings and, he added, the Church of England is not disposed to reject its own 39 Articles of religion. This is followed by a comment from the Revd Mr Berry of the Congregational Union that 'one can only hope for important results'.[3] A certain Mr Robert Perks, an eminent layman of the Methodist Church, is quoted as saying that he considered the reunion of the two Churches as 'the end of the Church of England'. He thought that 'Anglican ministers would have to be re-Ordained, that they would have to accept the roman Credo and become part of the Roman Church'.[4] A correspondent of the Catholic News Service wrote that 'English Catholics, however strong their desire to see their separated brethren united in Catholic unity, are unanimous in stating that this cannot be conceived of without the Anglicans accepting in their entirety the teachings of the Catholic Church. On the Anglican side, moreover, one can see no sign whatsoever, however small it may be, of a wish to accept the teachings of the Catholic Church, such as are promoted by the Holy See. Their bishops are strongly critical, in their statements to the Press, of the attitude of the Protestant Archbishop of Canterbury, who has encouraged the conversations at Malines.'[5]

In the issue of February 1924 of the review *The Month*, Fr J. Keating S.J. published an article entitled 'Clearing the Air' in which he proposed as a preliminary condition for reunion that those 'who desire to belong to the Church must believe that God instituted an infallible Church to teach and govern mankind in matters spiritual until the end of time, and that that Church is ours'. The author added that 'whatever the results of

---

1. *A propos de "Conversations de Malines" : Une lettre pastorale du Cardinal Bourne et un article du "Month"*, published in *La Semaine Religieuse de Paris*, April 1924, pp. 566/568.
2. The 'Church Association' was a society formed in 1865 during the ritual controversies by several leading Evangelical churchmen to maintain the Protestant ideals of faith and worship in the Church of England.
F.L. Cross and E.A. Livingstone, *Oxford Dictionary of the Christian Church*, 2nd Ed., (Oxford: Oxford Univ. Press, 1983).
3. *La Semaine Religieuse de Paris, Op. Cit.*, p. 567.
4. *La Semaine Religieuse de Paris*, p. 567.
5. *La Semaine Religieuse de Paris*, p. 568.

CONTROVERSY GROWS AS CONVERSATIONS ARE MADE PUBLIC

Malines, there is no doubt that the discussions in the Press and in public will bring about a better understanding of the nature of the Church of Christ, such as is taught in Catholic theology, and a definitive recognition of the impossibility of 'corporate reunion' with Rome.[1]

In the April issue of the American catholic revue *America*, Fr Wilfred Parsons S.J. gave an overall view of the Conversations from the point of view of Cardinal Bourne's Lenten pastoral, and tried to clarify for the American public the distinct groupings within the Church of England. 'There are, broadly speaking, three parties to the discussion, the Catholics, the Anglicans, and the non-conforming Protestants. Among Catholics there is only one stand on doctrine, whether at Malines or at Westminster, but certain differences as to procedure. Among Anglicans there are widely differing viewpoints on doctrine and severe conflict as to procedure. The Protestants, far apart on doctrine and on procedure, have little in common with the other two parties, except, among some of them, a certain vague desire for the union of Christendom. The greater number of Protestants in England and America have been frankly hostile to any parleying with Rome.'[2] Fr Parsons was obviously not hopeful of any useful outcome to the meetings as, in the same article, he ventured that Bourne's Lenten letter had written the last chapter in the discussions about the 'conversations of Malines'.

A similar pessimism and indeed cynicism can be read in an undated article (but probably written around April 1924) prepared for *The Tablet* by Oldmeadow but never published, as Cardinal Bourne had written from Rome asking that further comment on the Conversations should be suspended. The proof edition is conserved in the documentation at Archbishop's House, Westminster.[3] Oldmeadow's prognosis was that 'there can be "nothing doing" beyond some more snug little private chats in a snug little private sitting-room. It is interesting: but it is not Reunion.'

(iv) Cardinal Mercier's Pastoral Letter.

On the other side of the Channel, Cardinal Mercier had already found himself under increasing pressure due to these Anglican and Catholic revelations and reactions in England. As a result, he issued a Pastoral

---

1. *La Semaine Religieuse de Paris*, p. 568.
2. *Canterbury and Malines*, Wilfred Parsons S.J., '*America*', 5th April 1924, p. 587.
3. Archdiocese of Westminster Archives, Ref. No. 124/4/2.

'A BROTHER KNOCKING AT THE DOOR'

Letter on the 18th January 1924. This Pastoral, entitled *Conversations de Malines*, was read in all Churches of the Archdiocese on Sunday, 3rd February 1924.[1]

In the Pastoral, Mercier justified what had taken place at Malines, and expressed his intention of continuing the Conversations with a view to realizing that unity willed by Christ. The Cardinal rejected in very straightforward language the criticisms which had been directed at the idea of holding meetings with the Anglicans:

> 'A great nation was, for more than eight centuries, our beloved sister; this nation gave the Church a phalanx of saints whom to this day we honour in our liturgy; it has preserved astonishing resources of Christian life within its vast empire; from it numberless missions have gone out; but a gaping wound is in its side. We Catholics, kept safe, by the grace of God, in the whole truth, we lament the criminal sundering which tore it away, four centuries ago, from the Church our Mother; and there are Catholics who, like the Levite and the Priest of the old Law, reproved by our Divine Saviour in the parable of the Samaritan, would have a Catholic bishop pass by, proudly indifferent, refusing to pour a drop of oil in this gaping wound, to tend it, and try to lead the sick man to God's house whither God's mercy calls him. I should have judged myself guilty, if I had been so cowardly.'[2]

The important points which were expressed in the Pastoral were:-
 (a) that the 'Conversations' were *not* 'negotiations' - he stressed that they were, and had been from the very beginning, *private*, because for 'official' talks one needs a mandate or authorization to speak on behalf of someone. Neither of the two sides involved in the Conversations had such a mandate. He made the point, however, that the Pope knew about the meetings and had given them his blessing;[3]
 (b) that it was indeed their privilege to be involved in such an opening of the way for a spiritual rejuvenation in both Churches;

---

1. Bivort de la Saudée, *'Documents sur le Problème de l'Union Anglo-Romaine: (1921–1927)'*, Bruxelles 1949, p. 140/152.
2. *'Les "Conversations de Malines"'*, Cardinal D.J. Mercier, Malines 18th January 1924, Part II, p. 9.
3. Bivort de la Saudée, *'Documents sur le Problème de l'Union Anglo-Romaine'*, p. 143.
'... il nous suffisait de savoir que nous marchions d'accord avec l'autorité suprême, bénis et encouragés par Elle.'

(c) that in order to have even a possibility of reunion, it was necessary to have great faith in God's mercy and help.

Frere emphasises this last point as being one of the great assets of the Cardinal's character,[1] talking about Mercier's 'largeness of heart' and remarking that reunion would be easy if it depended only on faith and charity and not also on points of doctrinal belief. It was the head and not the heart which was obstructing reunion.

On the whole, Cardinal Mercier's Pastoral letter was very well received. Apart from some minor criticisms regarding individual words in the text (such as describing the Church of England as 'Protestant'), both Portal and Halifax were pleased with it.[2] Even in Rome, the Pastoral was well received, and Mercier told Halifax in a letter of 7th February 1924[3] that he had received a very favourable letter from Cardinal Gasparri in Rome. Then on the 24th March 1924,[4] the Pope himself gave a guarded

---

1 Frere, *Recollections of Malines*, p. 50.
2. Only to Portal did Lord Halifax express his hesitations about some points of the Cardinal's letter: 'I have told the Cardinal how much his letter gave me pleasure but to you, my dear friend, I dare admit to you that I would have preferred that certain things be omitted or that certain things have been said differently'.
Letter of Halifax to Portal, 7th February 1924, Portal Papers, Paris.
3. Bivort de la Saudée, in his book *'Anglican et Catholique'*, p. 116, says that Mercier wrote to Halifax on the 7th February 1924, recounting a letter he had received from Cardinal Gasparri: 'From Rome I have received an excellent private letter from Cardinal Gasparri; this confirms the encouragements of the first, but the Holy See does not wish to take an official attitude for the moment.'
However, Rogert Aubert, in both *'Collectanea Mechliniensia'*, t. 52, 1967/1, p. 52, and also in *'Bulletins de l'Académie Royale de Belgique'*, Bruxelles 1967, p. 112, reports that Mercier wrote to Rome asking Pius XI to confirm his approval, and that Cardinal Gasparri replied on 10th January 1924 with two letters in the same dispatch. These two letters are published in full by R. Aubert in the *'Bulletins'*, pièce annex XXVI, pp. 152/153.
(i) The first letter dealt with the Pastoral Letter of 18th January 1924, and Gasparri tells Mercier that the Pastoral had been well received, but that the Pope did not see the necessity of giving any further official recognition, and that Mercier should carry on the way he was going.
(ii) The second letter, which arrived with the first, was a disclaimer that the Holy See had anything to do with the missing phrase in a translation of the Pastoral Letter which appeared in *'Osservatore Romano'*. The missing part was the one which referred to the Holy See's approval of the Conversations.
4. Pope Pius XI's discourse included the following passage which, although far from specific, gives an open approval to those Catholics who engage themselves in preparing the way for reunion by rectifying prejudiced opinions and explaining the (Catholic) faith: 'In quo catholicis omnibus gratiam habebimus maximam, quotquot dissidentibus a se fratribus, divina gratia instincti, ad germanae adeptonem fidei viam munire contemderint,

but definite approval in a discourse which he addressed to the cardinals gathered at the termination of a 'secret' Consistory.[1] The following day, Gasparri wrote to Cardinal Mercier[2] confirming the approval which the Pope had expressed at the Consistory. One must surely note that these three publications (that is, the Christmas letter of Davidson, Mercier's Pastoral Letter, and finally the Pope's public approval in Consistory), following so closely on one another, gave the whole affair not only a full airing, but also a definite semi-official, if not official atmosphere.

(v) The Malines Conversations – official or not?

That not everyone was in favour of this aura of officialdom being given to the Conversations is illustrated by one incident which is related by Bivort de la Saudée. In the translation of Cardinal Mercier's Pastoral Letter which appeared in the *Osservatore Romano*,[3] the phrase '... we proceed with the agreement of the supreme authority, blessed and encouraged by Her' was omitted.[4] In France, the Dominican publication *Revue des Jeunes*, printed the Pastoral Letter, whereas in England members of the same Order were forbidden to publish anything on the

---

(Footnote no. 4 continued from previous page.)
praeiudicatas convellendo opiniones, integram tradendo catholicam doctrinam ...
Note: R. Aubert in *'Bulletin'*, gives the date of the Consistory as 26th March 1924. This date is incorrect cf. *Acta Apostolicae Sedis.*, Rome 1924, t.XVI, pp. 134/124.

1. A *Consistory* is a solemn assembly of all the cardinals present in Rome, presided over by the Pope. This assembly normally considers some of the more important matters concerning the government of the universal Church. The Consistory of April 1924 was a "secret" or "ordinary" Consistory for the nomination of new cardinals. The allocutions of the Pope at such Consistories are subsequently published in the official publication of the Holy See, the *'Acta Apostolicae Sedis'*.
For a fuller explanation of Consistories and their different types, cf. 'New Catholic Encyclopedia', Washington 1967, Vol. 4, p. 217.
2. Bivort de la Saudée, *Documents sur le Problème de l'Union Anglo-Romaine*, p. 117.
The last letter from Gasparri found in the Malines Archives by Aubert was dated 13th March 1924. But Aubert explains that Saudée consulted these archives at the time when Mercier's Secretary was still alive, so he may have got this information from him.
3. *'Osservatore Romano'*, 7th February 1924.
4. R. Aubert, *Bulletin*, pièce annexe XXIV, pp. 149/151.
This is the text of a letter from A. Sordet CSSR, a friend of Mercier in Rome, explaining the discrepancy. He tells Mercier not to worry about it: '... it is simply the daily gaffe which the editors of the Osservatore are wont to make ... I really ought to issue an official communiqué to say that the Holy See is not responsible for the stupidities of the Osservatore'.

CONTROVERSY GROWS AS CONVERSATIONS ARE MADE PUBLIC

subject of reunion without the special permission of the Superior General in Rome.[1] Fr Vincent McNabb O.P., the eminent Dominican writer, replied to a letter of Abbé Portal in the following terms:

'You suggest my writing in *Blackfriars* an article on Cardinal Mercier's Pastoral. I would willingly do so, but there are difficulties which perhaps you or His Eminence might help to remove – let me explain.

I have several times already been denounced to Rome for what I have written on the subject of Reunion. Indeed both myself and my Dominican brethren in England have been threatened with punishment on account of my writings. I have no great wish to know who is the very energetic person that watches everything I write – whoever he (or she) – for it was once a SHE and not a HE – is, he or she succeeds not merely in misleading himself but in misinforming the authorities in Rome. The last denunciation occurred only a few weeks ago. It was based on my alleged contumacy in having, as they thought, republished in my book *From a Friar's Cell* an article which had already been denounced. But they thought wrongly, because I had *not* republished the article – the matter was very painful. As an old Irish Catholic my respect for Rome is so congenital and deep seated that I am pained when some ill-informed people send the Sacred Congregations, and even the Cardinal Secretaries of these Congregations – on wild-goose chases.

However the upshot of the matter is that I am not allowed to write anything on Reunion unless it is personally approved by the Master General of the Order in Rome.

You will see from this how difficult it is for me to give any written support to what I consider the classical and historical Pastoral of Cardinal Mercier. Perhaps His Eminence could do something in Rome in order to allow at least one (Irish Catholic) theologian to express one side. Perhaps I might be told what I have said that *was wrong*. I am perplexed to know where I am wrong; as I am too loyal a Catholic to hesitate about withdrawing it. I am all the more perplexed because the only alleged mistake I was finally charged with was to have called 'Rome, the Mother Church of the Church of

---

1. Bivort de la Saudée, *Documents sur le Problème de l'Union Anglo-Romaine*, p. 119.

England'. Yet Wiseman calls Rome the Mother Church of the Lutheran Churches! His Eminence, therefore, might find it possible to do something in Rome towards allowing me to express one view – his own view – on the subject of Reunion.
Perhaps he could express a wish to me personally, or to the Master General that I might write on his Pastoral. Otherwise I cannot see that anything can be done.
I hate tittle-tattle and Roman gossip: but someone suggested that one of the chief movers in denouncing me is Dom S. Langton OSB, chaplain to Cardinal Gasquet ...'[1]

In a further letter of the 20th April 1924 addressed to Mercier, McNabb complains that none of the English Catholic Press was giving a favourable account of the Pastoral Letter. His Anglo-Saxon sense of fair play comes out when McNabb continues by stating that 'it might even seem regrettable that only one view of this action should be allowed publicity, and that the other side, based on documents and couched in temperate language, should be denied publicity. It is the traditional custom of Rome in all matters of moment to ask for a *Votum* on each side of the question. A seeming departure from this wise and just tradition may be difficult publicly to justify'.[2]

These incidents can be seen as indications of a mounting hostility towards the Conversations from some Catholics, and efforts by unseen hands to suppress or at least minimize any impression that there was official sanction on the part of the Pope or Roman Congregations.

---

1. Letter of McNabb to Portal, 18th February 1924, Archdiocese of Malines Archives, File 27, B.2.
Also contained in this file, is a copy of a 22 page article by McNabb entitled 'Cardinal Wiseman and Cardinal Mercier on Reunion' which was written but never published (File 27, B.1). McNabb in fact, submitted his article to the Master General in Rome, Fr Lewis Theissling OP, who told him to present the article to Cardinal Bourne. The Dominican General would only consent to its subsequent publication on condition that Cardinal Bourne approved of it (File 27, C.5). The Cardinal, who consulted with Bishop Bidwell, thought the article 'mischievous and misleading', and stated that he thought 'no useful purpose would be served by its publication' (File 27, B.5).
2. Letter of McNabb to Mercier, Archdiocese of Malines Archives, File 27, A.5.

7

The Fourth 'Conversation' and an examination of the discussion papers.

(i) The fourth Conversation gets under way.

Lord Halifax, impatient for the next meeting and becoming anxious lest the connections with the Roman Catholics weaken through lack of contact, decided to make arrangements for a private visit to Malines towards the end of April 1924.[1] He took with him his son Edward and his good friend Lord Hugh Cecil,[2] and it would seem that he wished to introduce these two to Cardinal Mercier as his own possible successors in the Conversations. It must be borne in mind that Halifax was of an advanced age – 85 years old – by this time. In a letter just before he left for Malines, Halifax mentions the possibility of discussing the powers of the Episcopacy and of the Pope during the next Conversation.[3]

The dates of the next Conversation kept being postponed for various reasons. It had first been thought to hold the fourth meeting on 8th and 9th October 1924, but the Dean of Wells, Dr Robinson, had an accident in August, and this incapacitated him for a couple of months. Then the meeting was fixed for some time in January 1925, but Dr Robinson's

---

1. The real reason for this visit was not only to meet with Portal and arrange the topics for discussion at the next meeting, but to decide how they should deal with Dr. Gore's attitude to the Conversations. In a letter of the 14th February, Halifax describes Gore as 'annoying', and ventured the opinion that Gore would continue to be annoying until the end of his days. In particular, Halifax took exception to Dr Gore's suggestion of discussing 'merits and indulgences' instead of concentrating on more fundamental points such as 'the Church'.
Letter of Halifax to Portal, 14th February 1924, Portal Papers, Paris.
2. Halifax gives a short description of Lord Hugh Cecil for Portal to pass on to Cardinal Mercier, so that he would know something of the background of his guest. Lord Hugh Cecil was the younger brother of Lord Salisbury and Viscount Cecil, both of whom had been members of the previous British Government. Lord Hugh Cecil was himself a Member of Parliament representing Oxford, and his family was in direct line from the famous Minister of Queen Elizabeth I. Halifax describes him as a pious, thoughtful, practising member of the Church of England. Letter of Halifax to Portal, April 1924, Portal Papers, Paris.
3. Bivort de la Saudée, *Anglicans et Catholiques*, p. 120.

health and Dr Gore's prospective absence abroad in the Far East caused the date to be postponed again. Concurrently there were considerable difficulties arising in the Church of England about the changes in the Book of Common Prayer, particularly concerning the arrangement and order of the prayers in the Communion Service. Some friends, including Lord Hugh Cecil, requested Halifax that any further Conversations be postponed till after June 1925 when the Prayer Book discussion would be concluded.[1]

Halifax, however, was not idle during all this time. In November 1924 he paid a visit to the Abbé Portal in Paris, and both then proceeded to Malines for another private visit to Cardinal Mercier. It was during this time that the question of 'corporate reunion' emerged. In a letter to Halifax dated 13th December 1924, Mercier mentioned that he would be leaving for Rome on the 21st of that same month. Halifax therefore suggested to the Cardinal that he should ask the Pope for an expression of his desire for 'corporate reunion' of the two Churches. Mercier replied that if the Pope thought such an expression of corporate unity would not disturb or be disagreeable to the Archbishop of Canterbury, then he (Mercier) thought that the Pope would not object to making such an appeal.

Halifax, having returned to England by this time, tried to persuade Archbishop Davidson to write directly to the Pope regarding this matter of an appeal for 'corporate reunion'. Davidson replied to Halifax by letter on 1st December 1924, a letter which was so full of doubts and hesitations that the primary purpose for which Halifax had wished the letter to serve, namely, corporate reunion, was completely destroyed.[3] Davidson wrote that he saw great difficulties and risks in writing to the Pope on the subject of 'corporate reunion', and stated that he felt that he

---

1. Bivort de la Saudée, *Anglicans et Catholiques*, p. 120.
2. Because of the delays, Halifax began considering the possibility of having some kind of meeting at his own home between Anglicans and Roman Catholics, and he actually approached both Archbishop Davidson and Cardinal Bourne with this suggestion. Both of these personages expressed their opposition to the idea. Halifax reported to Portal about the archbishop's reply: 'He is opposed to meetings at my home with your people ... And, but this is only for you, Cardinal Bourne, whom I have also seen, he also thinks that this is not a good time for such meetings'.
Letter of Halifax to Portal, 15th June 1924, Portal Papers, Paris.
3. Letter of Davidson to Halifax, 1st December 1924, Malines Papers of Lord Halifax, File A4 271, Box 5.

could not in conscience follow Halifax's suggestion as this would be making him go further that he would wish to go. He had no objection, however, if, in writing to Cardinal Mercier, Halifax informed the Cardinal that the Archbishop of Canterbury was a prudent man (Davidson noted pointedly to Halifax that 'you might be able to find a stronger phrase'), and that contacts with theologians and the general feeling in England led him to believe that it would be unwise to take any initiative on 'corporate reunion' until many more consultations and explanations had been exchanged. It would also be very helpful if the Pope, instead of calling for individual conversions to the Roman Church, substituted a call to the whole Anglican Church, inviting them to consider 'corporate reunion'. This would then be totally in keeping with the spirit of the Lambeth Appeal. However, it showed Mercier, to whom Halifax sent a copy of the letter, that it was useless to push too hard. In this latest letter of the Viscount to Cardinal Mercier, Halifax explains that the Archbishop of Canterbury was 'very unwell, and I really am anxious about him. He says that he hopes he is mending but that he has been and is "overwhelmed with inexorable and urgent work".'[1] As regards a call from the Pope for corporate reunion, Mercier told Halifax that it was not the opportune time, but perhaps there would be a possibility later on in the year, during the second part of the first Vatican Council, which the Cardinal fully expected to re-open that year.[2]

Lord Halifax was not the only member of the Conversations team who was maintaining contact. Bishop Gore kept in contact with Pierre Batiffol and Hemmer, and on the 28th September 1924 he visited them

1. Letter of Halifax to Mercier, 19th December 1924, Archdiocese of Malines Archives, File 18, No. 16.
2. Letters of Halifax to Portal, 1st & 10th January 1925, Portal Papers, Paris. Bivort de la Saudée's account of this question of 'corporate reunion' is misleadingly reported in his book *Anglicans et Catholiques*, pp. 122/124. He gives the impression that the idea of 'corporate reunion' arose as a result of Cardinal Mercier's letter to Lord Halifax of 13th December 1924, in which Mercier first mentions that he was going to Rome on the 21st December 1924. This would obviously have been an excellent opportunity to ask the Pope for some sort of gesture of favour towards the Anglicans, as, for example, a mention of 'corporate reunion'. Then we have Halifax writing to Davidson, and sending a copy of Davidson's letter to Mercier on 19th December 1924. Considering the state of the postal services of the time, and also the caution with which Archbishop Davidson normally approached such topics, the time scale of this correspondence is improbable!
In fact, the whole issue of 'corporate reunion' had been under discussion since Halifax's letter to *The Times* of 22nd February 1924.

in Paris while returning from his vacation.¹ During this brief visit, the most important thing discussed was the importance of having a properly prepared agenda. Batiffol suggested the topic of 'the Episcopacy, its constituted rights and its functions'. Dr Gore, who had read Mgr Batiffol's recently published book *Le Siège Apostolique*² during his vacation, suggested that something be prepared on the development of dogma regarding the Apostolic See. All agreed on the necessity of fixing the subjects as soon as possible. Dr Gore then suggested that Dr Kidd be in charge of contacting the English members and for arranging with Cardinal Mercier a date for the next Conversation. The arrangements for the Fourth Conversation were now taking shape. We can note also a letter from Mercier to Batiffol on the 16th February 1925, in which he proposed the week of the 17th May as the date for the next meeting, and asked him to contact Hemmer and Portal. He mentioned that 'the Paris group' were in charge of studying the question of the Episcopacy from the historical and juridical points of view, and that Mgr Van Roey would approach the question from a theological point of view.³

The Conversations were eventually resumed, and the ten participants again met at Malines, on the 19th and 20th May 1925. There were no new members of the groups, and so the representatives were the same as those of the third meeting, namely, Cardinal Mercier; Dr Walter Frere, Bishop of Truro; Dr Charles Gore, former Bishop of Oxford; Dr Armitage Robinson, Dean of Wells; Dr Kidd, Warden of Keble College at Oxford; Mgr Van Roey, Vicar General of Malines; M. Portal, Congregation of the Mission; Mgr Pierre Batiffol, Canon of Notre Dame at Paris; M. Hemmer, Parish Priest of La Sainte-Trinité at Paris.

Dean Robinson's journal describes a private discussion he had with the Abbé Portal even before the meetings had begun. Evidently the Dean thought that the Conversations ought to come to an end. The journal reports: 'Lord Halifax in the next room to me, with only a door between, has been reading out in loud and clear tones to the Abbé Portal my letter to him in which I said the Conversations ought to come to an end! Then long talk in French which was beyond my hearing while they both

1. Bivort de la Saudée, *Anglicans et Catholiques*, p. 126.
2. Mgr Pierre Batiffol, *Le Siège Apostolique*, Paris, 1924.
3. Bivort de la Saudée, *Documents sur le Problème de l'Union Anglo-Romaine*, p. 153.

agreed how wrong it was of me, I suppose. I caught the little Abbé as he said Good night, and brought him in here and did my best French on him to show him why I was right, and to make him understand that I am not irreconcilable! He says that if the Conversations are suspended people in France will say there has been a rupture and nothing has been done at all, and the enemies of goodwill will rejoice.'[1] In proposing an adjournment of the Conversations even prior to the beginning of this fourth meeting at Malines, Armitage Robinson was clearly reflecting the view of the Archbishop of Canterbury. Dr Davidson was under severe critical pressure in England following his public statement on the Conversations, and the Prayer Book discussions were now being further complicated by the implication that they were linked with Malines.

The programme for the 19th May involved two sessions or *séances*, one beginning at 10 a.m., and the second at 4 p.m. The first séance involved the reading of a paper entitled *The Episcopacy and the Papacy from a theological viewpoint*,[2] by Mgr Van Roey. This paper had been circulated to members of the group as early as April 1925, (as indeed had all the papers, with the notable exception of that delivered by Cardinal Mercier the following day), and so the Anglicans considered it more of a précis of Catholic doctrine than a proposition to be discussed fully. There were a number of points, however, which they raised either for clarification or for explanation.

The content of Van Roey's paper was divided into three main sections: first, teachings on the Episcopate; secondly, teachings regarding the Pope; thirdly, the question of Papal Infallibility. In dealing with these, Mgr Van Roey tried to indicate the degree of certitude attached to each, i.e. whether the teachings concerned defined truth of Faith, or whether they involved merely non-defined truth but matters that were theologically certain, or whether the teachings constituted merely a disputable theological hypothesis.

During the discussion which followed the reading of Van Roey's paper, there were four main points on which clarification was required:

1. Journal of J. Armitage Robinson, 18th May 1925, p. 1.
Note: Robinson mistakenly writes the year as '1924' instead of 1925, as the content and dates clearly indicate.
2. Lord Halifax, *Original Documents*, pp. 159–174.
3. Bivort de la Saudée, *Anglicans et Catholiques*, p. 128.

(1) Regarding the question of the power of a bishop outside his own diocese, Van Roey had given as an example the circumstance of a metropolitan bishop of a province, who, 'under the title of charity', could intervene officially in the difficulties of another bishop. Dr Kidd proposed as possible examples the historical facts that Bishop Athanasius ordained priests outside his own diocese, and also the action of Saint Epiphanius at Antioch, but Batiffol and Hemmer rejected these as examples of legitimate action, regarding them rather as examples of bishops intervening unlawfully in other dioceses, interventions which, moreover, had unhappy results.

(2) Dr Gore then raised a question which had been dealt with in the third paragraph of Van Roey's paper, and said that Catholic theologians had admirably expressed the position of episcopal power and its extremes, but this had not stopped the continued development of papal power and its intrusion into what were properly episcopal domains. As proof of this he cited the text of the oath which each Bishop had to make to the Pope, adding that 'the realities, ... are more to be considered than the words'.[1] Gore's main objection seems to have been that this oath deprived the bishop of the normal exercise of his rights in his relations with the Pope. Cardinal Mercier immediately replied that in his eighteen years as a bishop, he had never once experienced a pontifical intervention, not even during the War.

(3) In that part of the paper which dealt with the powers of the Pope, namely sections 8, 9 and 10, the following two lines provoked some discussion: 'His acts do not derive from any superior authority here below; they carry within themselves a value which belongs to acts of a supreme power'.[2] Gore and Batiffol both agreed that there were certain ecclesiastical rights which ought to be respected in all cases, but Hemmer was of the opinion that one of the essential functions of the Holy See was to be able to step in or intervene in any circumstance in which the well-being of the Church was concerned, and that respect for 'the holy canons' should not be such that this power is blocked or impeded. Mgr Van Roey agreed that his original text could perhaps be capable of more than one interpretation, and agreed to re-phrase this section. This he did, and he presented the following re-worked version in the afternoon session: 'His acts carry within themselves a value which belongs to acts of a supreme authority; they are conditioned, however,

1. Lord Halifax, *Original Documents*, p. 52.
2. Lord Halifax, *Original Documents*, p. 168.

FOURTH 'CONVERSATION' – EXAMINATION OF DISCUSSION PAPERS

by divine right as by the natural law, and the ordinary government of the Church requires that they be based on already established canonical discipline'.[1]

(4) The last point which was raised regarding this first discussion document, was a request for clarification as to what exactly were the conditions which had to be fulfilled in order that the Pope might make an infallible pronouncement. Mgr Van Roey replied by enumerating the four classic conditions for an infallible pronouncement, that is, when the Pope is:

– acting as Doctor and Pastor of the Universal Church;
– intending to use the plenitude of his power and making this intention known;
– pronouncing on a matter of Faith or Morals;
– and imposes it on all as binding.

This first session concluded at 1 p.m.

The second session opened at 4 p.m., the afternoon of the 19th May. Apart from the alterations of the small part of Van Roey's text, already mentioned, the whole of the afternoon session was dedicated to the reading and discussion of a paper read by M. Hemmer, which was entitled *Relations between the Pope and the Bishops from an historical viewpoint*.[2] This was a long paper (53 pages in Halifax's book of original documents), in which Hemmer traces the relationships of the members of the hierarchy from the beginnings of the Church up to the present time. It was not a complete history, of course, but more of an outline, and he concerned himself only with the Western Church, leaving the Eastern Churches out of the discussion.

When the reading was finished, Dr Gore remarked that it was evident that much of the development in the Roman Church throughout the ages had been providential, but he insisted also that there was much in Anglicanism, in the Orthodox Churches and even in Protestantism, which belonged to the spiritual elements of early Christianity as expressed in the New Testament, and which was also included in the best of modern sentiments, criticism, and democratic tendencies, elements which had been more or less eliminated by the Roman Church.

---

1. Lord Halifax, *Original Documents*, p. 54.
2. Lord Halifax, *Original Documents*, pp. 187–240.

Dr Kidd added that on the Anglican side, they must recognize that the Church of Rome is a Church which had reformed itself at the Council of Trent, but he could not help deploring the massive centralization which had taken place since that time. There was no doubt, he continued, that the Papacy was the cause of unity, order, and spiritual independence of the Church, and it could be no longer held that the Papacy always acted on behalf of its own interests, but rather, with the exception of a very few occasions, it had always acted for the good of the Church. He concluded by remarking that he saw the hopeful beginnings of a de-centralization process.

Dr Frere sympathized with what had been said, and added that he fervently believed that if reunion could be brought about, the Church of England could contribute an immense spiritual richness to the Church.[1] With this, the discussion and the session ended.

(ii) **Cardinal Mercier's surprise presentation.**

The third session began the next morning, the 20th May, at 10 a.m. This was the session in which Cardinal Mercier delivered the famous paper on *The Anglican Church, united not absorbed*,[2] which caused such a stir among the participants. In a sense, it was an answer to the implicit ques-

---

1. Bivort de la Saudée remarks in a footnote that Dr Robinson, the Dean of Wells, in a note, dated at Malines the 19th May 1925, and shown only to M. Portal, had written the following lines which show the difference in mentality between the Catholics and the Anglicans:
'There are conclusions deduced from certain premises. We distrust logical conclusions AS SUCH. Moreover, we do not accept all the premises. Furthermore: we see the actual system of the Latin Church as the result of the isolation of the Latin element of Christianity which has developed in its own way. The Church has arrived at a point of practical incomprehension of the Greek and Anglo-Saxon elements and has developed to a point that we see now which we cannot accept as definitive. We appeal for a wider and more comprehensive idea of the Catholic Church.
We have the feeling that, through Providence, we exist in order to bring this witness. If our position can be understood it is scarcely by anyone but ourselves. It constitutes a protest in favour of freedom of spirit, a protest against rules set down by deduced logic, in a world where there are other things than logic. From an ecclesiastical point of view, we are a very turbulent group. In a full and comprehensive Church we must have our place, but not more. We have to be an element which stimulates thought and movement; but our eccentricities will find their counter-balance in other elements. Our exclusion (from the Church) is bad for us, even if we dare not think so; it is certainly bad for the Church considered as a whole'.
Cited by Bivort de la Saudée, *Anglicans et Catholiques*, p. 132.
2. Lord Halifax, *Original Documents*, pp. 241–261.

tion which is always present at meetings of namely, how far is the other side prepared to go in order to meet us?

This was a question which the Cardinal had obviously posed to himself sometime beforehand. His experiences during and immediately after the Great War, his contact with the Anglo-Saxon democracies – especially in America – undoubtedly had some considerable influence on him. There were obvious benefits which a reunion with the Church of England and the Anglican Communion would bring to the Catholic Church, their varied experiences, their Anglo-Saxon spirit, the geographical spread and influence of the British Empire and the United States. These elements of breadth and richness, however, would be endangered if Anglicanism were merely absorbed into the Latin framework of the Church of Rome. Roger Aubert offers another possible explanation when he points out that the Cardinal had been greatly surprised at the position the Anglicans had taken over the issue of the 'pallium', which had arisen at the 2nd Conversation, and that he began to realize the importance of the historical aspects which would present themselves in the practical matters of a reunion.[1]

(iii) Genesis of the Cardinal's Paper.

Whatever possible explanations there might be as to the Cardinal's motivation, there is no doubting the facts. In October 1924, Cardinal Mercier had asked Dom Lambert Beauduin OSB,[2] a Benedictine monk of the Abbey of Mont César in Louvain, to write a paper from a historical point of view on a possible reunion between the Anglican Church and the Roman Catholic Church. Dom Beauduin worked on this project while he was teaching at the College of San Anselmo in Rome, during the winter of 1924/25, and he sent the finished *Memoire* to Mercier on 31st January, 1925.[3]

Mercier was very pleased with the *Memoire*. He told Beauduin in a letter

---

1. Aubert, *Bulletins*, Classe de Lettres, p. 119.
2. Dom Lambert Beauduin OSB (1873–1960) was a notable ecumenist of the time. It was he who in 1925 founded the ecumenical monastery of Amay in Belgium, later transferred to Chevetoque, which includes monks of both Latin and Oriental Rites.
3. Aubert, *Bulletins,* pièce annexe XXX, p. 156.

of 15th February 1925,[1] that it was a real revelation to him. Although he had never lost hope in the Conversations, he had nevertheless thought that reunion would be impossible except perhaps in the very distant future. Now he had great hope in the present! 'And so, my dear friend, thanks to you, we exit from a dream. We enter now into the domain of a hopeful reality, even if not yet accomplished fact'.[2]

But before he presented Beauduin's *Memoire* at the Conversations, Mercier wanted to ensure that Rome was in accord with the principles outlined in the *Memoire*. He asked Beauduin, therefore, to approach Cardinal Gasparri regarding the matter, but Beauduin replied that he thought it would be better to give the paper to an Anglican who would then propose it to Rome. Beauduin thought that the Anglicans had more chance of getting the paper accepted by Rome than the Catholics would.[3]

However, Mercier never went any further with the matter, and on the 20th May 1925 he presented Beauduin's *Memoire*, introducing it as coming from a Roman canonist, but he made it quite clear that he was speaking privately and was in no way implicating the Holy See in these opinions.[4]

In fact, it would seem that the Cardinal was taking a tremendous responsibility on his own shoulders by offering this *Memoire* for consideration by the Anglicans, for the contents of the *Memoire*, as we shall see, went much further than anything which had ever been proposed before, particularly coming from a personage with as high an office and of such weighty authority as Cardinal Mercier. Mercier, however, was no doubt recalling the letter of 30th March 1923 which he had received from Cardinal Gasparri in reply to Mercier's own letter of 1st March 1923. Mercier's letter had been addressed to the Pope, and accompanied a copy of the Memorandum[5] issued at the end of the 2nd Conversation. In this reply, Gasparri had said: 'The Anglicans can rest assured that the Holy See will make all possible concessions in order to facilitate the

1. Aubert, *Bulletins*, pièce annexe XXXI, pp. 157/158.
2. Aubert, *Bulletins*, pièce annexe XXXI p. 158.
3. Aubert, *Bulletins*, p. 121.
4. Frere, *Recollections of Malines*, p. 56.
5. Lord Halifax, *Original Documents*, pp. 79/82.

FOURTH CONVERSATION – EXAMINATION OF DISCUSSION PAPERS

reunion so desired. Personally, I share the impression that a first reading of the Memorandum had suggested to Your Eminence'. The idea contained in the Memorandum of the 2nd Conversation was that the See of Canterbury should be placed in a position analogous with that of the old Patriarchates, that is, the continuance of certain of their own rites and customs, vernacular in the liturgy, communion under two species, and a married priesthood.[1] So, perhaps Mercier was confident that he was expressing more or less views which would be acceptable at Rome.

(iv) Examination of the Cardinal's Paper.

We pass now to examine the *Memoire*[2] itself, to see what exactly were the propositions offered by Mercier to the Anglicans.

The first part of the paper contained Beauduin's attempt to show that in the pre-Reformation Church in England, ever since the time of St Augustine, the Archbishop of Canterbury had enjoyed a Patriarchal jurisdiction, conferred on him by the Pope by the sign of the pallium. He compared this situation with the Uniate Churches of the East, and found a parallel. Therefore, suggested Beauduin, this would be a means of reunion without absorption; the Church of England could come into communion with the Church of Rome and still retain its rite, language, customs, etc., by the recognition by Rome of its Uniate status, and by the acceptance of the pallium from the hand of the Pope by the Archbishop of Canterbury.

It will be instructive if the major conclusions reached by Beauduin are examined in closer detail:

(a) That there does exist a method or formula for reunion of the two Churches which avoids the absorption of one or other of them, and which will safeguard the internal autonomy of each Church while at the same time maintaining the unity of the universal Church.
(b) That if ever there was a Church which by its origins, history and customs, has the right to concessions regarding autonomy, it is the Church of England.

---

1. Aubert, *Bulletins*, p. 105.
2. Full text of the Memoire taken from Lord Halifax's book *The Conversations at Malines (1921–1925), Original Documents*, is appended as Appendix 4.

(c) That the Archbishop of Canterbury would be re-established in his traditional rights as Patriarch of the Anglican Church, after having received the pallium from the Pope. This would give him complete power over the interior organization of the Church in England, such as that enjoyed by the Patriarchs of the Uniate Churches.

(d) That the Latin Code of Canon Law would not be imposed on the Anglican Church just as even now it does not apply to the Oriental Rites.[1]

(e) That the English Church would have its own proper Liturgy, which is, in fact, the old Roman Liturgy of the 7th and 8th century.

(f) That the traditional Sees of the English Church would be preserved, and the new Catholic ones, created since 1851 (such as Westminster, Southwark, Portsmouth, etc.) would be suppressed. Evidently, remarks Beauduin, this would be a serious measure, but no more serious than when Pius VII demanded the resignation of all the French bishops and suppression of dioceses in France when he concluded the Concordat with Napoleon.

(g) The major problem which Beauduin foresaw was the question of whether or not the Patriarch would have the same standing or status as a Cardinal. He resolves this problem, however, by suggesting the creation of a new order of Cardinals, namely, Cardinal-Patriarchs. Beauduin points out that it was only in the 8th century that the order of Cardinal-Bishops had been created, which was several centuries after the creation of Cardinal-Priests and Cardinal-Deacons.

The Anglicans present at the 4th Conversation were quite taken aback by the contents of this paper which the Cardinal had read, as Frere reports, 'all this took our breaths away, especially as it seemed to lead up to a proposal for a Canterbury patriarchate'.[2] But, not having been given the text of the Cardinal's paper, there was no possibility of it being fully discussed. The only comment came from Dr Gore who said that any consideration of reunion must include not only the archbishops and bishops of England, but also those of India, America, etc., who were in communion with the Church of England. Joseph Kempeneers, the biographer of Van Roey, notes that the Catholic participants were also taken

---

1. Cf. *Codex Juris Canonici*, (Vatican: Libreria Editrice Vaticana, 1983), Canon No. 1. This would allow the possibility of having married clergy, as in the Eastern Churches, but under certain strict conditions. It would not allow for married bishops.
2. Frere, *Recollections of Malines*, p. 56.

by surprise by Mercier's *Memoire*, and expressed their own reservations about its contents. He does not, however, cite any sources for this statement although it would seem to be a reasonable supposition. The only verifiable reaction was the decision of the participants that Mercier's *Memoire* should not be included as part of the *procès-verbaux* of the Conversations.[1] This later became a source of contention between Van Roey and Halifax.

(v) Concluding presentations by Dr Gore.

As there was no discussion after the reading of Beauduin's *Memoire* by Cardinal Mercier, the participants moved on to the next topic, and Dr Gore read his paper which was entitled *On Unity with Diversity*.[2] His objective was to show a means of uniting with Rome, in a sort of "corporate union" of the two Churches, while each Church has the rights to profess its own doctrine, yet safeguarding the communion of the Church by a common, fundamental faith.

Gore based his theory on the fact that St Cyprian, at the Council of Carthage in A.D. 256, while regarding the re-baptism of returning heretics as essential, nevertheless refused to judge, much less to excommunicate anyone who thought differently from himself on this question. By contrast, Pope Stephen, his contemporary in Rome, had declared that once baptism was administered it remained valid forever. The Pope pronounced his opinion, and even threatened to excommunicate any bishop who denied the lasting validity of baptism.

Gore concluded concerning Cyprian that, 'his insistence on this duty of tolerance was based on the principle that there are certain fundamental conditions of Catholic communion, but these conditions should not be extended beyond the certain warrant of Scripture. Beyond this lies the

---

1. J. Kempeneers, *Le Cardinal Van Roey en son temps (1874–1961)*, (Bruxelles, Oeuvres Pontificales Missionnaires, 1971), pp. 82–83.
2. For some unexplained reason Dr Gore's paper *On Unity with Diversity* was not published together with the other documents in Lord Halifax's book, *The Convesations at Malines (1921–1925) Original Documents*. The original English version is to be found in Walter Frere, *Recollections of Malines*, (London: Centenary Press, 1935), pp. 110–119. The French version is published by Bivort de la Saudée in *Documents sue le Problème de l'Union Anglo-Romaine, 1921–1927*, (Paris, Librairie Plon, 1949), pp. 225–232.

region in which it must be allowed to hold different opinions or follow different practices, without breach of 'communion' or 'unity'.[1]

This brought Dr Gore to the point where he now had to ask himself what would be the norms of these fundamental doctrines, in other words, what would be *de fide*? Gore pleaded that there should be the widest toleration of differences between Churches, both in doctrine and practice, on the basis of agreement over the necessary articles of Catholic communion.

He then drew on a distinction made by Fr Alois Janssens,[2] a professor of Theology at Louvain, between *fundamental de fide truths*, and *de fide truths* which are not considered fundamental.[3] As an example of a fundamental 'de fide' truth Fr Janssens cited the Godhead of Christ, and as an example of a non-fundamental *de fide* truth, he mentioned the Infallibility of the Pope. Both, of course, were *de fide* truths, both were revealed, and belief in them was required by the authority of the Church. But there were differences. That Christ is God is a fundamental, indeed *the* fundamental dogma of the Christian Faith. It has always been explicitly held. There was no development in this doctrine, but only in its terminology. The infallibility of the Pope, on the other hand, has admitted of a true development, a real doctrinal progress. It had been held but implicitly in the first three centuries and had been doubted afterwards, even until the time of the first Vatican Council. The Irish bishops who said in their catechism: 'this (i.e. the infallibility of the Pope) is a protestant invention', apparently did not as yet believe the infallibility of the Pope.[4]

On the basis of this distinction, Dr Gore went on to try and draw the following conclusion: 'Fundamental doctrines are those which have

---

1. Frere, *Recollections of Malines*, p. 111.
2. Fr Alois Janssens was a priest of the Scheut Congregation, a professor of Theology at the Scheut Theologicum of Louvain. He played a large 'behind-the-scenes' part in preparing the Conversations of Malines. He was an intimate friend and advisor of Lord Halifax, and helped him in the theological discussions which arose as a result of the Malines meetings. A good example of this will be found in his Memoranda, now published in '*Ephemerides Theologicae Lovaniense*', January/March 1967, pp. 234/235, where he tells of explaining the question of "praeambula fidei" to Lord Halifax.
3. Viscount Halifax, '*Further Considerations on Behalf of Reunion*', London 1923, pp. 58/59.
4. Viscount Halifax, '*Further Considerations on Behalf of Reunion*', p. 58.

always been held and believed in the Church in substance. There has been no development in the doctrine but only in the terminology.'[1] This is, in effect, the 'Canon' of Christian doctrine proposed by St Vincent of Lérins.[2] Dr Gore then quotes John Henry Newman as supporting this theory: '... every Catholic knows that the Christian dogmas were in the Church from the time of the Apostles; that they were ever in substance what they are now; that they existed before the formulas were publicly adopted, in which, as time went on, they were defined and recorded'.[3]

Now these statements, continued Gore, meant (to the Anglican mind) that dogmas such as Papal Infallibility, the Immaculate Conception, the definition of Transubstantiation, the definition of Purgatory, did not belong to the substance of Faith, and yet the Roman Catholic Church imposes these dogmas as a condition for membership.

Here Dr Gore reached the crux of his paper. He appealed as an Anglican who wished to see the Church of England and the Orthodox Church reunited to the See of Rome; he explained that the obstacle was those dogmas which the Catholics claimed to be part of the essential Faith, but which seemed to the Anglicans to conflict with history and with truth. 'It seems to us illegitimate to yield that faith which we give to the fact of the virginal conception of Our Lord, or his resurrection, or his ascension, to the immaculate conception of Mary. The former group of accepted facts rest upon original witness and good evidence: the latter on nothing that can be called historical evidence at all. But to believe in a fact on the mere ground of *a priori* reasoning as to what is suitable, without any evidence of the fact, seems to us to alter the fundamental character of the act of faith. It also makes with the other doctrines just specified, a claim for the authority of the Church as centralized and absolute, which the ancient Church never made. It frees it from all those restrictions of universal agreement and unvarying tradition

---

1. Frere, *Recollections of Malines*, p. 115.
2. The 'Vincentian Canon' was the three-fold test of Catholicity laid down by St. Vincent of Lérins in his *Commonitorium* (II,3), namely '*quod ubique quod semper, quod ab omnibus creditum est*', (what has been believed everywhere, always, and by all). By this triple test of ecumenicity, antiquity and consent, the Church is to differentiate between true and false traditions.
Cross and Livingston, *Oxford Dictionary of the Christian Church*, 1966, p. 1443.
3. John Henry Newman, *Tracts Theological and Ecclesiastical*, p. 287.

and scriptural authority – which in our judgement make the act of faith rational.'[1]

Gore concluded by asking if the idea was wholly impossible that, with a view to the corporate reconciliation of the Orthodox Communion and the Anglican Communion, the Roman Church could be content to require not more than the acceptance of those articles of faith which fall under the Vincentian Canon?

When Dr Gore had finished his paper, Mgr Batiffol went immediately into the presentation of his paper, which was a reply to that read by Gore. In the course of his presentation, Batiffol answered some of the specific questions or problems posed by Dr Gore. Schematically, these dealt with the following points:

(a) One seems to wish, in order that a truth be *de fide* that it be universally agreed, have constant tradition, be founded on Scripture, and that anything founded on inference be excluded. In this case the dogmas defined by the early ecumenical councils, such as the Nicean 'consubstantial', the Ephesian 'theotokos', etc., do not fulfil the conditions. Do we have to reject Nicea and Ephesus therefore?[2]

(b) Regarding the assertion that we place the Immaculate Conception on the same plane as the Ascension or the Resurrection, Batiffol replied that we give the same assent to these dogmas, but not because of the same criteria. On the one hand we have an affirmation of the Church, and on the other hand an inference sanctioned by the authority of the Church.

(c) Answering the question whether the Church will accept corporate reconciliation on a basis of the *de fide* truths of the Vincentian Canon, the Monseigneur replied in the negative. He gave the following reasons for his answer:

   i) As he had already explained, this Canon cannot be taken at its face value, at least in its conception of the development of dogma. In the perspective of development, none of the articles of faith of the ecumenical councils adapt themselves to the Vincentian Canon.

---

1. Frere, *Recollections of Malines*, p. 117.
2. Bivort de la Saudée, *Anglicans et Catholiques*, p. 147.

ii) The Church has never considered definitions of faith as provisional, but as revealed truths, and obligatory. The Holy See cannot accept that some dogmas be accepted while others are denied.[1]

(d) Batiffol concluded by remarking that it had been said by some that the Faith had become more complex or complicated in virtue of having to have certain aspects emphasized in order to combat heresies. He then quoted Joseph de Maistre, whom Newman cites as one of the inspirers, together with Moehler, of his theory of development, who had no hesitation in saying, 'The Faith, if the sophist opposition *(des "novateurs")* had never forced it to evolve, would be a thousand times more angelic'.[2]

The morning session then finished at 1.30 p.m.

The fourth session was held in the afternoon of the same day, between 3.30 p.m. and 5.30 p.m. Mgr Batiffol concluded his paper, but there was little discussion. Dr Gore said that he had no wish to return to the discussion which had taken place in the morning. He still held that there were possibilities of resolving the difficulties, but he had no idea at the moment where to look.

Armitage Robinson noted in his journal that he was delighted by the paper which had been delivered by Dr Gore. He wrote that Dr Gore, delivering his paper in English, while recognising the ability and clarity with which the completeness of the Roman system had been expounded by Monseigneur Van Roey, deplored the fact that it found no place for certain elements of the Christianity of the New Testament which were not only true and essential, but corresponded more particularly with conceptions of the present times. Gore cited in particular the principles of criticism and the ideals of democracy. The journal states: 'The system had proved too narrow for the needs of Christendom. The Orthodox Churches of the East and the Anglicans had elements to contribute without which the Church could not attain full Catholicity.'[3]

Robinson also noted his own contribution to this particular topic, after Dr Gore asked him to comment. 'I gradually poured out a good deal, and

---

1. Bivort de la Saudée, *Anglicans et Catholiques*, p. 148.
2. Bivort de la Saudée, *Anglicans et Catholiques*, p. 150.
3. Journal of J. Armitage Robinson, 19th May 1925, p. 2.

got at last to telling them that the completeness of the system literally terrified me. You have shut us out; is it good for us? Is it good for you? Can you do anything to find a remedy? Or must we wait till you yourselves have found the need of a decentralisation and such a further recognition of local self-government as will make our position better understood?'[1] The Dean concluded by noting that the others knew that he spoke from the heart, and they understood what he meant. He thought that the Abbé Portal was pleased with his contribution, and, although the Cardinal said but few words, they all showed sympathy and understanding.

Two questions were then posed by the Anglicans: (1) Could they have copies of the *Memoire* that the Cardinal had presented? (2) Would it be advisable to publish something regarding the Conversations? Cardinal Mercier was agreeable that they should have copies of the *Memoire*, but was opposed to the publication of any report.

The fifth and last session at 7.15 p.m. was a very brief affair lasting only 45 minutes, and was dedicated to the reading of a summing-up of positive statements which the Anglicans had prepared and which regarded the relationship between the Pope and the Bishops (a suggestion of composing a corresponding summary of criticisms was not accepted). Briefly, this summary read as follows:

The Pope is historically Primate of the Church, but
1) the authority of the Pope is not separated from that of the Episcopacy;
2) he can claim, however, to occupy a position in regard to all other bishops which no other bishop claims to occupy in regard to him;
3) the exercise of the Primacy has varied in past times and makes it difficult to define the respective rights of the Holy See on the one hand, and the Episcopacy on the other.

With this summing-up, the *procès-verbal* was accepted and the fourth Conversation of Malines terminated.

---

1. Journal of J. Armitage Robinson, 19th May 1925, p. 2.

FOURTH 'CONVERSATION' – EXAMINATION OF DISCUSSION PAPERS

(vi) The 'human' factor versus the official.

It is obvious from the comments and correspondence between the participants that these meetings at Malines contributed very substantially towards the good relationships and indeed friendship between the members. There was a clear distinction between what went on in the conference room, that is to say the 'official' exchanges, and the humour and banter which was shared outside on a purely human level. The exchanges between Dr Gore and Mgr Batiffol during this fourth Conversation was the nearest they came to a really heated discussion, although as Frere noted 'the discussion waxed hot at times without ceasing to be quite friendly ... Bishop Gore as protagonist (and others as well) felt that he had said at last, with an explicitness which would have been previously impossible, what he felt bound to say'.[1] It did underline the significant differences in approach and belief, what could be accepted and what could not – by either side, but even this did not impinge afterwards on the good-humour and banter which were the order of the day. Dr Frere recounts one illuminating incident as indicative of this spirit of friendship:

'I remember going out with Bishop Gore for a short walk before our morning meeting; as we got outside we found a Rogationtide procession on its way through the parish. So we joined in and followed for some time until it was time to get back to our gathering.

At *déjeuner* subsequently Batiffol said to the Cardinal, "Eminence, do you know that there were two Anglican bishops following in the Rogationtide procession this morning?"

The Cardinal in his grave way said "Then indeed we are coming nearer to unity."

"Yes," said Batiffol, "but does Your Eminence know that they didn't follow the procession the whole way?"

"Ah?" said the Cardinal.

"No, they left just before the prayers for the Pope."

This scandalous misstatement was drowned in roars of laughter; in fact we had left in the middle of the invocation of Virgin Martyrs.'[2]

Of the Anglican participants at the fourth Conversation, it was Dr Gore who felt the most disappointed. He had strongly made his point in the

---
1. Frere, *Recollections of Malines*, p. 57.
2. Frere, *Recollections of Malines*, pp. 52–53.

paper he delivered for some sort of distinction to be made between degrees of adherence to different dogmas, but the replies he had received did not encourage him at all. He acknowledged the suppleness of the Roman Catholics on almost all questions of organization, but saw no hope of concessions on any matter of dogma. In a letter to Halifax on the 25th May 1925, Gore summed up his feelings in stating that because, '... the R.C.s showed themselves quite unrelenting on the dogmatic issue (which in my judgement dominates all else), we put ourselves in a false position in continuing conferences for the present. On the heading of organization they showed themselves fairly concessive: on the heading of dogma they showed themselves not only unconcessive, but, in my judgement,...they made the discussion on the grounds of Scripture and antiquity more hopeless than ever. I have told the Arch. [bishop] my opinion, but said that I did not think my colleagues agreed.'[1]

Archbishop Davidson, while noting Dr Gore's comments, thought that there should be one more Conference followed then by a pause for assessments by both sides. The Archbishop of Canterbury also agreed with Cardinal Mercier's proposal that there should be no more publications about the Conversations till both sides had completed their respective assessments.

Lord Halifax concurred with the Archbishop and the Cardinal, and he suggested November 1925 as an appropriate time for a fifth Conference. In a letter to Portal he explains: 'It seems to me that ... we ought to have another conference in November so that we can prepare and edit a report for the ecclesiastical world on your side and on ours of what has been happening at all our meetings ... After that there should be an interlude so that one can talk and discuss about what we did. One should envisage a certain uproar, but this is necessary and will be fruitful'.[2]

---

1. Letter of Gore to Halifax, 25th May 1925, Malines Papers of Lord Halifax, File A4 271, Box 5.
Halifax's comment on Dr Gore reflects his exasperation: 'Gore has been in every way exasperating, and I had great fear of what might result from it. Thanks be to God, the danger was dispelled, but! but! One should never chase tigers with a companion such as he'.
Letter of Halifax to Portal, 29th June 1925, Portal Papers, Paris.
2. Letter of Halifax to Portal, 4th July 1925, Portal Papers, Paris.

8

Preparations for a fifth 'Conversation', Mercier's interventions against Woodlock. The death of Mercier and then of Portal, and the effect on the fifth and final Conversation.

(i) Preparations for a fifth Conversation.

When the fourth Conversation had finished, Lord Halifax was anxious to press on with the organization of the following one, urging that another Conversation be held in the autumn of that same year (1925). Halifax foresaw the next meeting as one where the results of all the previous conferences could be summarized and any measures of agreement then published by both the Archbishop of Canterbury and the Cardinal Archbishop of Malines.

Archbishop Davidson, despite the voiced opposition of Bishop Gore to a continuation of the Conversations, wrote in a positive strain on the 1st August 1925 to Cardinal Mercier agreeing that there should be at least one further meeting at Malines. His letter was, however, guarded on several points. Beginning his letter with fulsome praise for the Cardinal and the participants at the Conversations, he noted that whilst the meetings had brought about a better and more sympathetic understanding of the position of each side, he could not agree with the Cardinal's expression that they had made 'progress in agreement'. 'In fact', continued the Archbishop,

> 'In studying the papers before me, I do not find any indication of a readiness on the part of those whom Your Eminence associated with yourself at Malines to show or suggest the possibility of any modification by re-statement or otherwise of what are commonly regarded as irreducible doctrinal requirements to which expression has been given ... I need not remind Your Eminence that on all these questions there was not merely verbal discussion, but that literary contributions of the most valuable kind were made available. I have myself studied both the record of the Conversations and the material furnished to aid them. Your Eminence will I think agree with me when I say that they

afford no evidence of a departure on either side from the doctrinal principles which you or we maintain.'[1]

The Archbishop continued by declaring that he was in favour of a further meeting under the presidency of Cardinal Mercier, but that he thought the task of this fifth meeting should be to draw up a statement (or statements) as to the points on which misunderstanding had been removed and also those points which remained as obdurate difficulties, among which, he twice emphasized, was the question of the Papacy.

The Cardinal responded on the 25th October 1925 to Davidson's letter with a long reply. Mercier began by expressing some disappointment with Davidson letter,

> 'When I first read it, your letter caused me a certain uneasiness. I was not sure that I had grasped its inner meaning. The document was inspired by an unaltered goodwill, all appreciations on the past were encouraging, but reflections on the present situation and on future developments seemed to betray a shaken confidence.'[2]

The Cardinal continued by urging the Archbishop not to be over-influenced by those external pressures from either those who thought their differences should be resolved more quickly nor those who thought the differences were insoluble,

> 'You must, no doubt, meet with the same restlessness on the part of inveterate optimists and obstinate pessimists among your own flock; they wish to obtain from us a sudden solution, and, if they could, they would urge us to end the matter promptly. Do you not think it would be weakness on our part if we gave way to these solicitations? We have responsibilities which our followers do not share and do not always understand. Our situation imposes upon us the duty to consider the general situation from a higher standpoint, according to deeper supernatural standards. The direction of consciences entrusted to us allows us to act with authority'.[3]

1. Bell, *Randall Davidson*, pp. 1293–1296.
2. Letter of Mercier to Davidson, 25th October 1925, Malines Papers of Lord Halifax, A4. 271, Box 7.
3. Letter of Mercier to Davidson, 25th October 1925, Malines Papers of Lord Halifax, A4. 271, Box. 7

PREPARATIONS FOR A FIFTH 'CONVERSATION'

Cardinal Mercier continued his letter by agreeing to the proposal for another meeting, concurring with a wish expressed by Lord Halifax that it should be arranged for the first fortnight in January 1926. He also concurred with the suggestion of Archbishop Davidson that the meeting should concern itself with drawing up two statements, one outlining the conclusions already reached, and the second on disputable points only partially considered, but he ventured to suggest that when it came to publication, only the first statement should be released to the public. Explaining his reasoning, the Cardinal said that it was his opinion that any negative conclusions would only provoke polemic in the press and re-awaken animosities.

(ii) Fr Woodlock enters the scene again.

During the intervening time and with a view to continuing to keep the reunion issue to the front of the public mind, Lord Halifax accepted to give a speech at the Anglo-Catholic Congress at the Albert Hall on the 9th July 1925. On receiving a draft copy of Halifax's proposed speech, Archbishop Davidson protested that the Viscount had not made clear in the text that he was speaking for himself and not for the body of Anglicans, and Halifax adjusted his speech accordingly to make it clear that his address was from a personal point of view, adding that he was sure that the Archbishop would dissent both from his words and his conclusion.

Among the audience at the Albert Hall on 9th July was Fr Francis Woodlock SJ. In the course of his speech Lord Halifax, without giving any indication of its source, took one of the themes of Cardinal Mercier's Memorandum from the fourth Conversation – that dealing with the historic claims of the See of Canterbury throughout a thousand years. Reunion, he claimed, was not a case of 'absorption' of the Church of England, but rather the union of the two Churches under the primacy of the successor of St Peter, the Bishop of Rome. Woodlock took grave exception to that part of the speech where Halifax had stated that reunion did not imply the rejection of the historic claims of Canterbury, and took his case to the public domain in a series of letters and articles to the religious and national newspapers. Abbé Portal warned Halifax in a letter of the 27th July 1925 that; 'I have read his latest [letter] in the *Church Times*; it is essential to avoid all controversy with him and especially any comparison between him and Cardinal Mercier;

his goal is obviously to get Cardinal Mercier to respond, whereas good politics demand that he remain silent for the present. There is no doubt that Cardinals Merry Del Val and Gasquet are behind Fr Woodlock and push him. They know fine well that the Pope and Cardinal Gasparri are favourable to Cardinal Mercier, but its the old story once again, and we know very well how that ended in '96.'[1]

Fr Woodlock did not limit his campaign to the press, but wrote directly to Halifax about the claims made in the Albert Hall speech. In a letter of the 30th July 1925 to Halifax, the Jesuit tried to explain to the Viscount precisely the points of his objection.

'... You speak of me as if I were opposed to corporate reunion; but I am no more opposed to that idea than I am to that of a single republic of all the nations of Europe! Both notions *may* be realized some day, but not in my lifetime or in yours ... Coming back from Malines, Your Lordship's words bore an emphasis which no disclaimer could remove. Your audience must have gathered from your words that there were hopes of great concessions in the case of a corporate return of England to communion with the Pope, and the unfortunate phrase about the claims of Canterbury had to be at once noted and the false impression corrected. The *Church Times*, in its leader, quotes my words and insinuates that I and Cardinal Mercier have different views on the point of the catholicity of Anglicanism ...It is hard that Your Lordship can only read into my words the desire to thwart your efforts for corporate reunion. I cannot but think that, outsider though I am, I know the temper of the Anglican Establishment better than does Your Lordship.'[2]

Lord Halifax's reply to Fr Woodlock was both short, and final.

'I acknowledge receipt of your letter because I do not want you to think I bear any grudge against you, or am either hurt or surprised by what you say. You do not believe in the possibility of corporate reunion and what you desire are individual conversions. I do believe in corporate reunion and I do not desire individual conversions. That

---

1. Letter of Portal to Halifax, 17th July 1925, Malines Papers of Lord Halifax A4 271, Box 7.
2. Letter from Woodcock to Halifax, 30th July 1925, Malines Papers of Lord Halifax, A4 271, Box 7.

PREPARATIONS FOR A FIFTH 'CONVERSATION'

sums up the whole matter between us and there it must stop. I am glad to know that all your co-religionists are not of your way of thinking.'[1]

The criticisms enunciated by Fr Woodlock and others in England (including Canon James Moyes, a former participant of the Anglican Orders Commission), quickly spread to the Continent via the French Jesuit periodical *Études*, and Portal noted in two letters of the 6th and 16th August 1925 that: 'the fact that *Études* accepts the prose of Fr Woodlock seems to indicate that the attack against Malines becomes more generalised',[2] and also '... Fr Woodlock SJ is the mouthpiece of a group of opponents who agitate greatly among catholics ...'[3] The Viscount himself seems to have had a mixed reaction to the controversy with Woodlock and his followers because although he saw the strength of the reaction as indicating a certain fear on the part of their opponents ('our war against the English Catholics, led by the Jesuits, begins to develop. The fact bears witness that they are afraid, which is an agreeable thought').[4] At the same time he expressed a sense of regret that the controversy had begun at all ('I cannot tell you how much I detest all such controversy, such as this one, but it is the fault of Fr Woodlock, not mine').[5]

That the growing controversy was having an effect both on Cardinal Mercier and in Rome itself is indicated in a letter from a friend of Halifax's, Hoffman Nickerson, who had just returned from a visit to Rome. He wrote on the 18th September 1925, telling the Viscount that:

'... You will remember that early in the Spring in talking with Cardinal Mercier I thought I could trace a distinct falling back from the original position as sketched out two years ago, i.e. that terms might be offered to the Anglicans which would give them a sort of uniate status, and I think I suggested to you at the time that perhaps the Vatican had "put the brakes on him" – to use an Americanism.

---

1. Letter of Halifax to Woodcock, 1st August 1925, Malines Papers of Lord Halifax, A4 27a, Box 7.
2. Letter of Portal to Halifax, 6th August 1925, Malines Papers of Lord Halifax, A4 217 Box 7.
3. Letter of Portal to Halifax, 16th August 1925, Malines Papers of Lord Halifax, A4 271, Box 8.
4. Letter of Halifax to Portal, 19th August 1925, Portal Papers, Paris.
5. Letter of Halifax to Portal, 25th August 1925, Portal Papers, Paris.

This impression was strongly reinforced at Rome. There Gasparri received me with an almost startling absence of preliminaries. I was amazed at his accessibility. Whereupon he rose and bowed me out immediately as soon as I mentioned the word reunion! I don't believe I was with him five minutes, certainly not much more ... In view of Cardinal Mercier's letters, together with the other documents I had with me, all this did not altogether come up to our expectations ... Unfortunately Gasquet still seems to be considered a first rate authority on Anglicanism and Anglican affairs.'[1]

The mounting pressure on Cardinal Mercier was verified by Portal: '... the Cardinal is violently attacked by the Flemings who use everything for ammunition, including all that is supplied to them by the English Catholics'.[2]

Cardinal Mercier was at this time under great pressure at home because of the linguistic difficulties in Belgium, what later came to be known as the 'Flemish Question'. Nevertheless he sprang to the defence of his friend Abbé Portal when Fr Woodlock made the mistake of repeating some mis-reported words of Portal which had been taken from a talk given during a meeting organized by the Belgian Benedictine Dom Lambert Beauduin in Brussels on the subject of unity. Mercier, in a letter dated 26th October 1925, accused Woodlock of misrepresenting Lord Halifax and of misquoting Portal, and insinuated that in doing so he was attacking the whole effort for reunion which the Conversations at Malines represented. Further, the Cardinal suggested, Fr Woodlock was venting his grievance at not being invited to contribute his own experience and advice.[3] The Belgian Cardinal sent this letter to the editor of *The Tablet* for publication, and he also sent a copy to Lord Halifax asking him if he would have it published in *The Times*.[4]

1. Letter of Nickerson to Halifax, 18th September 1925, Malines Papers of Lord Halifax, A4 271, Box 7.
2. Letter of Portal to Halifax, 24th September 1925, Malines Papers of Lord Halifax, A4 271, Box 7.
3. Letter of Mercier to Woodlock, 26th October 1925, Malines Papers of Lord Halifax, A4 271, Box 7.
4. Letter of Halifax to Portal, 29th October 1925, Portal Papers, Paris.'The Cardinal has written a letter to *The Tablet* in order to put Fr Woodlock in his place concerning his letter to *The Tablet* of the 10th October, and another long and completely admirable letter to the Archbishop of Canterbury. The letter to *The Tablet* I am sending to the editor of *The Times* requesting, as asked by the Cardinal, that it be published'.

PREPARATIONS FOR A FIFTH 'CONVERSATION'

The editor of *The Tablet*, Ernest Oldmeadow, on receipt of Mercier's letter, immediately took it to Cardinal Bourne, the Archbishop of Westminster, and this resulted in an urgent letter from Bourne to Mercier on the 29th October. This important letter not only points out the impropriety of a Roman Catholic Cardinal publicly chastising a priest of his own Church in the press, but further takes issue with Cardinal Mercier over keeping the English hierarchy and particularly the Cardinal Archbishop of Westminster in the dark about what was really happening at Malines. Cardinal Bourne wrote as follows:

'The Editor of *The Tablet* has thought it his duty to refer to me, as principal Trustee of that paper and as Archbishop of Westminster, Your Eminence's letter to Father Woodlock for which you ask publicity in *The Tablet*. I feel obliged to say that it would be a grave error of judgement, productive of serious harm to religion, to publish a letter of this kind. The publication would be injurious to Your Eminence, for it is quite contrary to English usage for a Cardinal thus to reprimand a Priest in the public press – and, further, it would accentuate the mischief which Anglican exploitation of the "Malines Conversations" has already undoubtedly done to the cause of the Catholic Church in England.

Your Eminence has kept honourably the silence imposed upon or accepted by you. But it is manifest that the same discretion is not being observed by Anglicans, and they openly declare that the views on the Holy See held at Malines are not the same as those taught by us in England. The Abbé Portal is allowed to speak in Belgium, and we are not allowed even to have an accurate account of what he actually said. The Anglicans are treated as friends – we, the Catholics of England, apparently as untrustworthy.

I am powerless to intervene, for Your Eminence has thought well to leave me – who after all am the principal Catholic prelate in this country and your colleague in the Sacred College – absolutely in the dark. It would have surely been but right and seemly that Your Eminence should have stipulated from the outset that there should be no secrets from me. Yet with the exception of Your Eminence's communication at the end of 1923, I have been treated as if I did not exist. The Archbishop of Canterbury has been given the fullest information of the proceedings at Malines – I have been excluded from all such knowledge and thereby a grave wrong has been done both to me and to the interests of the Catholic Church in England.

'A BROTHER KNOCKING AT THE DOOR'

Your Eminence, I have been patient and have kept silence, with the result that I am quite unable either to correct or to control free-lances like Fr Woodlock who has many sympathizers both here and in Rome.

Had I in a matter affecting Belgium acted towards Your Eminence and the Belgian Bishops, as Belgium has now acted towards us in a matter most profoundly affecting the Catholic Church in England, there would have been just cause of complaint. We have never done so.'[1]

On receipt of Cardinal Bourne's letter, Mercier immediately sent a telegram to Halifax asking him not to publish his letter in *The Times*, and Canon Dessain, the Cardinal's secretary, followed this up by a letter to both Halifax and Portal explaining that Mercier wanted some time for reflection on the matter in the light of the English Cardinal's reaction. The editor of *The Tablet* even went to Malines himself to try to resolve the difficulty between the journal and the Belgian cardinal, but without success. Oldmeadow wrote on the 18th November 1925 to Canon Dessain that 'after making so long a journey to compose the difference between Cardinal Mercier and *The Tablet*, I am disappointed to find that it has been aggravated ... It is true that I expressed my regret for having allowed Cardinal Mercier to be named in this paper by Father Woodlock; and it is also true that I promised to continue seeking a formula of regret such as would be satisfactory to His Eminence'.[2] Oldmeadow continued by promising to try to seek a draft formula to rectify the matter, but in the end Cardinal Mercier decided 'for the sake of peace' not to pursue the matter any further.

This incident, and particularly the exchange of letters between the English and Belgian Cardinals, exemplifies an important difference in viewpoints between the two church leaders. Cardinal Bourne, although he had acknowledged in earlier correspondence to Oldmeadow that he had known about the Conversations from the beginning, obviously felt

---

1. Letter of Bourne to Mercier, 29th October 1925, Archdiocese of Westminster Archives, 124/4/1.
2. Letter of Oldmeadow to Dessain, 18th November 1925, Archdiocese of Westminster Archives, 124/4/1.

that he should have been kept informed of all the developments of the subsequent meetings at Malines, and felt hurt that whereas the Archbishop of Canterbury was 'fully informed', he, the principal Roman Catholic prelate in England, was not. Cardinal Bourne obviously saw himself as the Roman Catholic equivalent of the Archbishop of Canterbury, whereas Cardinal Mercier clearly saw the Pope as Canterbury's equivalent, and it was Rome that he kept informed of all the developments, not Bourne. The information given to Cardinal Bourne, both by Halifax and Mercier, was seen by them as a matter of courtesy, and not as a matter of essential and diplomatic importance. The motivation of the two Malines conversationalists was unlikely to have been the same, as Lord Halifax would have been extremely cautious in his approach to the Westminster Cardinal in the light of his past experiences, whereas Cardinal Mercier was clearly not alive to the multiple sensitivities of the English Church situation.

Despite his protestations to Mercier, Cardinal Bourne did not exert any overt opposition to the Conversations, but it was obviously central in his list of preoccupations. In preparation for an audience with Pope Pius XI which took place on 15th December 1925, Bourne noted a number of points which he wished to discuss with the Pontiff in an *aide-memoire* which remains in the Archives at Westminster. These include: (1) setting aside the English Roman Catholic hierarchy; (2) re-opening the issue of Anglican Orders; (3) effacing of Papal Infallibility; (4) if (Anglican) orders were recognized and teaching authority placed into the episcopacy, the Anglicans would have gained all they wish; (5) the Archbishop of Canterbury as *Papa alterius orbis*.[1]

(iii) The death of Cardinal Mercier in January 1926, and of Portal in June 1926.

In the meantime, the preparations for the fifth Conversation were proceeding. Archbishop Davidson wrote to Cardinal Mercier on the 9th December 1925 expressing his pleasure at the resumption of the interrupted 'conversations', now scheduled for 25th January 1926, but adding his caveat about the proposed publication of the record of the meetings.

---

1. *Aide-Memoire* of Cardinal Bourne, 14th December 1925, Archdiocese of Westminster Archives, 124/4/1.

'I have myself considered with the utmost care the opinion expressed by Your Eminence about what should be contained in, or omitted from, any published record. Unless I misunderstand you, your opinion is that the record, while it tells of the endeavour, successful as I hope, to remove or diminish misunderstandings upon several points of difference between us (points which though important are minor), should make no reference to the larger and more fundamental question or questions upon which no approach to agreement has been made or appears possible. I refer especially to the vital question of the Papacy ... Is there, or is there not, a Vicar of Christ upon earth, who possesses *jure divino* a distinctive authoritative position in relation to the whole of Christendom? ... I claim to know something about the Church and People of this Country, and I have no hesitation in saying that to publish a record or summary of the discussions without making outspoken reference to that great unremoved mountain of difficulty would be worse than useless. The outcry which would immediately arise would certainly retard instead of promoting the cause for which we care – the cause of removing misunderstandings and contributing to the wider reunion of Christendom.'[1]

Cardinal Mercier replied to the Archbishop on the 22nd December, agreeing that something should be included in the eventual statement about the divergence on the question of Papal Primacy, but that the exact compilation should be left to the discussion of the group at Malines. By this time, however, the Cardinal was ill from cancer, and it was only a few days afterwards that Halifax received the news that Mercier would not be able to attend the meeting, and that Mgr Van Roey would preside.[2] In a series of letter to Abbé Portal, Halifax expressed his increasing concern for the Belgian prelate, and asked Portal to join him in visiting their dying friend and to seek his benediction.[3] In the same letters of the 18th January, he told Portal that he wanted to ask Cardinal

---

1. Letter of Davidson to Mercier, 9th December 1925, cited in Bell, *Randall Davidson*, vol. 2, pp. 1297/8.
2. Letter of Mercier to Halifax, 21st December 1925, Malines Papers of Lord Halifax, A4 271, Box 7.
3. Letter of Halifax to Portal, 16th January 1926, two letters on the 18th January 1926, Portal Papers, Paris.
In both the letters of the 18th January, Halifax made the common mistake of many at the turn of a year in dating these letters '1925' The contents, however, referring to the illness of Mercier, make it clear that they are in fact of January 1926.

PREPARATIONS FOR A FIFTH 'CONVERSATION'

Mercier if he would write to the Archbishop of Canterbury, to the Pope and to Cardinal Bourne urging them to continue the work which he had begun for the cause of reunion. By the evening of Wednesday, 20th January 1926, Portal, Halifax and Hemmer were in Brussels where they were told that the Cardinal wished them to be present at the Mass to be celebrated in the Cardinal's hospital room the following morning. The meeting of these friends is described touchingly in Lockhart's biography of Lord Halifax, but the Viscount, despite the weakness of the dying Cardinal, pursued his goal by asking if Mercier would write letters to the Pope, Bourne and Davidson. It was at this last encounter that Cardinal Mercier gave Halifax his episcopal ring as a memento, and after Halifax and the others had departed, Cardinal Mercier dictated his final letter to the Archbishop of Canterbury.[1] There is no indication of letters to either the Pope or Cardinal Bourne, which were probably never written, because Halifax had already intimated to Portal that he was prepared to go to Rome himself to deliver such a letter addressed to the Pope but instead he returned to England. Two days later the Cardinal Archbishop of Malines was dead.

With the death of Cardinal Mercier, one of the main inspirers and key sustainers of the Conversations was removed. Archbishop Davidson, whose anxieties about the continuation and publication of the Malines reports we have noted, became even more hesitant about the continuation of the meetings. He was at this period deeply occupied in the revision of the Book of Common Prayer and its passage through the British Parliament, and was against anything which would disturb or distract from this process.

The period immediately following the death of Cardinal Mercier was an anxious time for Halifax and Portal. Who would now preside at the

---

1. Cardinal Mercier to the Archbishop of Canterbury, Bruxelles: 21 January, 1926.
'Monseigneur,
During the trial which Divine Providence has sent me these last weeks, it has been a great comfort for me to receive a visit from our venerable friend Lord Halifax. I have learned from him of your continuing desire for union; I am happy of this assurance, which gives me strength during these present hours.
"Ut unun sint," it is the supreme wish of Christ, the wish of the Soverign Pontiff, it is mine, it is yours. May it be realised in its fulness.
The expressions of sympathy which Your Grace has sent me have touched me deeply; I thank you from the bottom of my heart, and assure Your Grace of my religious greetings.
+ D.J. Card, Mercier, Arch. de Malines.'
Cited in Bell, *Randall Davidson*, vol. 2, p. 1926.

Conversations? Portal visited the Papal Nuncio in Paris, Mgr Cerretti, who reported to him that opposition to the Conversations was strong. Much now depended on the Pope and whoever he would nominate as successor to Mercier and Archbishop of Malines. Cerretti thought that Cardinal Bourne would not oppose the Pope's wishes, but that Bourne was not the man to preside. It should be someone with status and influence.[1] In a further letter of the 20th February 1926, Portal reported to Halifax that the Flemings in Belgium were causing many difficulties for Mgr Van Roey, and they were pushing for the appointment of Mgr Ladeuze, the Bishop of Namur, as the new Primate of Belgium.[2]

The appointment of Mgr Van Roey as the new Archbishop of Malines in March 1926 was greeted with relief by the two friends, because they understood well the significance of the appointment. Portal informed Halifax that he had heard that 'Cardinal Bourne, the Jesuits and all their habitual adversaries had tried to block the nomination',[3] and Halifax was able to report that 'I hear on indisputable authority that the Pope took a very strong line that the Conversations at Malines should not end, and was very stern about Mgr Van Roey's appointment, and this despite all the opposition that was made to that appointment in order to put an end to what Cardinal Mercier had begun'.[4] Further encouragement arrived with the news that the Archbisop of Cambrai, Mgr Jean Chollet, had successfully proposed a resolution of tribute from the French episcopate to Cardinal Mercier for his work for reunion.

The fifth Conversation was now re-scheduled for the end of June 1926, when Abbé Portal became ill and died in that very month. The venerable Lord Halifax was so devastated that he did not have the energy or will even to attend the funeral of his closest friend. To his son he wrote that with Mercier and Portal now dead, the next should be himself and that would make the trio complete. The fifth Conversation was now

---

1. Letter of Portal to Halifax, 22nd January 1926, Malines papers of Lord Halifax, A4 271, Box 8.
2. Letter of Portal to Halifax, 20th February 1926, Malines Papers of Lord Halifax, A4 271, Box 8.
3. Letter of Portal to Halifax, 19th March 1926, Malines papers of Lord Halifax, A4 271, Box 8.
4. Letter of Halifax to J. Armitage Robinson, 24th March 1926, Malines Papers of Lord Halifax, A4 271, Box 8.

PREPARATIONS FOR A FIFTH 'CONVERSATION'

rescheduled yet again, the new dates being 11th and 12th October 1926.[1] When this last meeting was held under the presidency of the new Archbishop of Malines, Mgr Joseph Van Roey, it turned out to be a rather cursory affair, its main objective being to draw up a Report of all the previous meetings. It was proposed that there be two Reports, one from each of the participating sides, with the Roman Report placing more emphasis on the positive aspects of points of agreement from the meetings, but complementary to the Anglican Report. The first day was spent drawing up the Anglican Report and the second on the Roman Report, both sides agreeing on the contents. It was also agreed that both Reports should be published in their original language, but not including the various papers which had been delivered. The tenor of this final meetings is described by Halifax's biographer as having 'a little of the depressing atmosphere of a liquidation'.[2]

(iv) **Problems which hindered publication of the two Reports.**

The one objective which now remained to Lord Halifax was to see to completion the publication of the two Reports. He reported to his son Edward that he returned from Malines much happier than he when he went. Halifax expected that the Reports would be in print within a reasonably short period of time, certainly for Christmas, but he did not forsee the various difficulties which now began to present themselves. Both of the Reports would have to be published together, as, at least in Halifax's mind, 'the French document, with its greater emphasis upon what had been agreed, put the English document into a better perspective'.[3]

In England, Archbishop Davidson began to show even greater reluctance to involve himself in the publication of anything connected with Malines, and was uncomfortable about the Reports finding their way into the public forum. The reason was the ongoing controversy about the Revised Prayer Book and its passage through Parliament. Although entirely unconnected with the happenings at Malines, many of the more protestant-inclined members of the Church of England were linking the

---

1. For some unknown reason, G.K.A. Bell gives the date of the fifth Conversation as 25th October 1926. The correct dates are 11th and 12th October 1926.
Bell, *Randall Davidson*, vol. 2, p. 1300.
2. Lockhart, *Charles Lindley Viscount Halifax*, vol. 2, p. 332.
3 Lockhart, *Charles Lindley Viscount Halifax*, vol. 2, p. 333.

revision of the Prayer Book with the Conversations, and Davidson saw that the publication of the Malines Reports at this particular time would simply increase these suspicions. He wrote to Halifax about the amount of adverse correspondence he was receiving on both these issues, and pleaded for extreme caution on any public statements which concerned Malines. His fears were reinforced by a letter from Lord Hugh Cecil, who had read the draft versions of a Malines report which the Anglican participants had prepared, and which itself was not very pleasing to Davidson. Lord Hugh intimated that he thought the report would be beneficial from the point of view of Christian Unity but feared, 'any publication about Malines will frighten some people just now ... what people fear is that Malines is meant to lead to our all going over to Rome as a body. And any reminder of Malines is therefore unfortunate, just while the Prayer Book revision is going on ... some Protestants will now certainly say that Malines and P.B.R. [Prayer Book Revision] are two parts of the same conspiracy'.[1]

Halifax himself became ill shortly after the turn of the year, and was not disposed to re-enter the fray till April 1927. In May he received a letter from Bishop Gore which gave him further cause for concern about publication of the Roman part of the Malines Report. Gore wrote that he had been to Paris and seen both Hemmer and Batiffol, and they informed him that since Cardinal Mercier's death the Pope's sympathy with the Conversations was gone, and that Cardinal Bourne's influence was now in the ascendancy. Gore told Halifax that Batiffol was clearly nervous about the publication of the Malines Report and wanted only the English edition printed without any preface from the Archbishop of Canterbury, as this might give it a quasi-official character. Hemmer, reported Gore, was not in agreement with Batiffol. Dr Gore added that he personally did not think that the Anglican Archbishops would consider writing an introduction for the publication of the Report till the Prayer Book controversy was over.[2] In another letter a week later, Dr Gore advised Halifax not to publish anything about Malines on his own account, despite the delays.[3]

---

1. Letter of Lord Hugh Cecil to Davidson, 11th December 1926, cited in Bell, *Randall Davidson*, vol. 2, p. 1300.
2. Letter of Gore to Halifax, 31st May 1927, Malines Papers of Lord Halifax, A4 271, Box 9.
3. Letter of Gore to Halifax, 3rd June 1927, Malines Papers of Lord Halifax, A4 271, Box 9.

PREPARATIONS FOR A FIFTH 'CONVERSATION'

Having taken stock of the situation, Lord Halifax decided to take the bull by the horns and write directly to the Archbishop of Canterbury. On the 6th June 1927, he wrote as follows:

'I have been expecting and hoping since your Grace's last letter to see the introductory words your Grace was to put to our memorandum of what had been said and done under the presidency of Cardinal Mercier at Malines, but nothing appears, and instead I hear rumours of the publication of the memorandum being put off till the question of the acceptance of the "deposited Prayer Book" has been settled. In other words the work of the last six years in regard to reunion and Cardinal Mercier's efforts to promote that reunion which had raised so many hopes are to be jeopardized in order to avoid possible local difficulties which are feared in regard to English Church affairs.
That delay, as I have feared all along would happen, has been utilized by those, like the English Roman Catholics, Cardinal Bourne, etc. who have disapproved of Cardinal Mercier's action, to make difficulties in the way of such reunion as had been the object of the Malines conversations and to play into the hands of those at Rome who were hostile to them.
Further delay would add to the difficulties which have been and are now being made and I for one may be obliged to publish some account of what has really passed in order to counteract the sort of impression which those, whose interests are confined to individual conversions and have no interest in the Church of England, and the reunion of Christendom, are trying to create.'[1]

Walter Frere had also been busy trying to convince Archbishop Davidson to hasten with the publication of the Report, but without success. Frere reported to Halifax on the 7th June 1927 that he was thinking of going to Paris to visit Batiffol and Hemmer and 'see what was the matter'. Frere told Halifax that this impressed the Archbishop more than all the correspondence he had received. About Hemmer and Batiffol, Frere stated that 'they have been got at by the English Romans and are being tempted to hold the whole thing up'.[2]

In fact it was not Frere who went to Paris to 'see what was the matter',

---
1. Letter of Halifax to Davidson, 6th June 1927, Malines Papers of Lord Halifax, A4 271, Box 9.
2. Letter of Frere to Halifax, 7th June 1927, Mirfield Deposit, W.H. Frere, 1.6/1 Malines.

but Lord Halifax himself. Despite his advanced years – he was by now 88 years old – on 17th June he found himself in Paris visiting Hemmer and Batiffol. He wrote again to Archbishop Davidson on the 25th July 1927 reporting that:

'The situation at Rome, owing to Cardinal Bourne and Cardinal Gasquet's actions (I should say intrigues) is that the Pope's mind has been changed and that a message has been sent to Archbishop Van Roey that the Conversations at Malines must cease and that those (the Frenchmen) who took part in them must not publish their report as had been agreed to at our last meeting at Malines and which, if there had not been all these delays, would have been in the hands of the public by now.
The French, Hemmer (who is most friendly – and much annoyed) wished *both* accounts, theirs and ours, to appear together as had been agreed, said quite clearly they could publish nothing themselves. Privately, I think Hemmer for one would not be sorry if someone took the bull by the horns and published what they are forbidden to do.
I saw him and Mg. Batiffol several times. Batiffol had seen and had a long conversation with the Pope, but as your Grace knows, Portal did not trust Batiffol as he did Hemmer. The other Frenchmen I saw were all most sympathetic and did not conceal their annoyance at and dislike of the action at Rome. The new Archbishop of Malines, though an excellent man, was not one, they all said *"who will fight"* or would concern himself much about anything outside his own diocese. Therefore, if anything has to be done it must be done here – in England – with *an eye* to France.
They all agreed that it was imperative that there should be an authoritative and complete statement of the results of the conversations at Malines with a view not only to the present but to the future.'[1]

It was this trip to France that decided Halifax's mind to publish the Reports himself. It was obvious that both the Anglican and Roman Church authorities had vested interests in delaying publication, and, in fact, on the Roman side, of not proceeding at all. In a telegram to Dr Kidd dated 27th July 1927, Halifax made clear his intention: 'Must beg you not to communicate with our colleagues or the Archbishop. Have

1. Letter of Halifax to Davidson, 25th July 1927, Malines Papers of Lord Halifax, A4 271, Box 9.

PREPARATIONS FOR A FIFTH 'CONVERSATION'

purposely avoided saying anything to them as to my intention in order that the responsibility and blame if there is any be mine. I purposely don't and will not ask their consent'.[1]

Halifax's determination to publish both the Reports was reinforced when he finally received the French translation of Robinson's Malines paper from Batiffol who emphasized that any publication should exclude introductions from either Davidson or Van Roey. Batiffol informed Halifax that he had spoken with both Van Roey and Bourne at Louvain, and they felt that this was the only way of saving some of Cardinal Mercier's work.[2] In August Halifax was again in correspondence with Archbishop Davidson, presenting his case for the quick publication of both Reports, Anglican and Roman. Having first given a summary of the situation as seen by Halifax, the Viscount continued '... under the existing circumstances it is absolutely necessary and due to Cardinal Mercier and the Abbé Portal that the French Report should be published with ours, and that at once. Such a publication would be as welcome to our friends abroad as it would be distasteful to Cardinal Bourne and our opponents'.[3] Threatened with an unofficial publication by Halifax, the only concession that the Archbishop was able to extract from Halifax was that nothing would be published before the Parliamentary vote on the Revised Prayer Book due in December of that year.

In November Halifax paid a visit to Rome to try to find out what was the current attitude of the authorities concerning the efforts for reunion, conscious that the Bishop of Namur had withdrawn his permission for the monks of Amay, the Belgian monastery which had been founded to work for reunion, to continue publication of their ecumenical review *Irenicon*. In Rome, through the good offices of Cardinal Ceretti, the former Nuncio in Paris, he was able to obtain an audience with the Pope, who gave him his blessing, but Halifax – to his disappointment – was not able to speak to Pius XI about the Conversations at Malines as he wanted to. Cardinal Ceretti, in arranging the papal audience for him, had

---

1. Telegram of Halifax to Kidd, 27th July 1927, copy in Malines Papers of Lord Halifax, A4 271, Box 9.
2. Letter of Batiffol to Halifax, 30th July 1927, Malines Papers of Lord Halifax, A4 271, Box 9.
3. Letter of Halifax to Davidson, 10th August 1927, Malines Papers of Lord Halifax, A4 271, Box 9.

therefore asked him to submit a written paper in advance, which Halifax did. Ceretti explained to Halifax that audiences were usually short, and so consequently there was no possibility of discussions. However, when Halifax described the meeting later he said '... the Pope was very kind and gave me his personal blessing, as I knelt, and blessed my work'.[1] An account of his trip to Rome was published as part of a small pamphlet entitled *Notes on the Conversations at Malines* which appeared in print on the 6th January 1928, and Cardinal Merry del Val immediately took exception to the description of the audience and to many of the points contained in the *Notes*. To Fr Woodlock he wrote: 'Halifax was not granted a private audience, nor do I believe for a moment that H.H.[His Holiness] "extended his blessings to his work for reunion" – I do not believe either that "the Holy See requested a paper" from him, as he says in his Introduction. I suspect Card. Ceretti, who knows little of these matters, asked him to write a statement, especially in view of his not having obtained a private audience ... Halifax avoided Cardinal Gasquet and myself, though we both know him.'[2]

On the 15th December 1927, the House of Commons of the British Parliament rejected the Revised Prayer Book by 238 votes to 205 votes,[3] and Halifax now felt free to proceed. He sent advance copies to all the participants of the Conversations, and despite the protests and hesitations of almost all of them, the Reports appeared before the public in January 1928 under the title *The Conversations at Malines*. During the same month was published the Papal Encyclical of Pius XI, *Mortalium Animos*, dated 6th January 1928, in which the Pope condemned certain unnamed movements involved in the efforts for Christian unity and reiterated in strong terminology the doctrine of Papal Supremacy. Halifax maintained that the Encyclical was directed at the World Conference on Faith and Order which had met in Lausanne in August of the previous

---

1. Letter of Halifax to Davidson, 11th November 1927, Malines Papers of Lord Halifax, A4 271, Box 9.
2. Letter from Merry del Val to Fr Woodlock, 18th January 1928, Jesuit Archives, Farm Street; London, Ref. BH/6.
3. The debate was marked by a lack of understanding and clarity about the issue of the Revised Prayer Book, as evidenced by the many speeches on the theme of 'No Popery'. The Members of Parliament were not convinced that the Prayer Book's recognition of many Anglo-Catholic practices was not a capitulation to Rome. In the eventual vote, all Roman Catholic M.P.s abstained.
David L. Edwards, *Leaders of the Church of England 1828–1944*, (London: Oxford University Press, 1971), p. 252.

year, but there was no doubt that parts of *Mortalium Animos* could be applied to Malines, and, as though to emphasise the point, the *Osservatore Romano* announced on 21st January 1928 that there were to be no further Conversations.

In one final attempt to break what he saw as 'the conspiracy of silence which certain people in authoritative quarters had set up against the Conversations',[1] Halifax proceeded to publish a fuller version of the 1928 booklet which included all the papers presented during the Conversations, including the 'unofficial' memorandum of Lambert Beauduin read by Cardinal Mercier at the fourth conversation, omitting only Dr Gore's paper which Halifax had evidently mislaid. In the face of protests by all his fellow 'conversationalists', and in blatant disregard for any possible breach of copyright, this appeared in print in February 1930 under the title *The Conversations at Malines 1921-1925, Original Documents*. From the various letters of protest which resulted from this final publication by Halifax, the ones from Hemmer and Van Roey make clear their anxiety about the inclusion of the *Memoire* read by Cardinal Mercier at the fourth Conversation, *The Anglican Church United Not Absorbed* which, as they rightly explained, was not part of the official agenda, but it is clear that they were concerned about possible reaction from Rome, particularly following *Mortalium Animos*. It was Van Roey's letter of protest, published in Belgium and reprinted in the English Press, which finally revealed the author of this *Memoire* as being Dom Lambert Beauduin, the Benedictine founder of the abbey at Amay which works for ecumenism.

---

1. Letter of Lord Halifax to *The Times*, 27th February 1930.

9

Reflections on the importance of the Conversations in the history of Anglican/Roman Catholic ecumenical relations, their contemporary context, and the particular influences of the personalities involved.

(i) Objectives of the Conversations.

When we begin to analyze the Conversations at Malines, we can recognize immediately their importance in the fact that they were the first direct discussions between Anglicans and Roman Catholics in over three hundred years. They also preceded a process of dialogue between the Anglican and Roman Catholic Churches which was re-opened following the Second Vatican Council (1962–67).[1] The historic setting-up of the ARCIC (Anglican/Roman Catholic International Commission) discussions following the meeting in 1966 between Michael Ramsey, then Archbishop of Canterbury, and Pope Paul VI, can perhaps be viewed as a indirect consequence of the 1921–25 Conversations. These important and on-going ARCIC discussions began with precisely the same objectives as had the participants at the Malines Conversations, to promote a better understanding of each other's ecclesiological position, and to prepare the way for closer co-operation with the eventual objective of reunion. Whereas the Malines Conversations began as a tentative and private initiative of individuals such as Portal, Halifax and Mercier – only gradually taking on a semi-official character – the ARCIC talks were totally official from the beginning, with full and authorized representatives from both Roman Catholic and Anglican Communions. On the Anglican side, moreover, care was taken to nominate representatives who would adequately represent the various 'tendencies' of thought and belief within that Church, Low Church, High Church and Broad Church.

---

1. 'Among those in which some Catholic traditions and institutions continue to exist, the Anglican Communion occupies a special place'.
Decree on Ecumenism (*Unitatis Redintegratio*), *The Documents of Vatican II*, Ed. Walter Abbott SJ, (New York: Herder & Herder, 1966), p. 356.

REFLECTIONS OF THE CONVERSATIONS ON ECUMENICAL RELATIONS

The idea of 'corporate reunion', the vision proposed by Halifax, Portal and Mercier in the 1920's and so vigorously opposed by many of the English Roman Catholic church leaders and their representatives in the Roman Curia, is now accepted as part of the official goal of the present Anglican/Roman Catholic discussions.

It is necessary to look in closer detail at some of these elements of the particular times, situations and personalities of the Conversations, inserting them into their historical context, and to try to assess the nature of the difficulties which faced the meetings at Malines.

(ii) The historical context and theological stance of both Churches.

The period of time in which the Conversations took place was one of considerable change. The trauma of the First World War (1914–1918), with the participation of many hundreds of thousands of men and women in war situations, either on the battlefield itself or in the home industries, had caused a social upheaval in British society marked by significant change. There was an almost universal desire for peace and equality among the population in the aftermath of the horrors of war, qualities which were not well reflected in the structure of post-war British society. The social and political philosophies of Socialism and Bolshevism were making their mark on the political structures, as was the extension of the franchise to women. Many of the returning British soldiers had fought in France and Belgium alongside troops from those lands, the majority of whom were Roman Catholic, and their common experiences had helped to qualify some of the religious prejudices which were held on both sides. Of particular note is the fact that many of the military chaplains during the conflict found themselves out-of-touch and isolated, and had been found wanting by the troops.[1] Where the combatants at the front lines had sought simple reassurance and certainty from their religious leaders, they often found much uncertainty and doubt among the padres.[2] In the face of intolerable suffering and

---

1. The difficulties of army chaplains in particular during World War I is well illustrated by Alan Wilkinson, *The Church of England in the First World War*, (London: S.P.C.K., 1978), pp. 136–152.
2. The Anglican chaplains, in particular, reacted strongly against the Chaplain-General, an Evangelical ex-missionary bishop called Taylor-Smith. A much more broad-minded bishop, Llewellyn Gwynne, had to be re-called from Khartoum to be their pastoral leader in France.
David L. Edwards, *Leaders of the Church of England 1829–1944*, p. 245.

carnage, many of the Anglo-Catholic chaplains increasingly adopted the Roman custom of praying for the dead and of celebrating Requiem Mass for the deceased to which the more protestant-minded clergy were opposed, implying as it did the doctrine of purgatory. As W.S.F. Pickering comments, 'Churches which had something comforting and hopeful to offer, some action that could be embarked upon, were at a great advantage over those which remained silent and only proclaimed doctrines that seemed cold and remote'.[1]

One of the major causes of this uncertainty and doubt among a considerable number of the clergy was the after-effect of the Modernist movement which had greatly affected the thinking about traditional beliefs and especially about the Bible in both the Anglican Church and the Roman Catholic Church. Modernism was more a school of thought than an organized movement, but its effects were felt within all Christian Churches of Europe from the late 19th century until the 1920s. Its source was to be found in the aftermath of Darwin's theory of evolution and the consequent controversies on the relationship between science and religion, and the new rational approach to Biblical criticism originating in the German universities. This led to a new seeking for the truth of the Biblical stories and to a diminution of the accepted total historicity of the biblical narratives. The publication in November 1889 of a book entitled *Lux Mundi: A Series of Essays in the Religion of the Incarnation*, edited by Charles Gore, was an important turning point in the opening-up of theological thought in the Church of England. At the time of its publication it raised great controversy. The objective of these Oxford essayists was to reconcile the theology of the Tractarians with modern critical scholarship, and the contents tended to emphasise God's immanence, make ample use of evolutionary ideas, and adopt a critical approach to the Old Testament. Owen Chadwick describes Charles Gore's own contribution on *The Holy Spirit and Inspiration*, as advancing the theory that 'inspiration is compatible with the opinion that Jonah and David are rather dramatic narrators than history. He used the term myth. A myth is not a falsehood. It is an apprehension of faith by a child or a primitive people, a faith not yet distinguished into the constituent elements of poetry and history and philosophy'.[2]

---

1. Pickering, *Anglo-Catholicism*, pp. 46–48.
2. Chadwick, *The Victorian Church*, vol. 2, p. 101.

REFLECTIONS OF THE CONVERSATIONS ON ECUMENICAL RELATIONS

The publication of *Lux Mundi* marked an important step in the development of theological thought within the Church of England, and although it caused distress to older Tractarians such as Henry P. Liddon and to Lord Halifax and his circle, the majority of Anglo-Catholics gradually saw it as a way of progressing to a reconciliation of traditional beliefs and the demands of reason. Although Charles Gore and his collaborators in Oxford (the 'holy group') initiated this thrust of new theological thinking, Gore himself never moved much beyond these principles of what he himself termed 'liberal catholicism'. When a new generation of younger theologians, under the influence of continental modernists, extended these critical principles to the Creed and denied the historicity of some of the miracles of the New Testament, it was Gore who sought their condemnation. Both Gore, by then Bishop of Oxford, and other Anglo-Catholics vigorously defended the Creed against the Modernists. Archbishop Randall Davidson negotiated a compromise resolution at the meeting of Anglican Bishops in April 1914, and the issue eventually subsided.[1] This spirit of compromise of the Archbishop of Canterbury showed itself again in the case of Herbert Hensley Henson's nomination as the Bishop of Hereford by Lloyd George in 1917. In the face of an outcry about the liberalism of the nominee, Davidson eventually, after much persuasion, convinced a reluctant Henson to make a declaration of theological orthodoxy before the Archbishop would give approval to his appointment. We can see from these indications that the Church of England tried to adapt itself to the new spirit of theological thinking, and tried to contain and direct it within fairly extensive parameters.

In France, Alfred Loisy (1857-1940), a student of the famous historian Louis Duchesne (1843-1922) who also participated as a member of the Anglican Orders Commission, used Duchesne's principles of historical criticism and applied them to the Bible. In doing so, he called into question certain traditional interpretations and raised the problem of the compatibility of some traditional Catholic beliefs with modern exegetical criticism. In 1893 Pope Leo issued the encyclical *Providentissimus Deus*, which reaffirmed the traditional belief of the Bible's historical inerrancy, and Loisy was consequently deprived of his teaching post in Paris. His ideas on the development of understanding of Christian dogmas and their compatibility with reason found an echo in other

---

1. Edwards, *Leaders of the Church of England 1819–1944*, p. 242.

'A BROTHER KNOCKING AT THE DOOR'

Catholic scholars, principally George Tyrrell SJ and Baron Friedrich von Hügel. The Modernist movement was condemned by two papal documents of Pius X, the decree *Lamentabili sane exitu* (July 1907) and the encyclical *Pascendi* (September 1907), and an anti-Modernist oath was required from all clergy. Both Loisy and Tyrrell were excommunicated. Previous to these papal declarations, however, it is important to note that Cardinal Mercier offered Fr Tyrrell a refuge in his diocese when the Jesuit was expelled from his Order in 1906, which Tyrrell subsequently refused.[1] This invitation by Mercier was later seen by some of his opponents in Rome as illustrating a sympathy with Modernism rather than as an act of charity to the dispossessed priest, and this suspicion of weakness towards the Modernists obviously played a considerable if unspoken role in the opposition of Merry del Val and Gasquet to the appeals of the Belgian Cardinal to Rome for support for his ecumenical initiatives in the Malines Conversations. Mgr Pierre Batiffol, who joined the Conversations at the third session, was another who, while not in any way aligned to the Modernists, wished to apply a moderate form of critical scholarship to biblical studies. He was constrained to follow the conservative lines of the Pontifical Biblical Commission.[2]

After the First Vatican Council, there followed a period of increasingly firm and more centralized control of the world-wide Roman Catholic communion. While Pius X was enforcing strict orthodoxy within the Roman Catholic Church, thereby curtailing the immediate influence of Modernism,[3] the Church of England was finding its own unique solution to the problem within its vision of 'comprehensiveness'. The result was that the theological thinking of the two Churches was moving in virtually opposite directions, and by the 1920s when the Conversations were in progress, there was little possibility of a meeting of minds among the

---

1. When Tyrrell was expelled from the Jesuits, no bishop in England would accept him into his diocese. Mercier wrote to Rome that he was willing to take him in Malines, and Cardinal Ferrata agreed on condition that Tyrrell would not engage in religious teaching or publications.
Robrecht Boudens, *Kardinaal Mercier en de Vlaasme Beweging*, pp. 267–268.
2. Vidler, *The Church in an Age of Revolution*, p. 187.
3. To the surprise of many the Roman Church advanced to the contest with Modernism more adequately armed and in better heart after the Council than before it. In fact she showed herself better able to deal with the crisis than the amorphous forces of Liberal Protestantism.'
Bernard & Margaret Pauley, *Rome and Canterbury*, p. 213.

theologians present at the third and fourth of the meetings. This may also partly explain the initial difficulty of Halifax and Portal in accepting Bishop Gore as a member of the Anglican side, knowing as they did his more liberal theological background and thought. It was Archbishop Davidson who insisted that Gore should join the Anglican group at Malines.

(iii) The differences in character and structure of the Anglican and Roman Catholic Churches.

Another significant difficulty which faced the participants at the Malines Conversations was the different ecclesiological structures of the Anglican and Roman Catholic Churches, and particularly the question of who exactly were the competent authorities who could give some measure of official authorization to the meetings.

[a] The Roman Catholic Church.

The Roman Church was a very clearly centralized and hierarchical structure, with ultimate and total authority exercised by the Pope. The declaration of Papal Infallibility by the First Vatican Council (1870), although clearly and firmly restricted to faith and morals, was seen and judged by many both within and particularly outside the Church as a further consolidation of the power of the Papacy. The unfinished Council left much of the interpretation of the Council's decrees to canonists and administrators, who generally used their influence to strengthen and centralize the power-centre of Rome.

A different question was that of who were the Pope's advisors and those to whom he delegated his decisions. In this matter the influence of the members of the Roman Curia played a vital role, particularly that of the Cardinal Secretary of State. Although many of the Popes and their Secretaries of State were former diplomats with considerable experience in the service of the Holy See, nevertheless when elected to office their immediate concerns became inevitably the pressing affairs of State and Church of their particular times. From 1870 till 1929 one of the major problems facing all the Popes was a settlement of the 'Roman Question', the need for some kind of territorial independence for the Holy See following the occupation of Rome in 1870 by the Piedmontese armies of Garibaldi, and the consequent loss of the Papal States brought about by the unification of Italy. The anti-clerical decrees issued by the liberal Piedmontese government, including the secularization of education, civil marriage and the dissolution of a number of monasteries, did not endear to the Holy See any movement which bore the name 'liberal'.

Having said this, there is very little doubt that the Holy See, through the positive opinions expressed explicitly by Pius XI, was in favour of opening some kind of dialogue and discussion with the Church of England. Nor is there any doubt that Cardinal Mercier kept the Holy See up-to-date with all the information about the proceedings of the Conversations. From the first moment that Mercier had put his proposal to Benedict XV in December 1920 (and not receiving any reaction, either positive or negative) to invite some Anglicans and then Orthodox for informal discussions at Malines, to the more straightforward and definite approval of Pius XI, both orally in 1921 and twice in writing in 1922, there was clearly a distinct approval by the highest authorities in Rome of the Conversations. This approval was supported and encouraged by the Cardinal Secretary of State, Gasparri. Despite the efforts of Cardinal Merry del Val and to a lesser extent Cardinal Gasquet, this papal approval continued until after the death of Mercier. It was only at this point that we can begin to see a shift in the Roman attitude, with the increasingly negative influence of the Archbishop of Westminster, Cardinal Bourne. Roger Aubert indicates perhaps more precisely the point at which attitudes in Rome began to change when he postulates that when the Church of England decided to participate in the Life and Work Conference at Stockholm in August 1925 (which the Roman Catholic Church did not approve of nor participate in), Pius XI decided that nothing further was to be gained from Malines, and the death of Mercier shortly afterwards merely confirmed his decision. It was perhaps time then to make some sign of benevolence towards the hardline conservative group within the Roman Curia grouped around Merry del Val, who were positively antagonistic towards the Conversations. Pius XI was aware that he needed the support of this curial group in order to make any progress towards the settlement of the 'Roman Question', and it is perhaps more surprising that the Pope had deliberately ignored their protests for so long in order to allow room for the Conversations to proceed at all.[1]

---

1. Aubert, *Le Cardinal Mercier et le Saint-Siège*, in *Bulletins*, pp. 124–126.

REFLECTIONS OF THE CONVERSATIONS ON ECUMENICAL RELATIONS

[b] The Church of England and Anglicanism.

The Church of England, although maintaining many visible structures similar to the Roman Catholic Church, operated within a very different sort of ecclesiastical organization. The break with Rome at the Reformation did not lead to immediate radical changes for the Church in England as it did on the Continent, and the organizational life of the provinces, dioceses, cathedrals and parishes continued much as they did before 1534. The maintenance in particular of an episcopal structure, together with the orders of priest and deacon, in conjunction with the emphasis on continuity of catholic and apostolic tradition within the National Church, gave a special imprint to the 'reformed' nature of the Church of England. With the rejection of any papal jurisdiction over the Church in England, supreme authority then became totally vested in the Crown as arbiter between bishops and Commons, and henceforth excluded the possibility of appeal to Rome. There was a strong identification of religion and nationhood which has continued to this day.

The main organizational structure of the Church of England as it eventually developed – particularly since 1867[1] – was that of the Synod, principally those of York and Canterbury, which included elected representatives of both clergy and laity, with periodic joint meetings which were called the General Synod. For important decisions pertaining to the whole of the Church of England, a two-thirds majority in General Synod of each of the Houses of Bishops, Clergy and Laity was necessary. A further conciliar-type structure was the Lambeth Conference, first called in 1867 when Archbishop Longley, then Archbishop of Canterbury, invited all the Anglican Bishops throughout the world to meet at Lambeth. These Lambeth Conferences have always

---

1. 'In the organization of Synodal order for the government of the Church, the Diocesan Synod appears to be the primary and simplest form of such organization. By the Diocesan Synod the cooperation of all members of the body is obtained in Church action; ... it is not at variance with the ancient principles of the Church, that both Clergy and Laity should attend the Diocesan Synod, and that it is expedient that the Synod should consist of Bishops and Clergy of the Diocese, with representatives of the Laity ... The Lay Representatives in the Synod ought, in the judgement of your Committee, to be Male Communicants of at least one year's standing in the Diocese, and of the full age of twenty-one'.
The Principles of Synodical Government, Committee Report 'A' of the Lambeth Conference of 1867, as cited in *The Anglican Tradition*, Ed. G.R. Evans & J. Robert Wright, (London: S.P.C.K., 1991), pp. 58–60.

been consultative. They do not legislate, make decisions or pretend to any form of jurisdiction over the various Anglican Churches throughout the world. Each Church of the Anglican Communion was regarded as autonomous in its own right. One of the consequences of this type of decentralized organizational structure was that there was no one person or body which could speak authoritatively for the whole Anglican Communion.

Hence we can see the difficulties facing Randall Davidson, the Archbishop of Canterbury, Primate of the Church of England and *primus inter pares* of the Anglican Communion, when he was called upon to give some kind of official recognition to the participation of the Anglican members at the Conversations of Malines. At the initial stages, and in consultation with the Archbishop of York, he felt reasonably confident of being able to extend his personal if hesitant approval, but if the Conversations had developed to a level which demanded a serious commitment to unity on the part of both Churches, he would have been aware that even he did not have the authority to commit the Church of England and even less the Anglican Communion to such a project.

The very nature of 'comprehensiveness' as claimed by the Church of England was a serious obstacle to any discussions whose objective it was to narrow the areas of divergence, and to refine and possibly define those areas of common agreement and belief. The existence of ecclesiastical parties within the Church of England which were extremely diverse in their views of the Church and yet all claiming loyalty to that same Church, made a consensus of belief – apart from the basic 'Lambeth Quadrilateral' – very difficult. These difficulties of both structure and agreement on common belief were fundamental obstacles to any Anglican ecumenical effort. As Paul Avis notes in his essay *What is 'Anglicanism'*, '... the example of the Church of England's failure to rise to the challenge of the ecumenical vocation by the persistent blocking of initiatives in the Church's synodical machinery of government leads us to conduct a searching questioning of Anglicanism's supposed "synthesis". The reality of the theological life of the Church of England ... gives little grounds for self-congratulation. The domestic traditions of churchmanship – the so-called ecclesiastical parties, High, Low and Broad as they were once known; now Catholic, Evangelical and Liberal – would seem to have largely gone their own way, taking care to reinforce their prejudices through party patronage of livings, partisan theological colleges, newspapers and journals. Internal ecumenism has been minimal'.[1]

Hence, when Lord Halifax first approached Archbishop Davidson concerning the possibility of establishing contact through discussions with the Roman Catholics at Malines, the Archbishop was acutely aware that the Viscount represented only that section of the Church of England known as the High Church or Anglo-Catholics. Even within this grouping, there would have been many who did not approve entirely of Halifax's very pro-Roman stance, and so it was a very small minority of Anglicans that Halifax would have represented. Nevertheless, it took great courage and endless diplomacy for the Archbishop of Canterbury to extend even the limited approbation to the Conversations that he eventually gave.

(iv) Important assumptions in the methodology of the Conversations, the themes chosen for discussion, and points approaching agreement and points of divergence.

[A] The approach of 'unity by convergence'.

One very notable point underlining the whole of the Conversations at Malines was the basic presupposition, adopted almost unconsciously by all the participants, that the ultimate objective of these initial steps was the healing of the rift between the Church of England and the Roman Catholic Church brought about at the Reformation, and to prepare the way for the reunion of both Churches as corporate entities. The notion of 'corporate reunion' as an ideal was for Lord Halifax from the very beginning the keystone to his efforts, but for Portal and Mercier it was the result of a process of conversion from the predominant Roman and Ultramontane view of reunion as 'submission'. Abbé Portal's acceptance of the value of corporate reunion is clearly rooted in his long-standing friendship with Halifax, going back to their days in Madeira, and it was Portal and Halifax together who communicated their enthusiasm to the Cardinal Archbishop of Malines when they first broached the possibility of meetings.

---

1. Paul Avis, 'What is 'Anglicanism?', in *The Study of Anglicanism*, edited by Stephen Stykes and John Booty, p. 409.

'A BROTHER KNOCKING AT THE DOOR'

This assumed objective of reunion between Churches, certainly at least by the original participants at Malines – Bishop Gore being perhaps the exception later on – was in considerable contrast to the methodology adopted by the Faith and Order commission in its preparation for their 1927 Lausanne meeting. Whereas, as we have seen, the Malines Conversationalists had no hesitation about tackling the major doctrinal differences between the two Churches from the very first encounter, the early stages of Faith and Order were almost purely descriptive, more a process of discovery of each other's doctrine and organization. This Faith and Order process could be seen as 'growing awareness', whereas Malines concentrated on 'growing convergence'.[1]

It is important to recognize this point, as it indicates a new methodology of approach wherein brothers of a common Christian faith seek together to discover both those values held in common within each other's beliefs and expressions of worship, and those areas of divergence which cause the separation. This search for 'unity by convergence' marks an important change in the ecclesiological vision of reunion, and it has now become the accepted basis of the current ARCIC discussions, as witnessed by the Malta Report.[2] The conversationalists at Malines never for a moment thought that they could achieve their desired objective of reunion of the two Churches immediately, but their wish was that they could clear some of the ground as a preparation for future, more official meetings at which competent experts might bring closer their goal of reunion. Neither Mercier nor Halifax nor Portal saw themselves as adequately prepared theologically or in the details of historical controversy to be adequate to the task which would be demanded of any subsequent and more precise 'negotiations'. Nor indeed were these three principal protagonists of one mind in their motivation for seeking some form of unity by convergence, because it is clear from the documentation that Cardinal Mercier never fundamentally understood the Anglican

---

1. 'It is hard to overestimate the importance of Lausanne in the growing awareness of each other's tradition and the establishing of a commitment to engage in theological discussion in the search for unity'.
Mary Tanner, The ARCIC Statements in the Context of Other Dialogues, in *Their Lord and Ours,* Mark Santer (Ed.), (London: S.P.C.K., 1982), p. 47.
2. *The Malta Report* (Report of the Anglican/Roman Catholic Joint Preparatory Commission after meeting at Gazzada, Huntercombe Manor and Malta), No. 3; as published in Clark & Davey, *Anglican/Roman Catholic Dialogue,* (London: Oxford Univ. Press, 1974), p. 108.

position, and he saw it simply as a means of bringing a schismatic body of Christians back within the fold of the Catholic Church. For Lord Halifax, on the contrary, it was to seek an honourable way of reconciling two 'Branches' of the one true Church. Despite the clear diversity of motivations, the methodology adopted by all and agreeable to all was the same – to seek unity by means of convergence. All three churchmen were, however, because of their friendship, sincerity and deep desire for the unity of Christendom, more than adequately prepared to engage themselves in the work of preparation for reunion, John the Baptists.

Once news of the proceedings at Malines became public knowledge, however, many people at large on both sides presumed that they were in fact 'negotiating' the reunion of the two Churches, and this led to much of the hostility to the Conversations. The personalities of the participants and their ability to represent adequately both Anglican and Roman Catholic positions then became a focus of much of the controversy.

[B] The idea of unity in diversity.

Another important element which emerged during the course of the Conversations was the notion of achieving unity without necessarily demanding uniformity. This was evoked most forcibly by the unexpected presentation of Dom Lambert Beauduin's memorandum by Cardinal Mercier during the fourth Conversation, *L'Église Anglicane Unie non absorbée*. The idea had already arisen during the course of the second Conversation, when Dean Robinson had expounded the historical claims of Canterbury to a semi-autonomous status, including its own liturgies and customs. The *Compte rendu* drawn up by the French-speaking group at the end of the second Conversation clearly notes that the desire to maintain the internal organization of the Church of England was one of the predominant concerns of the English-speaking group, and accepts this as very understandable 'because it is not a question of acquiescence of individual personalities to the Church of Rome, but a collective reconciliation'.[1]

---

1. 'The main concern of the Anglican Church is to preserve, as much as possible, its organization and its actual hierarchy, its rites, its discipline. Because it is not simply a return of individual personalities to the Church of Rome but rather a collective return, this preoccupation is completely natural'.
Halifax, *The Conversations at Malines – Original Documents*, (1930), Annex IV, p. 86.

'A BROTHER KNOCKING AT THE DOOR'

Following the various discussions on a possible Uniate status for the Church of England, it became clear to the Anglican participants that the Roman Catholics were open to many elements of diversity within a reunited Church, but were not to be moved on the essential points of Papal primacy and declared dogmas. As Dr Gore stated to the Archbishop of Canterbury following the fourth Conversation, 'the Roman Catholics showed a surprising concessiveness in matters of organization, but were adamant on dogmatic issues'.[1]

This theme of the possibility of the Church of England being accepted on a uniate basis similar to the autonomous Eastern Catholic Rite Patriarchates, with its own proper liturgies and customs, is worth examining a little closer.[2] It is not a new idea, as we have seen in the suggestions of Ambrose Phillipps de Lisle in his correspondence with Dr John Bloxam in 1841 (cf. Chapter 1), and has its roots even further back. In the memorandum of Beauduin however, as presented by Cardinal Mercier, it is not the *creation* of a separate uniate status for the Church of England, but rather a *claim* that it was already virtually a uniate church on historical grounds, lacking only the essential link of unity to the Bishop of Rome, the Pope. Beauduin's memorandum, consequently, was an event of primary significance among the various papers presented at Malines, possibly even as G.K.A. Bell noted, producing one of the most enduring results of the whole Conversations.[3] The historical basis of Beauduin's memorandum was challenged later by the Cambridge historian, Outram Evennet, who pointed out that the Uniate liturgies and disciplines of the Eastern Churches have an inherent right to a place within the Catholic Church, having grown up concurrently with their Latin counterparts; they were outside the Latin patriarchate but always in communion with it.[4] Evennet states clearly that there is no parallel between such Uniate Churches and the Church of England, whose latter-day liturgies were composed in direct antagonism to the

---

1. Bell, *Randall Davidson*, vol. 2, p. 1293.
2. The 'uniate' idea is still much to the forefront in ecumenical discussions today, having been mentioned informally by one member of the ARCIC discussions (cf. Bishop Christopher Butler, in *The Tablet*, 14th November 1970, pp. 1098–1099). In a more poignant way, it has been reviewed once again by Bishop Graham Leonard, retired Bishop of London, following the decision of the 1992 General Synod to accept the ordination of women (cf. *The Tablet,* 28th November 1992, p. 1495).
3. Bell, *Randall Davidson*, vol. 2, p. 1291.
4. Outram Evennet, *The Dublin Review*, No. 186 (1930), p. 246.

Catholic conception of the Eucharistic Sacrifice; whose discipline embraces not only the ordination of married men but accepts the marriage of bishops as well as priests; whose orders have been solemnly condemned as invalid ... and whose Catholic predecessors never enjoyed the patriarchal self-government of the great Patriarchs of the East.[1] It is noteworthy, nevertheless, that although Evennet shows convincingly the lack of substantial historical evidence for the existence of an English Uniate Church, he carefully avoids entering into a judgement on the merit of such a uniate scheme.

At the time of its original presentation at Malines, because it was an unforeseen presentation by Cardinal Mercier, the participants did not have time to study and evaluate Beauduin's paper properly, although as Walter Frere noted, 'it took their breath away'.[2] The uniate scheme of Beauduin's paper, however, centered on the bestowal of the *pallium* on the Archbishop of Canterbury by the Pope, symbolic of papal jurisdiction over the whole Church. Any acknowledgement of the Pope's authority or jurisdiction over the whole Church, apart from an honorary one, was the issue which really became the crux of the Conversations, and eventually proved to be the unresolvable point. The Dean of Wells stated quite clearly that the Anglicans could not accept the papal claim to 'universal jurisdiction', and at most would admit to a degree of 'spiritual leadership' for the Pope. Dr Gore, however, said that he could not even accept the term 'spiritual leadership', and would rather see it phrased as 'spiritual responsibility'.[3]

However, here again the new insights of the Decree on Ecumenism of the Second Vatican Council allow scope for further discussions on this topic by the ARCIC members.[4] Some of the implicit points of the Malines discussions can be seen re-emerging in another form from the Joint Preparatory Commission's commentaries; 'During the Commis-

---

1. Evennet, *The Dublin Review*, pp. 247–248.
2. Frere, *Recollections of Malines*, p. 56.
3. Halifax, *The Conversations at Malines – Original Documents*, (1930), pp. 48–49.
4. 'While preserving unity in essentials, let all members of the Church, according to the office entrusted to each, preserve a proper freedom in the various forms of spiritual life and discipline, in the variety of liturgical rites and even in the theological elaborations of revealed truth.'
Decree on Ecumenism (*Unitatis Redintegration*), Ch. 1, No. 4, in Abbott, *Documents of Vatican II*, p. 349.

sion's discussions, mention of the statement of the Pope and the Patriarch, and of limited inter-communion between Roman Catholics and Orthodoxy as set out in the Vatican Council's Decree on Eastern Catholic Churches, gave rise to a suggestion as to the possibility of a similar relationship between Roman Catholics and the Churches of the Anglican Communion'.[1]

[C] **Positive Emphasis on common beliefs.**

In contrast to anything anterior, the Conversations marked a significant milestone by taking as their starting point those elements of the Christian faith which both Churches held in common or where they could arrive at a measure of sufficient agreement. This can seem such a simple point, as it is the fundamental presupposition of most ecumenical encounters in present times, but it was not particularly notable in the controversialist atmosphere of the early twentieth century. This seeking of areas of agreement on common belief was proposed by Lord Halifax at the very first of the Conversations, and further meetings were conditional on their having uncovered sufficient areas of agreement to continue with any confidence to additional Conversations.[2]

It is remarkable to note how much the conversationalists found themselves being in 'substantial agreement' over, and particularly in the discussion on the sacraments. The *Compte rendu* of the first Conversation notes briefly, 'no difficulties concerning baptism',[3] and the discussions of confirmation produced little difficulty. On penance and extreme unction, the Anglicans noted a revival within their communion of the practice of the sacrament for the sick and acceptance of the need for confession for those in serious sin. Even on the potentially thorny question of the eucharist, there was agreement that by consecration the bread and wine became the body and blood of Jesus, but the Anglicans

---

1. Bishop Henry McAdoo, *Unity: An Approach by Stages?*, in *Anglican/Roman Catholic Dialogue*, Clark & Davey, p. 94.
2. 'The immediate goal of these meetings will be to see if, by the witness of those persons present, there exists sufficient agreement between the two Churches to justify both the present meetings and, perhaps later on, further meethings which can be agreed upon by our respective authorities'.
Halifax, *Conversations at Malines – Original Documents*, (1930), p. 10.
3. Halifax, *Conversations at Malines – Original Documents*, (1930), p. 13.

would not accept the Roman use of the term 'transubstantiation' as a description of this action.

Number 3 of the ARCIC Malta Report similarly begins by enunciating those elements of common Christian heritage; 'We record with great thankfulness our common faith in God the Father, in our Lord Jesus Christ, and in the Holy Spirit; our common baptism in the one Church of God; our sharing of the holy Scriptures, of the Apostles' and Nicene Creeds; our common Christian inheritance for many centuries with its living traditions of liturgy, theology, spirituality, Church order, and mission'.

At Malines, despite the disagreement on the interpretation of the role of the papacy, as already noted, even in this contentious area there were notable points of convergence on which the two sides could agree. The Anglicans enumerated the following five areas which would be acceptable as a basis for further development and discussion:

(1) That the Roman Church was founded and built up by St Peter and St Paul, according to St Irenaeus (*Adv. Haer*, III, 3,2).
(2) That the Roman See is the only historically known Apostolic See of the West.
(3) That the Bishop of Rome is, as Augustine said of Pope Innocent I, president of the Western Church (*Contr Julianum Pelagianum*, I, 13).
(4) That he has a primacy among all the bishops of Christendom; so that, without communion with him, there is in fact no prospect of a reunited Christendom.
(5) That to the Roman See the churches of the English owe their Christianity through 'Gregory our Father' (Council of Clovesho AD 747) 'who sent us baptism' (Anglo-Saxon Chronicle, Anno 565).[1]

(v) Points of major difficulty and disagreement.

Despite these notable 'areas of convergence', it did not take long for the participants to arrive at the major points of divergence, most of which had been anticipated by Archbishop Davidson and which he had emphasized in his letter to Cardinal Mercier of the 9th December 1925 wherein

---

1. Halifax, *Conversations at Malines – Original Documents*, (1930), p. 47.

he offered his overall reflections following the conclusion of the fourth Conversation. These were, principally, the claims of papal jurisdiction over the whole Church, and its consequence in the declaration of such marian doctrines as the Immaculate Conception, and also the claim to Papal Infallibility which emanated from the First Vatican Council.

The whole discussion on the papacy centred around three distinct issues:
(I) Relationship of the Pope to the bishops.
The first was the relationship of the Pope to the local bishops and their distinct autonomy. This point of divergence emerged particularly during the fourth Conversation in May 1925, and strong emphasis was placed by the Anglicans on the more collegial nature of the Eastern Orthodox Churches, where the local bishops are autonomous within their own diocese and the Patriarch is a *primus inter pares*. This arrangement would have been more acceptable to the Anglicans present, but the actual claims of the Papacy went far beyond recognition of a simple primacy of honour. It was clear that the Church of England would be opposed to the type of centralization which had occurred in the Roman Catholic Church in virtue of the nature of the Papal claims, and particularly the type of ultramontanism which had been evident since the First Vatican Council. In contradistinction to this, the Anglicans also recognized the historic claims of the See of Rome to some kind of primacy within a reunited christendom, and that the Church could not claim true catholicity until this became a reality under some acceptable form. The summary of points drawn up on this issue is a helpful synthesis:
1. The authority of the Pope is not separate from that of the episcopate; nor in normal circumstances can the authority of the episcopate be exercised in disassociation from that of its chief.
2. In virtue of that primacy the Pope can claim to occupy a position in regard to all other bishops which no other bishop claims to occupy in regard to him.
3. The exercise of that primacy has in time past varied in regard to time and place: and it may vary again. And this adds to the difficulty of defining the respective rights of the Holy See on the one side, and of the episcopate upon the other.[1]

---

1. Halifax, *The Conversations at Malines,* 1927 edition, p. 42.

REFLECTIONS OF THE CONVERSATIONS ON ECUMENICAL RELATIONS

Almost fifty years after Malines, the Second Vatican Council provided what might be the key to the difficulties expressed by the Anglican participants at the Conversations. As a completion of the work of the First Vatican Council, the Second Council underlined the importance of the collegial nature of the episcopate which, together with the Pope, was responsible for the *episcopè* (leadership) of service to the whole *koinônia* (community) of the Church. 'Vatican II placed this service in the wider context of the shared responsibility of all the bishops. The ARCIC commission sees from the teaching of these councils that communion with the Bishop of Rome does not imply submission to an authority which would stifle the distinctive features of the local Churches. The purpose of this episcopal function of the Bishop of Rome is to promote Christian fellowship in faithfulness to the teaching of the apostles'.[1]

(II) Dogmas declared by Rome as articles of faith.
Another central difficulty for the Anglicans at Malines was those articles of faith which had been proclaimed as dogmas by the Roman Catholic Church since the event of the Reformation, principally the marian dogma of the Immaculate Conception, together with the decree on Papal Infallibility. It was asked during the May meeting that, in the event of a reunion of both Churches, would it be possible for the Anglicans to exercise freedom concerning those doctrines which had been defined by Rome since the separation, and hence, without reference to those Christians of the Anglican Communion. The reply from the Roman Catholics was that the freedom which the Anglicans seemed to exercise in matters of belief appeared to them to be excessive, and this was not only a difficulty but a real hindrance to unity.[2]

This question developed into the wide-ranging discussion of which beliefs were fundamental *de fide* truths and which were non-fundamental *de fide* truths. The theological line taken by the Anglicans was that there were certain fundamental truths which every Christian must accept, and these are to be found in; Scripture, tradition, the Creeds, the teaching of the Fathers and the decrees of the first four Ecumenical

---

1. Van Dyke, *Growing Closer Together*, p. 155.
2. Halifax, *The Conversations at Malines*, 1927 edition, p. 38.

Councils. These were seen as 'fundamental' truths requiring assent of all Christians. Anglican theology, they explained, had this built-in distinction between fundamental and accessory truths. Could this formula not be acceptable to the Church of Rome in the event of reunion? The response given by Mgr Batiffol at Malines was that this would not be acceptable, because although Roman Catholics give the same assent to dogmas such as the Resurrection of Christ and the Immaculate Conception of Mary, it is not because of the same criteria. On the one hand there is an affirmation of the Church (the Resurrection), and on the other hand there is an inference sanctioned by the authority of the Church (the Immaculate Conception). The Holy See could not agree that some dogmas be accepted while others were denied.

At Malines this brought the discussions to a halt, as there seemed no way forward. Now we can see the same discussion being dealt with in the Malta Report, but this time on the basis of Vatican II's acceptance of a 'hierarchy of truths'. The Malta Report states clearly in No. 6 that, 'In considering these questions within the context of the present situation of our two Communions, we propose particularly as matter for dialogue the following possible convergence of lines of thought: first, between the traditional Anglican distinction of internal and external communion and the distinction drawn by the Vatican Council between full and partial communion; secondly, between the Anglican distinction of fundamental from non-fundamental and the distinction implied by the Vatican Council's reference to a "hierarchy of truths" *(Decree on Ecumenism, 11)*, to the difference between "revealed truths" and "the manner in which they are formulated" *(Pastoral Constitution on the Church in the Modern World, 62)*, and to diversities in theological tradition being often "complementary rather than conflicting" *(Decree on Ecumenism, 17)*'.[1] Despite the complexity of this question, once again we can see that a certain preparatory work was done at Malines in 1925.[2]

---

1. *The Malta Report*, No. 6, in *Anglican/Roman Catholic Dialogue*, p. 109.
2. It is interesting to note in this context, the comments of John Jay Hughes in his Chapter entitled 'post-mortem' following the publication of *Apostolicae Curae*. Hughes writes, 'One should always be suspicious of the claim that there is one single view on this or that question amongst Roman Catholics, and that deviation from this view is imposible – either because non-conformity is ruthlessly suppressed by a draconian system of discipline or automatically eliminated by the natural unanimity of catholic opinion. Roman Catholics are united in their common assent to the church's dogmatic teaching; and the body of doctrine officially taught by the church is considerably smaller than is often supposed, even by catholics'. Hughes, *Absolutely Null and Utterly Void*, pp. 232–233.

REFLECTIONS OF THE CONVERSATIONS ON ECUMENICAL RELATIONS

(III) The validity of Anglican Orders and some disciplinary matters. Also connected with the issue of Papal jurisdiction and authority was the whole issue of Anglican Orders. When Pope Leo XIII had promulgated the Papal Bull *Apostolicae Curae* in 1896 declaring Anglican Orders 'absolutely null and utterly void', there was great indignation and hurt felt by members of the Anglican Communion who, as was expressed during the second Conversation in March 1923, 'felt keenly that the mother Church had done a very grievous wrong to the daughter Church'.[1] The Anglicans felt that this should be rectified in some way, and Lord Halifax in particular hoped that the issue could be re-examined. The 1920 Lambeth Appeal, however, seemed to offer a new possibility of overcoming the great difficulty which *Apostolicae Curae* had imposed on recognition of validity of orders by the offer on the part of the Anglican bishops to accept a 'form of commission or recognition' from other Churches, where 'terms of union had been satisfactorily adjusted'. The Anglicans expressed the view that it was essential that part of the terms which the Church of England be allowed to retain would include their characteristic customs and rites, such as, (i) the use of the vernacular and the English Rite; (ii) communion under both kinds, and (iii) permission of marriage of the clergy. It was noted that the Anglican Bishops were setting a great example of Christian humility and making a real sacrifice for the sake of unity.[2]

Apart from the common adoption by the Roman Catholic Church since Vatican II of the first two of the Anglican demands, the Dogmatic Constitution on the Church (*Lumen Gentium*) has instigated a whole new dimension of thought on the nature of the Church, the priesthood and the sacraments. In the mind of some catholic theologians, this new line of theology warrants a re-opening of the investigation into Anglican Orders, but on this occasion by a joint-commission of Anglicans and Roman Catholics.[3] Important here is the point that this issue of reconciliation of Ministries is not a closed one, but open to possibilities of further investigation, just as was requested by Halifax.

---

1. Halifax, *The Conversations at Malines*, 1927, p. 22.
2. Halifax, *The Conversations at Malines*, 1927, p. 16.
3. 'The growing conviction that *Apostolicae Curae* did not say the last word on Anglican Orders, and that the verdict of seventy years ago will have to be critically re-examined, has its roots in the one-sided procedure adopted in 1896'.
John Jay Hughes, 'The Papal Condemnation of Anglican Orders: 1896', in *Journal of Ecumenical Studies*, Philadelphia, Vol. 4, Spring 1967, No. 2.

(vi) **The role of powerful individuals, and contemporary issues which impinged on the Conversations.**

In this final section we shall look at the part played by the major personalities involved in the Conversations, their particular strengths and weaknesses, and at some of the important issues which ran concurrently to the meetings at Malines.

(A) Lord Halifax

There is no doubt from what we have seen about Halifax's wholehearted dedication to the cause of Anglican and Roman Catholic reunion throughout the whole of his long life, but particularly in his campaign centred on Anglican Orders and in the Malines Conversations. If his commitment and allegiance were never in doubt, it is also clear that he has often been accused of naivety. Shane Leslie, in his book on Cardinal Gasquet, refers to Halifax as 'half a saint and wholly a busybody',[1] and this probably reflects well both the personal holiness of the man, and his persistence in encouraging and pestering ecclesiastical leaders of both Churches to commit themselves to moves – at times also to risks – for the sake of unity of Christendom, risks which diplomacy or discretion either caused them to hesitate over or to decline.

The main accusation which is cast at Halifax is that he was not representative of the Church of England as a whole, and that his 'party', the High Church or Anglo-Catholics, were only a small part of the Anglican church body. Certainly the vast majority of the English lay people would not have been in agreement with Halifax, but probably a reasonable minority of clergy would have had at least some sympathy with his ideals. It is not true to say that Halifax was unaware that he was not truly representative of the whole of the Church of England, and on more than one occasion he spoke of this fact. Before beginning the Anglican Orders campaign, when Abbé Portal first visited him in Hickelton, Halifax declared that he and those who sympathized with him only represented a comparatively small party in the Church of England. But he also observed that it was small groups who were generally the

---

1. Shane Leslie, *Cardinal Gasquet*, (London: Burns & Oates, 1953), p. 53.

initiators of great movements,[1] as he himself had witnessed at the beginning of the Oxford Movement. This was how Halifax and Portal saw themselves, as initiators of a movement for reunion which was based solidly on friendship and mutual acceptance. Neither expected to achieve the reality of union in their lifetime, but they could begin the first moves.

Halifax was driven always by the ideal of one united Christian Church, and he succeeded in a remarkable way by his enthusiasm and energy in shaping public opinion towards this goal. He drew the leaders of the Church of England with him in his prophetic vision, but, like all prophets, he was an uncomfortable figure to have around. Halifax's biographer notes that 'Halifax was always inclined to assume in others the same standpoint and premises as his own, and to be puzzled and indignant when these did not produce the same conclusions'.[2] Lockhart states that during the Anglican Orders campaign, 'the Archbishop's [Benson] position was totally different from Halifax's, and it must be admitted that not once, but many times, he tried to make this clear. Really he and the Cardinal [Vaughan], from their very conflicting points of view, were closer to each other than either was to Halifax. They, at any rate, spoke the same language and lived on the same plane. The language was that of common-sense, the plane that of practical politics'. The Viscount also on many occasions lacked a comprehension concerning practical affairs, and impatience with the delicacies of diplomacy in Church affairs. He considered the Prayer Book Revision 'a local affair' of the English Church[3] whilst Archbishop Davidson was struggling to have it accepted in Parliament. Halifax's vision of a reunited Church somewhat blinded him to the several important contemporary issues and difficulties which he regarded as peripheral.

(B) Abbé Portal

Abbé Portal's position was in a curious way similar to Halifax's, in that the main criticism levelled at him was that he did not know the Church of England as a whole, but only the Anglo-Catholic part of the Church,

---

1. Halifax, *Leo XII and Anglican Orders*, p. 101.
2. Lockhart, *Charles Lindley Viscount Halifax*, vol. II, p. 90.
3. Letter of Halifax to Davidson, 6th June 1927, Malines Papers of Lord Halifax, A4 271, Box 9.

to which Halifax had introduced him. This was the main criticism of first Cardinal Vaughan, and then both of Ernest Oldmeadow and Francis Woodlock, and they thought that he was being deluded by Halifax. The English Roman Catholics cast him in the role of a meddler in the religious affairs in England which were nothing to do with him, and there were occasional accusations of disloyalty. Merry del Val was in the forefront of those who thought he was disloyal to the Catholic Church, and was prominent in the efforts to interfere in Portal's ecumenical efforts.

It cannot be stressed too strongly how much Lord Halifax influenced and impressed Portal from their first meetings in Madeira. It was such as to change the vocation of the young priest from missionary to ecumenist, and to dedicate the rest of his life working for the reunion of the Churches. But Portal was an intelligent and optimistic person. He studied carefully the Church of England, its theology, its history, its aspirations, and he knew that his friend Halifax was not representative of the whole Anglican Church. As early as 1911, Portal was answering the charge that he did not fully understand the nature of the Church of England, a charge that on this occasion had been made by Wilfred Ward. He wrote to Halifax stating, 'W. Ward knew very well that this was not true, because I told him myself that we had no idea at all that union was going to come about today or tomorrow. I told him that I knew you and your friends were a minority. But what I maintained was that all great movements were produced by minorities. And the whole question was whether the elements which existed within the Church of England were strong enough to give birth to a movement of real importance capable of achieving some result within a given time. We said they were ... What you accomplished, along with your friends like Lacey, Puller, the Archbishop of York and others, proves that our opinion about the possibility of creating a large movement was correct. In spite of all the difficulties you met with you stirred up public opinion. What might you have done if you had received encouragement?'[1]

When, after *Apostolicae Curae*, Portal was obliged to terminate the *Revue anglo-romaine*, Portal opened his house in the rue de Grenelle as a meeting point where unionists could share ideas and study, and his

---

1. Letter of Portal to Halifax, 7th November 1911, Malines Papers of Lord Halifax, A2, 231.

objective was to try to provide facilities and to train a new generation who would continue the work for reunion.[1] With the apparent closure of the door to reunion with the Anglicans, Portal turned his attention to the Orthodox Churches of the East, and became very involved in developing relations with Orthodox theologians such as Iswolski, Berdiaev, Kartachev, and also with Laberthonnière, Maritain and Boegner. Régis Ladous has expressed to me the opinion that the Eastern Churches remained Portal's main interest even throughout his involvement in the Malines Conversations.[2] However, Portal's knowledge of and familiarity with the French and Continental Catholic Church was an invaluable source of information for Halifax, and the two friends acted as catalysts to one another. As a person, Abbé Portal was experienced by his friends as warm-hearted and broad-minded, at ease with people, especially the young, and ever anxious to bring the Church to the forefront of people's minds in a modern and relevant manner. His ecumenical efforts were based on the precepts of charity and understanding, and these he lived out till the end despite all disappointments.

(C) Cardinal Mercier

Undoubtedly the most eminent member of the Malines group was the Cardinal Archbishop of Malines himself, Désiré Joseph Mercier (1851-1926). A man of great intellectual ability, founder and rector of the Thomistic Faculty of Philosophy at the University of Louvain, it was not however his academic ability which had raised him to world prominence, but his steadfast defence of the Belgian people during the 1914–18 World War. His courageous stance against the excesses of the German troops and the injustices of the occupying government earned him an enormous respect and prestige both within his own country and among the Allied nations. At the conclusion of the war, Mercier found himself occupying a world stage, particularly following his visit to the United States in 1919. The warmth of his reception there, particularly from the many non-Catholics who turned out to greet him and listen to his talks, not only greatly impressed him but instilled in him the need to

---

1. 'I have formed a group of young clerics and laity who are studying particularly the religious elements of the English and the Russians.'
Ladous, *Monsieur Portal*, p. 410.
2. This was expressed during a personal discussion with Ladous in Oxford, 23rd July 1985.

work more for the unification of the Christian Churches. As we have seen, this led him in turn to propose to Pope Benedict XV his plan to invite some Anglican and Orthodox theologians to Malines in order to initiate discussions.

It must be said, however, that despite his sincere welcoming and great warmth to the Anglican participants at all the Conversations, Mercier did not at depth understand the Anglican mentality and sensibilities. A good example of this can be seen when the Cardinal wrote to Pope Pius XI on the 14th November 1922, requesting official approbation for the continuation of the Conversations, where, in the same letter, he asked the Pope to consider a papal proclamation of the mother of Jesus under the title of 'Mary, Universal Mediatrix', apparently unaware of the sensitivities of the Anglicans to other marian issues such as the dogma of the Immaculate Conception.[1] The Cardinal was also evidently surprised at how much emphasis the Anglicans placed on the historical aspects of the Church of England's continuity with apostolic tradition and with the pre-Reformation Church, although purged of its excesses. It was the issue of the *pallium* which caused him to ask Dom Lambert Beauduin to prepare his Memorandum for the fourth Conversation.

A particular cause of worry to the Cardinal and major distraction from his ecumenical endeavours at Malines during these years were the internal political and cultural changes then in progress in Belgium. Since the formation of Belgium as an independent nation in 1830, there had been a continual effort on the part of the Flemish-speaking peoples of the country to place their language and culture on a par with the mainly French-speaking governing culture. The German occupying-forces during the 1914–18 war, when it became clear that they could not win the war, tried to use the Flemish/French division to at least safeguard their influence in the country. During the course of 1917, efforts were made to use Cardinal Mercier to sound-out the Belgian government-in-exile about making a separate peace with Germany in exchange for German withdrawal from the whole country, but at the same time

---

1. Letter of Mercier to Pius XI, 14th November 1922, Archives of the Archdiocese of Malines, Box 1.
'I was profoundly happy to learn that Your Holiness had always had in mind and heart the holy cause of proclaiming Mary as universal mediatrix ...'

REFLECTIONS OF THE CONVERSATIONS ON ECUMENICAL RELATIONS

Berlin began a process of federalization of Belgium. In February 1917, the Germans erected a Council of Flanders, and decreed a separate administration for each linguistic area. Brussels became the capital of Flanders, and Namur the capital of Wallonie. In Flanders, teaching at all levels of education was switched from French to Flemish, of particular importance being the University of Ghent.[1]

Cardinal Mercier was bitterly opposed to these changes, partly because they were imposed by the occupying forces, but more importantly because he identified *la patrie* unconditionally with a unitary nation of Belgium. Indubitably his own French background and culture played an important part in his attitude. The mainly Catholic, Flemish-speaking, political parties, however, were quite happy with the new arrangement, and pushed for their retainment at the conclusion of hostilities. The Cardinal's opposition to the linguistic division of Belgium, and particularly to the introduction of Flemish in the schools and colleges, caused bitter dissension at all levels of society, and he was portrayed by the Flemings as anti-Flemish.[2] Mercier was more disappointed when a number of the Belgian bishops, particular those of Liège and Namur, decided to join with the Christian Democrats and support the educational policy of the Flemish-speakers.[3]

The effects of this 'Flemish question' very clearly impinged on the later stages of the Malines Conversations, when it became obvious that the English Roman Catholics were being fed ideas and information by the Flemish Belgians to use against Cardinal Mercier. Lockhart comments that Cardinal Gasquet, in criticizing Mercier's involvement in English

---

1. This policy of federalization was devised principally by Oscar, Baron von Der Lancken-Wakenitz (1867–1939), a German diplomat, who from 1914 onwards was chief of the political section to the Governor-General of Belgium, Baron Von Bissing.
H. Haag 'Le Cardinal Mercier devant la guerre et la paix', in *Revue d'Histoire Ecclesiastique*, 1984, LXXIX, p. 766.
2. As Boudens points out, many of the initial demands of Van Cauwelaert, the Flemish leader in the parliament, were fairly minimal: full use of Flemish in education (till then everyone was taught through French); legal and public services in Flanders to use Flemish; the division of the army into Flemish and Walloon regiments (previously the vast majority of officers were French-speaking, and often could not understand the Flemish-speaking soldiers); that personnel in the central administrations should be able to deal with any matters in the Dutch language.
R. Boudens, *Kardinaal Mercier en de Vlaamse Beweging*, pp. 196–197.
3. Dick, *The Malines Conversations Revisited*, p. 94.

church affairs, stated that he himself might as well go to Belgium and tell Mercier how to solve the Flemish question.[1]

Despite these internal political and cultural problems within Belgium, and even considering this evident blind-spot in Mercier's vision of the Belgian Church and nation, it was undoubtedly the Cardinal's personal holiness and international prestige which carried a major part of the burden of continuing the Conversations past a point at which others would have had to succumb.

(D) Archbishop Davidson

Archbishop Davidson's role during the Malines Conversations was an exceptionally delicate one. To begin with, the 1920 Lambeth Conference *Appeal to All Christian Peoples* had not been prepared with the Roman Catholic Church in mind, but rather addressed to those Churches who did not embrace episcopal ministry. Moreover the roots of this *Appeal* lay in the two interim reports of the preparatory commission (February 1916 and March 1918) set up jointly by the Church of England and the Free Churches to prepare for a world Conference on Faith and Order. Discussions with the Nonconformists were in progress throughout the period when the Conversations were continuing, and Davidson had to exercise his considerable diplomatic skills in maintaining a balance. Additionally, there was the pressing matter of the Revised Prayer Book, a long time in preparation, and now coming towards a definitive version for presentation in the British Parliament. The Archbishop was being almost continually pressed by the more extreme parties of the Church of England, and inevitably the pressures were in opposing directions. Davidson's declared objective during his term at Canterbury was to be as open and comprehensive as possible. He described the aims he had set himself as Archbishop of Canterbury in some notes which he dictated in January 1917. His aim, he said, 'if I were forced to put it in a single phrase... could be described as a desire to assert in practice the thoughtful and deliberate comprehensiveness of the Church of England, as contrasted with the clear-cut lines and fences of demarcation which mark the rulings of the Church of Rome, and the corresponding, though quite different, rulings of protesting sects in

1. Lockhart, *Charles Lindley Viscount Halifax*, vol. 2, p. 286.

REFLECTIONS OF THE CONVERSATIONS ON ECUMENICAL RELATIONS

England, Scotland, America, and presumably Germany in the 17th century and since'.[1]

The process of revision of the Book of Common Prayer demanded much of the comprehensiveness sought by Davidson. For a considerable number of years many of the High Church clergy had been pressing both in theory and by practice for Reservation of Holy Communion for the sick and for devotion.[2] The Prayer Book did not allow for this or for other Ritualist practices which were slowly making an impact on Anglican Church life. Davidson gave voice to his disappointment about this in the same notes by saying, 'I come to the question of boundaries of legitimate ritual variety, and here I must sadly confess to myself that, whether it be my misfortune or my fault, I have been quite unsuccessful in introducing a comprehensiveness of a reasonable and, in a large sense, law-abiding kind'. When a Joint Committee of Convocation of Canterbury had presented in 1915 its initial proposals for some changes to the Prayer Book, including a re-arrangement of the Communion Service, these proposals caused much alarm among Evangelical churchmen.

This was the on-going delicate situation concerning the various stages of the revision of the Book of Common Prayer which caused much anguish to the Archbishop when Lord Halifax wished him to commit himself more fully to giving official cognisance to the delegates at Malines, and when Halifax persisted in airing the nature of the Conversations to the general public by his various publications and speeches.

Nevertheless, it is to the credit of the Archbishop of Canterbury that he cautiously continued to support Halifax's efforts and that of the other Malines participants to the extent that he did, but by nature and by virtue of his office, he could never have shared the outright enthusiasm of either a Halifax or a Portal. Davidson's principal difficulty with the Malines Conversations seems to have stemmed from the fact that the initiative for the meetings came from private individuals who subse-

---

1. Bell, *Randall Davidson*, vol. 2, p. 795.
2. Anglo-Catholics had for a long time reserved communion for the sick and for devotion. However, article 28 of the 39 Articles denies any ordinance of Jesus allowing or ordering reservation. But the ancient Church allowed reservation at home, or for travel. The Book of Common Prayer orders reverent consumption of the Species.

quently requested official authorization. Even apart from the 'representativeness' of the particular individuals involved, this process was not to the Archbishop's liking. It was in sharp contrast to the process which was concurrently being used in preparation for the Faith and Order Conference being planned for Lausanne in 1927, where invited delegations, fully authorized by their respective Churches, were participating in the planning of the agenda. This was a methodology which Davidson understood, and where he felt the Church authorities had control. The initiative for and the process being used at the Malines meetings was one over which the Archbishop felt little control but growing responsibility. The consequence was an understandable uneasiness with Lord Halifax and his friends.

This is in no way to suggest that Archbishop Davidson was opposed to such meetings. On the contrary, he had already expressed himself as being entirely favourable to discussions with other Churches with a view to cooperation and understanding: 'My own feelings have always been strongly in sympathy with a desire, not only to confer with, but, so far as possible, to work with, Christians outside our own Church, and this, as I have always contended, can be done without any compromise of our own distinctive principles, if the difference between undenominationalism and interdenominationalism, is kept prominent and clear'.[1]

(E) Merry del Val

Probably one of the strongest personalities outside the meetings at Malines but who played an important part in bringing them to an inconclusive end was Cardinal Rafael Merry del Val (1865-1930). He went to Rome as a young man to begin ordination studies at the Scots College, but was entered into the *Accademia dei Nobili Ecclesiastici* (the training school for Vatican diplomats) by Pope Leo XIII personally. Even at this stage he was obviously intended for an ecclesiastical career in Rome. He had already been sent on diplomatic missions to London, Vienna and Berlin with the title of Monsignor before he was ordained to the priesthood at the age of twenty-three. He was consecrated as Archbishop at thirty-five years of age, and became Cardinal Secretary of State a mere three years later.

1. Bell, *Randall Davidson*, vol. 2, p. 797.

REFLECTIONS OF THE CONVERSATIONS ON ECUMENICAL RELATIONS

Such was his gratitude and respect for the figure of the Pope, and in particular towards Pope Leo XIII, that anything which detracted or diminished from the person or office of the papacy was to him clearly an aberration. During the campaign by Portal and Halifax on Anglican Orders, Merry del Val readily accepted Cardinal Vaughan's protestations that recognition of Anglican Orders would stem the flow of individual converts to Catholicism, and that what was necessary was an unconditional submission to the Holy See by Anglicans. The Anglo-Spanish Cardinal was the ultimate figure of ultramontanism.

What was decisive in both the Anglican Orders debate and during the Malines Conversations was that because of Merry del Val's position in Rome, he was taken as an expert and consultant in things concerning England and English Church affairs. His experience as Secretary of State to Pope Pius X and his involvement in the anti-Modernist campaign, left him with an abiding suspicion of any signs of Modernism, which, he suspected and had confirmed by Woodlock and others, was clearly evident in the Church of England. He was also the inside advisor at the Vatican for those ecclesiastics and lay people in England who were opposed to corporate reunion, as is evidenced by his correspondence with Vaughan, Moyes, Gasquet, Woodlock and Oldmeadow. Finding himself in such a pivotal position, the English-born Cardinal used it to the fullest in advancing his own conservative convictions. He was evidently unable to combine his own generous and loyal personality with a critical faculty of distinguishing the good faith and sincere convictions of people like Halifax and Portal. In the matter of reunion of the Churches, it would appear that Merry del Val was incapable of appreciating any other view but his own, and he was particularly depreciative of the part played by Abbé Portal, declaring him to be a disloyal catholic priest.

The indications are that the Curia Cardinal used his influence in Rome and elsewhere to stem any sort of favourable publicity or views given to the efforts of Halifax and Portal in favour of corporate reunion, by both encouraging Woodlock and Oldmeadow (in *The Tablet*) and the English and French Jesuits (in *The Month* and *Études*) to air their opposition, and, where possible, in silencing favourable opinions (Fr NcNabb in *Blackfriars*). The resulting one-sided publicity gave a misleading impression to the general public.

(F) Cardinal Bourne

Cardinal Francis Bourne (1861-1935), Archbishop of Westminster, is the one important figure on the English Roman Catholic side who emerges from the scenario of the Malines Conversations as having exerted a moderately sympathetic view of the meetings, although pessimistic about any possible outcome. The paucity of relevant archival documentation on the extent of the Cardinal's knowledge of, support for or opposition to the Conversations renders an accurate judgement of his position extremely difficult. On balance, it would seem likely that Cardinal Bourne knew from the beginning of Halifax's involvement in discussions with Cardinal Mercier, but that probably Halifax did not reveal to him the true depth or intention of the Conversations. This can be inferred from Bourne's own admission that Halifax had been to see him twice (29th November 1921, and again following the third Conversation in November of 1922,) about the Malines meetings, together with Bourne's letter from Rome to Oldmeadow on 6th February 1924 in which he stated that he had known of the Conversations all along. The question remains, however, as to whether this letter to Oldmeadow was meant to convey the extent of Bourne's knowledge, or whether it was intended to subdue the adverse publicity which the Conversations were attracting in the English press. The text of Bourne's letter of 6th February 1924[1] remains intriguingly ambiguous. When Cardinal Mercier's letter of 19th May 1922 addressed to Fr d'Herbigny is taken into consideration, wherein the Cardinal states that Cardinal Bourne had not known of the first Conversation on 6-8th December 1921, then the issue becomes even more confusing.[2] Finally we must consider Bourne's accusation of Mercier contained in his letter of the 29th October 1925, when Mercier had taken up arms against Fr Woodlock. In this letter, Bourne chides his Belgian colleague for keeping him 'absolutely in the dark' about the happenings at Malines. Bourne continued, 'The Archbishop of Canterbury has been given the fullest information of the proceedings at Malines – I have been excluded

---

1. Letter of Bourne to Oldmeadow, 6th February 1922, Archdiocese of Westminster Archives, 124/4/1.
2. 'I believe, nevertheless, that the Archbishop of Canterbury learned of it (the first Conservation) later on, whilst Cardinal Bourne remained in the dark, and, doubtless, remains still in the dark'.
Letter of Mercier to d'Herbigny, 19th May, 1922, Archdiocese of Malines Archives, Box 1.

REFLECTIONS OF THE CONVERSATIONS ON ECUMENICAL RELATIONS

from all such knowledge and thereby a grave wrong has been done to me and to the interests of the Catholic Church in England'.[1]

From the above exchanges, all that can be inferred is that Bourne knew of the Conversations, that they were taking place, but was not aware or certainly not fully aware of the extent or depth of the exchanges. The Westminster Cardinal began as sympathetic to the idea of the meetings, and seems to have maintained goodwill throughout the Conversations, despite the adverse publicity they increasingly received. It was only after the fourth Conversation that Bourne seriously began to question why he himself and the other English bishops were not involved, and his criticism and opposition slowly increased.

As John Dick points out, Cardinal Bourne himself later became involved in similar discussions with the Church of England from June to October 1931, meetings which were held this time in London. These further meetings were approved by Cosmo Lang, now Archbishop of Canterbury, and attended by Cardinal Bourne himself. They were not successful, and little has been heard of them since.[2]

Cardinal Bourne's role in the Conversations, therefore, cannot be said to be an opposing one, but neither can it be judged as constructive. At best it was a neutral one, one which hoped for the best but was not optimistic about the outcome. He did not continue the forthright ultramontane position of his predecessors at Westminster, and in some ways tried to tame and modify the criticisms of the more outspoken opponents of corporate reunion. There can be no doubt that he found himself and his position as leader of the English Roman Catholic community more and more vulnerable as the Conversations proceeded on their course, with no apparent serious effort being made by Malines or Rome to involve the English hierarchy in what could be potentially important decisions, as, for example, the proposed creation of an English Uniate Church, or even the possible abolition of the English hierarchy. In one sense, it can be said that Bourne was forced into taking a more critical attitude to the reunion efforts of Cardinal Mercier in order to become part of the decision-making process.

---

1. Letter of Bourne to Mercier, 29th October 1925, Archdiocese of Westminster Archives, 124/4/1.
2. Dick, *The Conversations at Malines Revisited*, p. 189.

'A BROTHER KNOCKING AT THE DOOR'

Each of these personalities connected with the Malines Conversations, both by their personal strengths and their weaknesses, helped to illuminate at that particular moment the grand vision of a united Christendom, while at the same time to expose some of the inherent weaknesses of ecclesiastical organizations guided by strong undercurrents of political expediency.

CONCLUSIONS

Towards drawing a conclusion on the Malines Conversations – success or failure?

(i) The primary objectives of Halifax, Portal and Mercier.

Throughout the history of the two great efforts of Portal and Halifax to initiate some kind of dialogue between the Church of England and the Roman Catholic Church (the Anglican Orders investigation and the Malines Conversations), the one constant and underlying objective expressed by both men on numerous occasions was that if they could just bring theologians of the two Churches together, in a cordial atmosphere, to share and learn from each other, this would be the advent of a new era in the relationship between both Communions. The subject decided upon (Anglican Orders) for their first attempt was not a felicitous choice, and was easily side-tracked by opponents into a one-sided investigation of the validity of Anglican Orders by a commission composed entirely of Roman Catholics. The ensuing result was the opposite to what was desired, and caused damage to Anglican-Roman relations instead of improving them.

The second attempt at establishing some kind of dialogue between the two Churches (the Malines Conversations), succeeded in achieving the original objective of Portal and Halifax, and over a period of four years maintained its own tentative momentum. In this achievement, it must be conceded that in establishing this first occasion of face-to-face discussions on the subject of reunion between the Church of England and the Roman Catholic Church for three centuries, the Conversations at Malines were a success.

Nevertheless, in the process of organizing these meetings, and particularly in seeking Anglican members who would be sympathetic to the cause of reunion, the representativeness of those attending the Conversations was clearly not adequate. It had of necessity to be restricted to those Anglo-Catholics who were considered open to such a venture, and did not in any way represent the other major parties in the Church of England. When the meetings were eventually made public, they were immediately denounced by the Evangelicals and more protestant-inclined Anglicans. Curiously enough, an almost similar accusation was made against the Roman Catholic members at Malines, in that they, although perhaps competent to expound Roman Catholic teaching, did not understand the English Roman Catholic situation, and hence were not suitable representatives for such discussions. Additionally, these meetings at Malines were inevitably seen as 'negotiations', and this produced a considerable element of fear in many ordinary members of both Churches that traditional views and values would be negotiated away.

From the standpoint of the present time, it is clear that the Conversations had very little possibility of arriving at any clear and positive outcome. The theological position of the Church of England and the Roman Catholic Church had not only been moving in opposite directions, pushed into action by the Modernist movement and its consequent theological conclusions, but had probably arrived at a point where there was no obvious meeting point on a purely theological level. Another consequence of this same Modernist Movement was to accentuate the structural divergences between the organization of the two Churches, moving the Church of Rome into a more defensive, centralized and theologically restrained mould and moving the Church of England in the direction of a more comprehensive, embracing and theologically permissive structure.

The various personalities involved in the Conversations all played important roles, both positively and negatively, but the undoubted central figure was that of Cardinal Mercier. It was the tremendous prestige and outstanding international reputation gained from his defence of the Belgian people and their interests during the Great War which gave the Malines Conversations an aura of importance which no other contemporary churchman could have given. The Belgian Cardinal's involvement and commitment to the Conversations automatically moved them in the eyes of many from the plane of 'private discussions' to a much more important and authoritative level which they never claimed to have.

These in-built defects both of membership and standing could not have been foreseen at the time, and it is to the credit of the participants that they continued with their meetings amidst the increasing clamour and

CONCLUSIONS

negative reaction of the period. Bishop Stephen Neill has offered the opinion that the importance of Malines has been enormously exaggerated,[1] while G.K.A. Bell thought that Mercier's memorandum had been the more memorable and lasting influence,[2] but the real success and importance of Malines should be judged not so much on its impact in its own historical period, important though that may be, but rather in its later consequences in the development of ecumenism.

(ii) Consequential successes.

The fact that the Conversations at Malines took place at all, probably produced their most enduring success. This can be clearly seen in three distinct areas:

(a) The Conversations allowed the Roman Catholic Church to 'test the waters' of ecumenical discussion without being totally or officially involved in their organization. Through the medium of Cardinal Mercier, acting in his own name but with a 'semi-official' blessing from the Holy See, the Roman Church, while officially banning the participation of Roman Catholics in any joint or collaborative ventures with other Churches and Communions such as the *Life and Work* or *Faith and Order* meetings, was able tentatively to involve itself in a similar venture. This tiny move was a real opening of doors in terms of future ecumenical relations.

(b) The method and process of discussion employed at Malines laid, in a very real sense, the groundwork for an acceptable methodology in ecumenical discussion which has become the norm of future meetings. The objectives of *unity by convergence*, an acceptable *unity in diversity*, and the *emphasis on common beliefs*, have all since become the basis of ecumenical discussions between the Church of England and the Roman Catholic Church, as evidenced in the ARCIC reports of Malta and subsequent meetings.

(c) The influence which the person and writings both of Cardinal Mercier and Lord Halifax and their ecumenical efforts had, long after their deaths, on Cardinal Angelo Roncalli, the future Pope John XXIII, while he was Papal Nuncio both in Paris and later in Brussels. Both Jean Guitton,[3] a student and disciple of Abbé Portal, and Mgr Loris

---

1. Stephen Neill, *Twentieth Century Christianity*, (1960), p. 353.
2. Bell, *Randall Davidson*, vol. 2 p. 1291.
3. Jean Guitton, *Dialogue avec les précurseurs*, (Paris: 1962), pp. 61. ff.

CONCLUSIONS

Capovilla,[1] secretary to Cardinal Roncalli, testify to the influence of the Malines personalities and their reunion efforts on the future Pope of the Second Vatican Council. It is surely more than conjecture to say that Mercier, Halifax and Portal could have been instrumental in setting the agenda for the historic Decree on Ecumenism which eventually emerged from the Second Vatican Council, or the event of Pope Paul VI's personal reception in Rome of the Archbishop of Canterbury, Michael Ramsey, in March 1966, thereby marking a new era in Anglican-Roman Catholic relations.

---

1. Cited by John J. Hughes in *Absolutely Null and Utterly Void*, p. 209.

Appendix 1
Letter of Cardinal Merry del Val

My dear Father Woodlock,

I have received your letter of 9th and the little book 'One God and Father of All', by Dr White and Wilfred Knox. The minutes of the Commission that sat in Rome before the Cardinal's meeting, presided over by Leo XIII in person, July 16th 1896, are in the archives of the Holy Office. I see no possibility of access being allowed to those records, nor can I in my position as Cardinal Secretary of the Holy Office permit my name to be quoted. But I may give you some information and facts which I can vouch for and which you may unhesitatingly assert. I was Secretary to the Commission and during the whole time before and after the Commission I lived in the Vatican in attendance on Leo XIII, in daily contact with him, and he had recourse to my services in connection with all Anglican controversy from beginning to end. The Commission had not to decide anything, but was summoned to examine the question, to discuss fully and freely all the possible arguments in favour of the validity of Anglican Orders, to study all the available documents in and out of Rome without any restriction or limitation. The archives of the Holy Office were open to the Commission, where the question had been thoroughly gone into centuries before by the greatest theologians of the day, since the time of Cardinal Pole, and where there was and is a copy of the Edwardine Ordinal of 1552, in English. So complete and deep was the study in the past, that Leo XIII declared to me after his decision that 'had he realised how fully and thoroughly the matter had been dealt with and settled in the past, he would not have allowed the reopening of the case'. And indeed the Commissioners had to recognise that, except for later documents confirming the previous decision, there was little that had not been considered. Leo XIII says as much in his Bull *Apostolicae Curae* see the paragraph *Quae cum ita sunt, non videt nemo ... etc,* page 267 of the *Acta Leonis* vol: XVI, 1896 where the Pope explains the reasons of his *maxima indulgentia*. It is most important that the Bull should be very carefully read. Every word of it was weighed and it clearly states the theological reasons for declaring the Orders absolutely invalid in the Catholic sense and for the purpose of a sacrificial priest-

APPENDIX 1

hood – *sacerdotium* – as distinct from *presbyter* in its merely etymological meaning.

Not the English Catholics, but a section of Anglicans raised the question and appealed to the Holy See for a fresh examination. With the Holy See English Catholics had always held Anglican Orders to be invalid and only defended their conviction when it was clamorously questioned by Lord Halifax and his followers. They were anxious in view of the controversy that the Pope should speak again, but there was no other desire on their part but a declaration of the truth after a full consideration of the facts and on the basis of unquestioned Catholic doctrine.

It is a striking fact, but a fact it is, which I have verified myself: whereas there are innumerable cases of doubtful ordinations in the archives of the Holy Office, extending over centuries, it is difficult to find an instance in which the reordination *absolute* has been prescribed. Wherever there was the slightest doubt of any kind, or for any reason, the answer has always been *reordinetur sub conditione* The one, I might say unique, case in which always unceasingly and without exception or hesitation, without fear of committing even a material sacrilege, the answer has been *reordinetur absolute* is the case of Anglican Orders. And why? Because the form of the valid sacrament had been changed and drawn up precisely to exclude the conferring of a sacrificial priesthood and as a consequence the Mass. It is idle of Dr White and Mr Wilfred Knox to refer to Eastern forms of ordination. That point was also examined by the Commission and by the Holy Office. In all Eastern forms of ordination recognised by the Church, there is always an allusion to the *sacerdotium*. The forms are simpler, simpler perhaps than the form of 1662, where mention is made of 'the office of a priest' though this was added a century after the Ordinal of 1552, and the addition shows the need of something more. If taken as it stands, and independently of the circumstances or of the meaning attached to the word 'priest', one can perceive the possibility of admitting the validity of that form. But it came too late, in any case and the established form had been purposely mutilated to exclude the sacrificial priesthood. The Eastern forms were and are simple, but simple from their origin, and not the result of a mutilation or change of doctrine, and they contain the essential elements.

It is idle and beside the point to argue as White and Knox do concerning the intention of the minister. It is contrary to truth to attribute to Leo XIII an error on this head, or to quote St Alphonsus and the common teaching of our Theologians. If a minister uses a valid form, it

APPENDIX 1

is most difficult, often impossible, to prove that his personal intention invalidated the sacrament, unless clear evidence is forthcoming and absolutely conclusive. But that is not the point here. If a minister uses a corrupt or mutilated form, the intention is expressed in the rite itself, viz. the intention of excluding the definite object and effect of the Sacrament. That is why in this case we often speak of the *intentio ritus* rather than of the personal and private opinions and intentions of the minister. This also is made clear in the Pope's Bull. There too is the answer to White and Knox's interpretation of the *Accipe Spiritum Sanctum* with the imposition of hands, which cannot be the form of conferring ordination unless the prayer or prayers accompanying explain for what precise purpose it is used, for we have the same words and imposition of hands for the diaconate etc., and the imposition of hands and an equivalent form of bestowing the Holy Ghost are found in the administration of Confirmation.

It is not true that the condemnation of Anglican Orders was based on the omission of the instruments in the Anglican Form. That omission constituted only a subsidiary argument as showing what the Reformers intended to exclude, viz. the *sacerdotium* and the Mass. All these points were discussed by the Commissioners. Those among them who were anxious to do their best for Anglican Orders, as far as I recollect, never went beyond pleading that those Orders might be considered doubtful and implying reordination *sub conditione*. They only repeated the standard Anglican arguments which fell before the arguments on the other side.

Puller and Lacey hovered round the Commission the whole time and put in every argument they could think of. There was never a fuller hearing of any case. When the Commission ended its debates, the minutes and reports were handed to the Holy Office, where they were examined. And then came the solemn meeting of all the Cardinals of the Holy Office at the Vatican in the Holy Father's presence. It was what we call a Feria V. Short of an ecumenical Council and a definition *ex cathedra* I suppose there is no more solemn form of procedure. It lasted two hours or more. The Cardinals were unanimous in declaring the Orders absolutely invalid. The Holy Father took further time to consider the matter and then drew up his dogmatic Bull, concerning a dogmatic fact, thereby involving indirectly if not directly his infallibility; for if with a given form before his eyes he cannot decide whether or not it contains the essential elements of a valid sacrament, what becomes of his infallibility? Policy or expediency played no part in the decision.

APPENDIX 1

Certainly not on our side. Indeed, if policy had come into the matter it would have been in the opposite direction, for the Pope would have been only too glad to remove an obstacle to reunion and the conversion of those who believed in the validity of their orders. Pressure was brought to bear on him in this sense and he was being constantly assured that if he found a verdict favourable to the validity of Anglican Orders or at all events to a conditional reordination thousands would submit to the Holy See. I can testify to this from personal knowledge. The Barlow case was discussed at the meetings of the Commission, but again only as a subsidiary argument. On this point a positive and absolutely certain conclusion could not be reached. It appeared to many as a waste of time, being an intricate historical and not a theological question. Just as in the past the great issue was the *defectus formae et intentionis*, 'intentionis' in the sense I have explained above. This is stated in the *Apostolicae Curae*, p. 266 cf. the Acta Leonis XIII. Here there was a clear theological issue with the unquestioned text of the Ordinal under consideration, together with the authoritative explanations of the new Ordinal by its compilers and by the Protestant theologians of the time. The Gordon case was decided on the same grounds as is evident from the decree of the Holy Office, the full text of which is not given by Eastcourt, if I am not mistaken.

There was nothing new brought up on the Anglican side and the arguments were those put forward with which you are well acquainted.

I have let myself run on and I must apologise for the length of this letter and for having repeated things that, I am sure, you know better than I do. Before concluding I should like however to call your attention to Father Vincent Hornyhold's pamphlet 'Catholic Orders and Anglican Orders. Catholic Truth Soc. 198. It is an excellent summary of the whole question. I have rarely seen a better one. If out of print, I think it would be useful to reprint it and to distribute it widely. It is in a great measure an answer to the misleading and false statements of the book by White and Wilfred Knox. I understand that Cardinal Gasquet's papers have been deposited at Downside. I know that there you would find the printed documents circulated by Puller and Lacey in Rome during the sittings of the Commission, together with the printed replies from the Catholic theologians. They are interesting and perhaps useful.

An interesting book, which I dare say you have read, published in 1926, (Longmans) is *The Story of the English Prayer Book* by Dyson Hague, a Protestant Doctor of Divinity and formerly a Canon of St Paul's. It frankly gives the history and purport of the English Ordinal

APPENDIX 1

and therefore entirely supports our assertion. I have only glanced at White and Knox's book, but my impression is that it is a very poor production, sophistical, and misleading, with false statements of facts and revealing often an *ignoratio elenchi*. It is rather late in the day to question even the presence of St Peter in Rome!

With every best wish, I am, dear Father,
Yours devotedly in Xt,
R. Cardinal Merry del Val.

January 16th, 1930.

[Text of unpublished letter of Cardinal Merry del Val to Fr Francis Woodlock, sj, dated 16th January, 1930 – Jesuit Archives, Farm Street, London, Ref. BM/6.]

Appendix 2

Statements agreed following the Second Conversation

15 mars 1923

In the autumn of 1921, Lord Halifax came to see me at Malines and asked me if I would be disposed to receive some of his friends, members of the Anglican Church like himself and desireous like he, to work for the coming together of the Anglican Church and the Roman Catholic Church. The moment was appropriate, he said, because 250 Anglican bishops, meeting in conference at the palace of Lambeth, had expressed in a very clear and explicit way their lively desire to see realised the catholic unity of Christianity.

With a grateful heart, I acquiesced to the confident request of Lord Halifax and of his companion, the abbé Portal.

We had a first meeting at Malines on the 6th and 7th December 1921, at which participated on the Anglican side Lord Halifax, Dr Armitage Robinson, the dean of Wells; Dr Frere, superior of the Resurrectionists; on the Catholic side there were the abbé Portal, Mgr Van Roey, vicar general of Malines, and myself.

This first conference, quite unofficial, affected us deeply with feelings of mutual esteem, of reciprocal confidence, of brotherly warmth, and rekindled our common desire to help, if possible, this coming together so desired by the Lambeth conference, and which today, more than ever before, is desired by all those who remain sad and often powerless witnesses of the demoralisation and the de-christianisation of society.

This need for unity was reinforced throughout our first meeting. We insisted on the necessity of a catholic unity which was visible, and on this our feelings were unanimous; then on the necessity of a spiritual primacy, which the Roman Church sees realised in the Successor of Peter. On this last point, we did not arrive at a positive unanimous conclusion; however, our Anglican friends did not reject a recognition of a spiritual supremacy of the Papacy. This question was suspended for the moment.

During the course of this first meeting, our Anglican friends renewed

APPENDIX 2

the declaration already made by the Lambeth Conference, in virtue of which the bishops and priests of the Anglican Church - all necessary conditions for reunion having already been previously established - would be willing to accept from the Roman Church whatever was judged necessary by Her for the validity of Anglican Orders.

Following our meeting of 1921, and during the course of 1922, Lord Halifax published an English translation of my Pastoral letter on the Papacy and the election of Pope Pius XI, and adjoined to it a very important introduction which constituted a new appeal for reunion.

In his encyclical *Ubi arcano Dei*, the Sovereign Pontiff has also issued a moving appeal for the realisation of the vow of Our Lord Jesus Christ: *Et alias oves habeo et illas oportet me adducere ... et vocem meam audient et fiet unum ovile et unus pastor.*

> 'Venerable Brothers, when, from this apostolic See, like an observer on the tower of a high fortress looking out on the world, We are saddened to see how many souls are still totally ignorant of Christ, or who distance themselves from the integral purity of His doctrine or the unity of His Church. How many sheep do not belong to that Flock which, by their divine vocation, ought to be theirs. The Vicar of Christ, who is the eternal shepherd of souls, fired by that zeal with which he himself had been engulfed, We cannot but recall and repeat those words which, so precise and full of love and compassionate pity, escape from His Heart: "And I have other sheep still, and I must lead them also". Our memory suggests to Us that we re-read also, with trembling happiness, the prediction of Christ: "And they will hear my voice and there will be only one Flock and one Shepherd".
>
> Please God, Venerable Brothers, - in union with You and with your diocesans, We will ask Him with all Our hearts and with all the ardour of Our prayers - that this consoling prediction so close to His Divine Heart may be soon fulfilled and that We might be the joyful witnesses of it.'

Our second meeting opened on the 13th and 15th March 1923. The members at this meeting were the same as that of the preceding one, but this time, not only had we Roman Catholics received written assurance that the Holy Father approved, encouraged and blessed us, but our three English confreres arrived with the approbation of the archbishops of

APPENDIX 2

Canterbury and York. These, having consulted the English bishops under their jurisdiction, sent them to Malines on their behalf.

This time, the question examined by us concerned this theme: supposing that an agreement of spirit might be arrived at on a doctrinal level. Under what conditions would operate such a union of the Roman and Anglican Churches?

The principle preoccupation of the Anglican Church is to safeguard, as much as possible, its organisation and its hierarchy, its rites and its discipline.

Because this would not be a matter of individuals returning to the Roman Church, but rather a collective return, this preoccupation is completely natural.

It is natural that the archbishop of Canterbury, considered by the bishops, the clergy, and by the faithful as their leader, should be able to continue to exercise that authority in their regard.

By means of this exercise, the rites and discipline would be sufficiently maintained. The entry as a group into the interior of the Roman Church would be facilitated.

Hence, the basic questions to be posed appear to be the following:

- Would the Holy See approve of the archbishop of Canterbury being recognised as Primate of the Anglican Church in union with Rome, he having accepted the spiritual supremacy of the Sovereign Pontiff and whatever ceremonial judged by him (the Pope) to be necessary for the validity of the consecration of the archbishop?
- Would the Holy See agree to invest the archbishop of Canterbury and the other metropolitans with the pallium as a symbol of their jurisdiction over their respective provinces?
- Would they allow the archbishop of Canterbury to apply to the other bishops the ceremony of validation accepted by the archbishop?
- Would they allow each Metropolitan to confirm and consecrate bishops for his province in the future?

Until such times as this fundamental question can be resolved, it would be unhelpful to continue our negotiations. If it can be resolved affirmatively, the way would be open to examine further questions of application.

APPENDIX 2

Accepted for submission to our respective authorities.
+ D.J. Card. MERCIER, Archevêque de Malines.
E. VAN ROEY, vic. gén.
PORTAL, prêtre de la mission
HALIFAX
J. ARMITAGE ROBINSON
WALTER HOWARD FRERE

The Anglican representatives, being in hearty agreement with the statement drawn up by his Eminence, desire on their part to sum up the position in the following terms.

As a result of the recent conversations at Malines it was agreed by those who were present that, supposing the doctrinal differences now existing between the two Churches could be satisfactorily explained or removed, and further supposing the difficulty regarding Anglican Orders were surmounted on the lines indicated in the Lambeth Appeal, then the following suggestion would serve as a basis of practical action for the reunion of the two Churches.

1. The acknowledgement of the position of the Papal See as the centre and head on earth of the Catholic Church, from which guidance should be looked for, in general, and especially in grave matters affecting the welfare of the Church as a whole.
2. The acknowledgement of the Anglican Communion as a body linked with the Papal See in virtue of the recognition of the jurisdiction of the Archbishop of Canterbury and other Metropolitans by the gift of the pallium.
3. Under the discipline of the English Church would fall the determination of all such questions as:
    (a) The English rite and its use in the Vernacular.
    (b) Communion in both kinds.
    (c) Marriage of the Clergy.
4. The position of the existing R.C. hierarchy in England with their Churches and congregations would for the present at any rate remain unaltered. They would be exempt from the jurisdiction of Canterbury, and as at present directly dependent on the Roman See.

APPENDIX 2

Accepted for submission to respective authorities.
+ D.J. Card. MERCIER, Archbishop of Malines.
E. VAN ROEY, vic. gen.
PORTAL, prêtre de la mission.
HALIFAX.
J. ARMITAGE ROBINSON.
WALTER HOWARD FRERE.[1]

---

1. Original text to be found in Lord Halifax, *The Conversations at Malines (1921–1925), Original Documents*, (London: Philip Allan & Co., 1930), pp. 83–88.

Appendix 3

Archbishop Davidson's speech to Convocation

From a Speech by the ARCHBISHOP OF CANTERBURY in the Upper House of Convocation on February 6th, 1924

Now, my lords, in writing to our Metropolitans about all these I took occasion, as your lordships will remember, to recount also the fact of conversations having been held under the roof of Cardinal Mercier, at Malines, between some of our Anglican theologians and certain theologians of the Roman Catholic Church, the conversations taking place under the Presidency of Cardinal Mercier himself ...

The controversy and even clamour which has arisen about these conversations, is due, I suppose, to the rarity of such incidents. It would be difficult, I imagine, to find a former occasion when opportunity has been given for quiet interchange of opinion or restatement of facts on the part of a joint group of expert theologians, Roman Catholic and Anglican. Accordingly, as soon as I had made public the fact that these informal conversations had been held (and I wished to make it public at the first available moment) the statement was twisted or exaggerated into an announcement that secret negotiations were in progress under the Archbishop of Canterbury's leadership for the reunion of the Church of England with the Church of Rome. As regards secrecy – an allegation upon which much has been made to turn – I took the first available opportunity, as I said, for publicly stating in the simplest way what had happened. This was on purpose to avoid the growth of misunderstandings based on ill-informed rumour which might become current. I told the story with absolute simplicity and straightforwardness. You may have seen that Cardinal Mercier in a Pastoral Letter published a few days ago, a copy of which he has kindly sent to me, has done the same, and I need hardly say that his narrative corresponds closely with my own.

So far as Convocation is concerned I should be quite satisfied to leave the matter there, for I have no reason to fear that there is the least misunderstanding on the part of any member of either House. But comments and criticism from outside have been abundant. The comments may be divided into three groups. There are, first, those (and they are very many) who, either in public speeches or in letters to myself, have

APPENDIX 3

expressed their complete satisfaction with what I have tried to do, and what I have abstained from doing. I have abundant letters to that effect from Anglicans at home and overseas, and from leading Scotch Presbyterians, from leading English Nonconformists, and from public men whose denominational position I do not exactly know. That is the first group. Then the second group of criticisms (if the word is not too mild) comes from men and women expressing a fear or an indignation based apparently upon some complete misrepresentation or misunderstanding of the facts. These denounce me as having 'betrayed the Church' or 'sold the pass' or 'bowed down to idolatry' or 'headed a secret conspiracy against the truth of God'. These have been widely circulated in various publications in this country. The best answer to these controversialists is silence, for it is impossible to deal with arguments based not on facts but on imagination.

There is, however, a third group, consisting of more or less thoughtful men and women, whose loyalty to Protestant principles makes them fearful of anything which looks to them like an approach towards friendship with the Church of Rome and who believe me to have harmed by my action or inaction the Church of England which they love. To these I should say something. It is against myself as a troubler of Israel that their shafts are directed sometimes in sorrow and sometimes in anger. Formal letters have been written to me, and to one at least of these, as coming from an important quarter, I wrote a careful reply, but the writer has not, to the best of my belief, fulfilled the intention he expressed to me of making the correspondence public.

Now, my lords, I find it difficult to understand how so mistaken a view of the facts has come about, for I tried in my public letter of Christmas to make as clear as I could what is really a very simple story. In case it may be helpful to any one who reads a report of what I am now saying I will here repeat the story in outline.

Some two years ago it came about almost fortuitously that a little gathering was arranged at which a few leading Roman Churchmen should meet a few Anglicans for conversation about the differences which separate our Churches. This was to take place under the hospitable roof of the venerable Cardinal Mercier at Malines. Though I had no responsibility with regard to this, it is doubtless the fact that had I desired to do so I might, so to speak, have stamped out the very suggestion of such a conversation taking place, however informally; or at least I might have refused to know anything whatever about it. Such action on my part – and this seems to me self-evident – would have belied the

APPENDIX 3

Appeal which the Lambeth Conference had made in the widest possible terms 'to All Christian People' for the furtherance of a wider unity of the Church of Christ on earth. It would, further, have been contrary to every principle which I have entertained in religious matters. I have always believed that personal intercourse is of the very highest value for the better understanding of matters of faith or opinion whereon people are in disagreement, however wide or even fundamental the disagreement may be. To me the quenching of smoking flax by the stamping out of an endeavour to discuss, thus privately, our differences would, I say unhesitatingly, have seemed to be a sin against God. What followed is thus described in my published letter to the Metropolitans:

> It was suggested that, with a view to a second visit the two English Archbishops might informally nominate delegates and might suggest the outline of discussion to be followed. I did not see my way to doing this (that is why I abstained from doing it) but in the correspondence which ensued I expressed my readiness to have official cognizance of the arrangements, provided that a corresponding cognizance were given by the Vatican. Satisfied, after correspondence, with regard to that point, I gave what was described as friendly cognizance to a second visit of the Anglican group to Malines in March 1923.

I have quoted these words to you because some discussion has arisen respecting them. I adhere to them exactly as they stand, and I am certain that their truth will not be contravened by anyone who is aware of all the facts. Cardinal Mercier, I need hardly say, confirms them absolutely in his Pastoral Letter, to which I would venture to refer your lordships.

After the second conference had taken place a wish was expressed on both sides that the number of those taking part in the conversations should be extended. The point at issue, or at least one of the great and far-reaching matters which I was anxious should be adequately handled was the question of Papal authority as a doctrine of the Roman Catholic Church. Feeling the importance of this I said that in my view it would be well that Bishop Gore and Dr Kidd, as two of our divines who had given closest attention to this particular subject, should be added to the group. I asked the five men who were, accordingly, going to Malines for the third group of conversations to meet me at Lambeth when, without giving any formal direction or insisting upon any particular Agenda Paper, I urged the necessity of its being made quite clear what is our

APPENDIX 3

well-established and coherent Anglican position as set forth by our great divines. This corresponds exactly to what we have throughout endeavoured to do in our conversations with our Free Church friends in England. I found everyone to be in complete accord with me on the matter.

The third conference, or rather group of conversations, took place, and there the matter remained, and there it stands now.[1] Let me repeat, for the reiteration of it seems to be necessary, that there have been no negotiations whatever. We are not at present within sight of anything of the kind. Cardinal Mercier emphasizes this as strongly as I do. There are whole sentences about it in his Pastoral. They were private conversations about our respective history and doctrines and nothing more. The critics of our action urge that before any such conversation can be rightly allowed to take place we ought to insist that the Church of Rome must confess the error of its doctrines and repudiate the Declaration about Anglican Orders. I think your lordships will agree with me when I say that to describe the conversations as being useless or harmful unless we secure such a preliminary surrender shows a fundamental misconception of what is meant by the sort of conversations which can be held in order to elucidate our respective positions. Where should we be, my lords, if, in all matters of controversy, conversations were to be pronounced useless or hurtful unless the conclusion or even conversion which on either side is hoped for has been already secured? Were we in this matter to reach at some future time a stage in which the word 'negotiations' would be appropriate I should certainly feel it to be essential that those who would then be going out as in some sense delegates or representatives of the Church of England should be men who represent the different points of view which have a legitimate place in the Church of England.

My lords, this repetition of the account I have already given of what has passed may seem to be – perhaps it really is – unnecessary. But I do want, if I can, to help those outside who are criticizing what I have tried to do or have abstained from doing, to realize the necessity of looking largely at the great question of the religious obligation which is ours at a supremely critical time in the history of the world. If the Church of Christ, interpreting that word in its widest sense, is to fulfil the trust given to us by our Divine Lord we have to see to it that, to the utmost

---

1. This speech was delivered prior to the fourth Conference held in May, 1925.

APPENDIX 3

extent possible, we should act together against the evil things which He bids us fight and conquer. The uniting of the forces of Christian men on earth may be a long, long way off. I think it is. But we must continually and prayerfully strive thitherward. And, while holding for dear life to what we solemnly believe to be true in regard to the presentation of the Gospel of Jesus Christ to mankind, we must beware – is it not so? – lest we turn a deaf ear, or a blind eye, to even the slightest movement in the direction of a truer understanding of the different aspects of the Divine message which at sundry times and in divers manners God has given to the sons of men.

Lord Halifax, *The Conversations at Malines 1921–1925*,
(Oxford: Oxford University Press, 1927).
Appendix II, pp. 50/59.

Appendix 4

The Anglican Church united not absorbed[1]

by ***[2]
Memorandum read by Cardinal Mercier.

INTRODUCTION

1. The fact that all bishops have equal rights has to be considered as something divinely established: one only, the successor of Peter, the bishop of Rome, is established as the supreme leader of the episcopal body and of the universal catholic Church. His episcopal jurisdiction extends to all the particular local churches without exception: *Episcopus Catholicus*.

2. However, human law, whether evolved by custom or based on something more positive, has allowed a hierarchy of jurisdiction to develop among the bishops and established relationships of superiority and of subordination: patriarchs, primates, archbishops, suffragans. In order to be legitimate and in conformity with divine law, these powers have to be explicitly established, or admitted implicitly, or legitimized *post factum* by the supreme power of which we spoke in number 1.

3. These two principles were perfectly applied in the establishment and in the subsequent history of the Anglican Church during the first ten centuries of its existence (594-1537). On the one hand, the constitution of this Church as an organism exercising great autonomy thanks to the dependence of the whole English episcopacy on the very effective and widespread jurisdiction of the patriarch of Canterbury. On the other hand, the most explicit recognition, both in theory and practice, of the

---

1. Author's translation of text of the Memoire taken from '*The Conversations at Malines 1921–1925*', Original Documents edited by Lord Halifax, London 1930, pp. 241-261.
2 At the time of publication of Lord Halifax's book *The Conversations at Malines 1921–1925*, it was not known that the author of Cardinal Mercier's Memoire was Dom Lambert Beauduin.

APPENDIX 4

supreme jurisdiction of the Roman Pontiffs, and the unquestioning subordination of the patriarchial power of Canterbury to the See of Peter. Because of this fact, the Anglican Church was known as *the most profoundly and faithfully Roman Church*[1] of either East or West.

4. In other words, on the one hand, the Anglican Church appears throughout its history not simply as a juxta-position of dioceses attached to Rome without any serious and effective hierarchical relationships among themselves, but as a strongly organised unity, compact and united, under the authority of the successors of St Augustine; this was an organisation so in keeping with the aspirations of this autonomous and island nation, proud of its notions of *self-government* and of *splendid isolation*.

On the other hand, there was never a Church so Roman in its origins, in its traditions, in its spirit, in its history; there was never a body so attached to the Apostolic See, the Mother-Church of all Churches, to such an extent that, four centuries after its separation, a writer could say: 'England is a Catholic cathedral inhabited by Protestants'.

5. Extensive internal autonomy and faithful dependence on Rome: such are the two characteristics of its history; these are also perhaps the basis of reconciliation. Our report envisages both these aspects as its objective.

First paragraph: Historical presentation of this double aspect: historical points.

Second paragraph: The possibility of a catholic statute for the present-day Church of England based on these historic facts: points of canon Law.

3. Conclusion

§1. – Historical points.

1. From the very beginning, St Augustine of Canterbury was appointed head of the Church of England by St Gregory the Great, who invested

---

1. All Italics are from the original text.

APPENDIX 4

him with the pallium, the sign of patriarchal power (*usum tibi pallii in ea ac sola missarum solemnia agenda concedimus* ...) (*Epist. ad Augustinum* quoted by the Venerable Bede, *Hist. Eccles. Anglorum* M.L., t. XCV, col. 69), comprising an effective jurisdiction over all the present and future bishops of the kingdom of England: '*Britannorum vero omnium episcoporum tuae curam Fraternitati committimus, ut indocti doceantur, infirmi persuasione roborentur, perversi auctoritate corrigantur*'. (*Epist. ad Aug.* M.L., t. LXXVII, col. 1192)

2. There can be no doubt concerning the effective consequences of this patriarchal jurisdiction. In fact, St Augustine wished to obtain further precision and asked if his power extended also over the bishops of Gaul, whom he doubtlessly visited when he travelled to Rome. St Gregory replied to him: *In Galliarum episcopos nullam tibi auctoritatem tribuimus, quia ab antiquis praedecessorum temporibus pallium Arelatensis episcopus recepit, quem nos privare auctoritate percepta minime debemus ... Ipse autem auctoritate propria episcopus Galliarum judicare non poteris; sed suadendo, blandiendo, bona quoque tua opera eorum imitationi monstrando...Britannorum vero omnium episcoporum tuae curam fraternitati committimus etc* ... It is therefore not a question of a position of honour or of fraternal influence: the Bishop of Arles in Gaul and the Archbishop of Canterbury in Great Britain exercised patriarchal power over all the Churches of their respective countries.

3. This patriarchal jurisdiction is conferred by a symbol as venerable as it is meaningful, the imposition of the *pallium*; and in order to understand the significance of the documents referred to in this report, it is important to grasp the full meaning of the rite of investiture which has been attached to this ceremony in the past. The *pallium* is a garment, a large scarf made of wool, which is worn around the neck and shoulders. The Pontifical *pallium* quickly adopted a deeper meaning: it symbolised the power of the Good Shepherd who takes the lost lamb on his shoulders and guards it tightly around his neck. Additionally, in order to communicate to a prelate his participation in the power of the supreme pastor, what more natural than to *clothe* him with the *garment* which was symbolic of the successor of Peter, the pallium: that is, a pontifical *investiture*. Already of ancient usage during the time of St Gregory the Great (see the letter to St Augustine mentioned above: *ab antiquis temporibus*), this symbol attracted great veneration during the middle ages. Woven from the wool of a lamb which had been solemnly

presented before the altar, it was blessed by the Pope in the Vatican Basilica on the feast of St Peter. The garment was then deposed on the tomb of the Prince of Apostles until such times as it was used at an investiture. When required, it would be delivered and imposed during three successive ceremonies. It is the sign of a supra-episcopal power, which cannot have its orgins outwith the tomb of the successor of Peter: *'in quo est plenitudo pontificalis officii cum archiepiscopalis nominis appellatione'*. Moreover, in consigning the pallium to Augustine, St Gregory told him: *'Tua vero fraternitas non solum eos episcopus quos ordinaverit fuerunt ordinati, sed etian omnes Britanniae sacerdotes habeat de Domino Nostro Jesu-Christo auctore subjectos'*. (*Beda. Hist. Eccl.* Lib. I cap. 29, M.L., t. VC, col. 69.)

4. In the annals of the Archbishops of Canterbury one finds frequent reference to the roman origin of this patriarchal power of Canterbury. One reads among others: *Effimus Lippe (+959) successor Odoni...ille petenti pallii causa Romam tendens, ubi Alpes conscendit, nimio evectus frigore interiit* (Mabillon, *Annales lib.*, 46, luca (1739), t. III, p. 518). The account of the life of his successor Dunstan begins likewise: *Dumstanum pallii cause Roman proficiscentem* ... (ibidem, p. 518). From Augustine right up to Cranmer, all the Archbishops of Canterbury received the pallium from the Sovereign Pontiff; most of them, following the ancient custom, travelled to Rome to receive it from the hands of the Pope himself. Before the ceremony of investiture, the archbishop exercised no patriarchal rights: the pallium invested by the Pope was like a sacrament of his supra-episcopal jurisdiction. So it was that an archbishop who had received the pallium from an anti-pope was not accepted as patriarch in England (Edwin Burton, *The Catholic Encyclopedia*, Vol. III, p. 301).

5. This patriarchal power of Canterbury, conferred on St Augustine by St Gregory, became increasingly a unifying principle within the Anglican Church. In 668, Pope Vitalien named to this See an oriental monk called Theodore, from Tharsis in Cilicia. He had spent many years in Rome, and was a person distinguished by his learning in both the divine and human sciences. According to his illustrious contemporary, the Venerable Bede, (675-735) (cf. *Histoire Eccl. Anglorum lib.*, 4 M.L., t.95, col. 171), he was for almost a quarter of a century one of the greatest archbishops of Canterbury, establishing a strong patriarchal foundation. He created new dioceses, naming and dismissing bishops,

APPENDIX 4

visiting the dioceses, convoking a patriarchal council of all the different ecclesiastical provinces. In short, he organised the Churches on the model of the orient, with the constant support of Rome for his effective and extensive patriarchal jurisdiction.

6. Two centuries later, Pope Formosus III (+896), in a letter addressed to the bishops of England, solemnly confirmed the patriarchal powers and threatened sanctions against those bishops who tried to extract themselves from this legitimate and full jurisdiction (an allusion to the archbishop of York who wanted to withdraw his metropole from this jurisdiction). In view of the importance of this document, we quote here the principal passage: (*Bullarium. Editio Taurinensis* 1857, t. I, p. 369):
... *Quis autem inter vos principatum tenere debeat, quaene sedes episcopalis ceteris praepolleat, habeatque primatum, ab antiquis temporibus notissimum est. Nam ut ex scriptis Beati Gregorii ejusque successoribus tenemus, in Dorobernia civitate (Canterbury) metropolim, primamquem sedem episcopalem constat regni Anglorum, cui venerabilis Frater noster Pleigmundus (890-914) nunc praeesse dignoscitur; cujus honorem dignitatis nos ullo pacto imminui permittimus; sed ei vices apostolicas per omnia gerere mandamus, et sicut Beatus Papa Gregorius primo gentis vestrae Augustino omnes Anglorum episcopos esse subjectos constitutis: sic nos praenominato Fratri Doroberniae seu Canterberiae archiepiscopo, ejusque successoribus legitimis eamdem dignitatem confirmamus; mandantes et auctoritate Dei et beati Petri apostolorum principis praecipientes, ut ejus canonicis dispositionibus omnes obediant, et nullus eorum quae ei suisque successoribus apostolica auctoritate concessa sunt, violator existat ...*

7. The following century, at the Council of Brandenford, in 964... the whole episcopate approved the decree of King Edward which ended the laws of persecution of his predecessor, and recalled St Dunstan to the See of Canterbury: *ut Ecclesia Christi in Dorobernia, aliarum Ecclesiarum regni nostri mater sit et Domina et cum suis omnibus perpetualiter sit ubique libera* (Mansi, A.C.C., t. 18-A, col. 476).

8. The whole life of St Anselm (+1109) attests to this same truth. The whole English episcopate assisted at his consecration in 1093 and proclaimed him *totius Britanniae Primatem* (one can see here that this was not a purely honorific title)(cfr. Mansi A.C.C., t. 20, col. 792).

At the Council of Rockingham in March 1094 (ibidem, col. 791) in

APPENDIX 4

the speech where St Anselm disclosed to the whole of the gathered episcopate his conflict with the King, he said: ... *nam cum nuper licentiam adeundi Urbanum sedis Apostolicae praesulem, juxta morem antecessorum meorum pro palii mei adeptione ab ipso postulassem ...*

At the Council of Bari (1098), Urbain II made Anselm sit beside him and his arch-deacon, saying: 'That he be part of our circle, he being in a certain way a Pope of another part of the globe': *Includamus hunc in orbe nostro, quasi alterius orbis papam* (Mansi, A.C.C., t. 20, col. 948).

There is an even more significant fact, and one which shows how effective and extensive was this patriarachal jurisdiction. Gerard, bishop of Hereford, was elevated in 1107 to the Metropolitan See of York, the premier See in Britain after Canterbury, and he sought to detach it from its dependence. Anselm wanted to require of the newly elected an explicit profession of obedience and submission, and was not content with that which had been professed by Gerard when taking possession of the See of Hereford. From this arose a conflict to which the King, happily, was able to find a conciliatory solution. Without making a new profession, the newly elected was able to repeat explicitly that made for Hereford: *Annuit Anselmus; et Gerardus sua manu imposita manui Anselmi, interposita fide sua pollicitus est se eamdem subjectionem et obedientiam ipse et successoribus suis archiepiscopatu exhibiturum quam Herefordensis Ecclesiae ab eo sacrandus antistes promiserat* (cfr. Mansi A.C.C., t.20, col. 1229).

9. In reality, there was nothing missing from this patriarchal jurisdiction. Numerous ecclesiastical benefices were withdrawn from the dependence of the local bishops and applied directly to the See of Canterbury. These exemptions were to the profit of the patriarchate. During the time of St Anselm, there were about 80 exempt benefices in the sense of which we have spoken. Several monasteries followed the same regulations.

10. Under the pontificate of Alexander III (1159-1181), the patriarchal rights of the See of Canterbury were violently attacked by the archbishops of York and London; the King, anxious to reduce the patriarch in order to weaken the Church (as would happen later with Peter the Great in Russia in substituting a Holy Synod in place of the patriarch of Moscow), supported all these pretentions. Archbishop Thomas, who was soon to die because of his zeal, defended the rights of his Church and excommunicated the insubordinate bishops and even the King

himself. Alexander III, by means of several Papal Bulls, confirmed all the rights and privileges of the Church of Canterbury: '*sicut a temporibus beati Augustini praedecessores tuos habuisse Apostolicae Sedis auctoritate constat*' (cfr. Mansi A.C.C., t. XXI, col. 871-872 and 899).

11. Do not these few historical facts which we have recalled, and to which others can be added, provide evidence for the two rules which we noted at the beginning? A Church strongly unified and organised under the effective patriarchal authority of the archbishop of Canterbury: the Anglican Church forms an historical and catholic homogenous unity. It cannot be absorbed or fused without losing a characteristic proper to its whole history. Additionally, from the very beginning this See has been strongly attached to the See of Peter. Invested with the symbolic mantle of the prince of Apostles, the Archbishop of Canterbury participates in the apostolic jurisdiction not only over the faithful but also over the Shepherds. Just as in olden times Elisha put on the cloak of his Master and discovered the breath of his spirit, so also Augustine and all his successors without exception went seeking in Rome, with the imposition of the pallium, confirmation of their patriarchal jurisdiction. This historical fact is so evident that, in all truth, an Anglican Church separated from Rome is above all a heresy of history.

In Brief: *An Anglican Church **absorbed** by Rome and an Anglican Church **separated** from Rome are two conceptions which are both equally inadmissible. We must therefore search for a formula between these two extremes, a middle way, the only historic way: an Anglican Church **united** to Rome.*

§2. – *A possible catholic status according to the given facts.*

According to the current Canon Law of the West, the title of Patriarch or of Primate is purely honorific, and does not comprise of itself any special jurisdiction (Can. 271). It was not always so. Historically, until about the XII century (and even later in certain Sees), the function of patriarch or primate entailed an effective and widespread jurisdiction as much over ecclesiastical provinces as of dioceses. Did this jurisdiction, a participation in the power of the Primate of the whole Church of Christ, carry simply the same name and especially was it as extensive in the Latin Church as in that of Byzantium? The greater proximity of

APPENDIX 4

Rome and the title of Patriarch of the West which the Sovereign Pontiff still officially bears today, diminished the utility and importance of this hierarchical grade and led gradually to its becoming atrophied. However, it is incontestable that, under the different name of Primate, the office did exist in the West as in the East and in a particular way, as we have seen, in the Church of England.

Let us look firstly from the point of view of the actual statutes of the Eastern Churches in union with Rome.

We shall see then what application can be made to the Church of England.

I. THE INTERNAL ORGANISATION OF THE EASTERN UNIATE CHURCHES.

The Patriarchal organisation is still in force in the Eastern Churches, as is well known. One can say that it is more effective in the Churches in union with Rome than in the separated Churches, where the intrusion of civil power and the lay element often renders it illusory.

As a concrete example, let us look at the organisation of the Catholic Melkite Church. The jurisdiction of the Patriarch, Mgr. Cadi, extends to all the Melkite faithful who lived in the Ottoman Empire in 1894, date of the concession of Leo XIII.

The Melkite Patriarch of Antioch (who also administers the two patriarchates of Jerusalem and Alexandria) counts within his patriarchate five metropolitans and seven bishops, and about 170 thousand faithful.

1. From the moment that the synod of bishops elected a new Patriarch, the newly elected would write a detailed profession of faith and send it to the Sovereign Pontiff, requesting the *patriarchal pallium* as a sign of apostolic investiture. Before receiving this investiture, the neo-elect would exercise no patriarchal power.

2. The following method is adopted for choosing bishops: the Patriarch proposes three candidates, from among whom the secular priests must choose. The one elected is then confirmed and consecrated by the Patriarch, without any intervention from Rome, which is not even informed of the election or consecration. No oriental bishop is proclaimed to the Consistory.

Concerning titular bishops, the choice of these is completely dependent on the Patriarch, with no intervention from or information to Rome.

3. At determined periods, the Patriarch convokes the archbishops and bishops for a patriarchal synod, which he directs and at which he presides. The decrees and decisions are subsequently submitted for approbation by the Holy See.

4. The Patriarch has the right of inspection and visitation in all the different dioceses. When serious measures are required, like the resignation of a bishop, the approval of the Synod is required.

5. The exemption of some important monasteries from episcopal jurisdiction is to the advantage of the Patriarch. These are called Stavropegic, that is to say, directly dependent on the Patriarch. Among the Melkites, five monasteries out of seventeen are stavropegic.

6. The patriarchal Churches have their own proper laws and customs, regulated by the Synods, including their liturgy and their works. In brief, they constitute, under the patriarchal authority, autonomous institutions with their own distinct organisation, but in communion and dependence on the Church of Rome.

7. Far from carrying any prejudice against this internal autonomy, Rome has assured the Eastern Churches of the conservation of their wide autonomy. The first article of the Code of Canon Law declares that the western legislation does not affect them and that the Catholic East conserves its own proper Laws and Institutions. The situation is similar for the liturgy and for all ecclesiastical organisations. Leo XIII expressed this in a marvellous way in his encyclical *Praeclara* of the 20 June 1894, and in the Constitution *Orientalium Dignitas* of the 30 November 1894. The basic line of the Roman Church is expressed as follows: 'The true union among Christians is that which the author of the Church, Jesus Christ, has instituted and which He desires: it consists in unity of faith and government. Neither We nor Our successors will ever suppress anything of your Law, the *privileges of your Patriarchs*, nor of the ritual customs of each Church. It has been and always will be in the thought and conduct of the Holy See to show itself *generous in concessions with regard to the origins and traditions proper to each Church*.

APPENDIX 4

II. APPLICATION TO ENGLAND.

1. There does exist, therefore, a Catholic formula for the union of the Churches which is not an absorption, but which safeguards and respects the autonomous and interior organisation of the great historic Churches, whilst at the same time maintaining their perfect dependence vis-à-vis the Roman Church, principle of unity for the universal Church.

2. Now, if there has ever been a Church which by its origins, its history, its national traditions, has the right to concessions of autonomy, it is the Church of England. We have demonstrated this sufficiently in our historical enquiry. The principle affirmed by Leo XIII and which applies to the Eastern Churches: 'There is and always will be in the thought and conduct of the Holy See to show itself generous in concessions with regard to the origins and proper traditions of each Church' can equally find its application to the Church of England.

3. In practical terms, the archbishop of Canterbury would be re-established in his traditional and effective rights as Patriarch of the Anglican Church. After having received his investiture from the successor of Peter, by means of the historic imposition of the pallium, he would exercise his patriarchal rights over the whole of the Church of England: the nomination and consecration of bishops; the convocation and presidence of inter-provincial councils; the inspection of dioceses; jurisdiction over the great religious institutions exempt of episcopal jurisdiction; in short, the internal organisation of a united Anglican Church, following the outline of organisation sanctioned and supported by Rome for the Eastern Uniate Churches.

4. The Code of Canon Law of the Latin Church would not be imposed on the Anglican Church. An inter-provincial Synod would establish its ecclesiastical law, which would subsequently be submitted for the approval of the Holy See and sanctioned for use in the Anglican Church. One knows quite well that the Eastern law is totally different from that of the Latin Church, except, as is obvious, in those points which pertain to natural or divine law. For example, if it were judged opportune by the Anglican Church, I would not hesitate in not imposing ecclesiastical celibacy in England no more than in the East.

5. The Anglican Church would also have its own proper liturgy, the Roman Liturgy of the VII et VIII centuries, such as was celebrated at

APPENDIX 4

that epoch, and which we can find in the Gelasian sacramentaries. Even today, there is a great movement in the Anglican Church to revive the beautiful classical Roman Liturgy which Rome, alas, has not conserved, but which the Anglican Church can restore with honour. As the cult towards Our Lady and the Saints is less exhuberant in the classical liturgy than in the present roman liturgy, there could be a happy balance there which would particularly assist the period of transition.

6. It is clear that the ancient historic Sees of the Anglican Church would be maintained, and the new roman Sees, created since 1851, would be suppressed, that is, Westminster, Southwark, Portsmouth, etc.

It is clear also that this is a severe measure; but we recall how Pius VII, at the time of the Concordat with France, suppressed all the existing dioceses in France and requested the resignation of all the bishops (more than 100).

7. One particular problem will arise, that of precedence: do the patriarchs have precedence over the cardinals? This is a serious question which could poison and compromise the negotiations, unless one decides to resolve it according to historic usage, of which we now propose some pointers.

a) It was solemnly decreed by several oecumenical councils (4th of Constantinople (869) in can. 21e (Denziger 341) and 4th council of the Lateran (1215) can. 5 (Denziger 436), that the four *effective* Patriarchs, that is, Constantinople, Alexandria, Antioch and Jerusalem, have the right to the first four places, in the order as indicated above, immediately after the Sovereign Pontiff of Rome. If, therefore, the full, effective patriarchal function is granted to Canterbury, then he should take his place among this category and occupy the fifth place among the Patriarchs, immediately after the Pope, and before the Cardinals. It is understood, of course, that these are only the grand Patriarchs, those who in former times had a patriarchal residence in Rome, for when they visited. From this arises the custom of the name of the patriarchal Basilicas: the Lateran was the residence of the oecumenical Patriarch, the supreme and universal Pontiff; at St Peter's was to be found the residence of the patriarch of Constantinople; at St Paul's, that of the Patriarch of Alexandria; at St Mary Major's, that of the Patriarch of Antioch; at St. Lawrence outside the walls, that of the Patriarch of Jerusalem. All these usages prior to the schism should be revived: and the archbishop of Canterbury must be assimilated among these four Patriarchs. However, it is clear that before the schism, the grand Patriarchs had precedence before the Cardinals.

b) But, having regard to the the views which have predominated since the XI century, it will be difficult to re-apply some of these ancient practices. One could perhaps draw inspiration from a practice which was applied at certain times where the high noble princes took their place immediately after the Dean of the Sacred College. The precedence was given to the Sacred College in the person of its Dean.

c) Finally, another system which had value at certain times: the grand Patriarchs took their position after the cardinal bishops, but before the cardinal priests and deacons.

d) An elegant solution would be to create an order of cardinal patriarchs, similar to the creation of cardinal priests and deacons in the VIII century. The fault of this solution would be that it is new, in an area where the Church is rightly traditional. Except for its novelty, the solution respects the lines of tradition.

Whatever might happen, let us not forget that these questions of precedence, because of what they symbolise, have a great importance and should be treated according to traditional principles.

PRACTICAL CONCLUSIONS

1. Union without absorption - this seems to us the formula for reconciliation. On the one hand, we have a religious society, the Anglican Church, exercising its own proper internal organisation, a moral body exercising its autonomy, its institutions, its laws, its proper liturgy, under the authority of its leader, the Patriarch of Canterbury. It lacks, however, the principle of unity and the foundation of infallible truth, that which Christ wished of the Church he had founded, that is, *unum ovile et unus Pastor*. On the other hand, we have the Roman Church, which also has its institutions, its law, its liturgy, in a word, its internal latin organisation; but what it possesses more than anything else in its leader is that principle of unity, the foundation of truth and apostolicity, the solid Stone (Peter) on which the whole Church of Christ is built. It is necessary, consequently, if the Anglican Church wishes to belong to this

APPENDIX 4

unique and visible society of Christ, that it establish between itself and the Roman Church this link of dependence and submission to the successor of Peter. In other words, it is necessary to become not *latin* but *roman*. In doing so, it may conserve all its internal organisation, all its historic traditions and its legitimate autonomy, after the example of the Eastern Churches, by establishing a strong and indispensible link of subordination to the universal Church, whose principle of unity is at Rome.

2. If the general principles indicated in this report can serve as a basis of a movement towards the union of the Churches, it will obviously be necessary to develop this work and to establish scientifically the various historical and canonical arguments. In view of the inevitable and probably very lively opposition which these new ideas can arouse, it is necessary, before making them public, to support and reinforce them with other considerations and developments which, from a theological and historical standpoint, are unassailable and to give them a precise and detailed form so that they be unequivocal. Such a work cannot be undertaken except by a group who can elaborate together a complete programme.

3. What will Rome think of this project? Obviously, it proposes a principle of decentralisation, which does not exactly conform to the actual tendancies of the Roman curia, a principle which will doubtlessly afterwards find other applications. But will this not be a good thing? Will Rome be of this opinion? No one can foresee the response to this question. Even if small things can sometime betray a grand design, two things should be noted:

a) In his apostolic letter addressed to Cardinal Pompili on the 5th May 1924 (A.A.S. 1924, p. 233), Pius XI, in recalling the glories of the Basilica of the Lateran, explicitly evoked the memory of the consecration of the monk Augustine by Gregory the Great. He added: 'This illustrious Pontiff then imposed the pallium on Augustine, and decreed that all the Churches of England already founded up till then and to be founded in future would be under the jurisdiction of the primatial Church of Canterbury.

b) Another significant fact is that, among *all* the Primates of the Catholic Churches, the Catholic Primate of Westminster, Cardinal

APPENDIX 4

Bourne, even if this title is of recent institution, is the *only* one who exercises truly patriarchal privileges in all the different ecclesiastical provinces within the kingdom of England, and this in virtue of the Apostolic Constitution *Si qua est* of 26th November 1911 (A.A.S. 1911, p. 554). He presides as of right at all the interprovincial synods of England; he has precedence over all the other metropolitans of the country, even within their own province; he wears the pallium, can erect his throne and have the cross carried before him in all the churches of England; he is the official representative of the whole Church in England before the Royal Court. 'Such a privilege, says one author, by its singularity, abnormality, amplitude, stands out clearly as an exception' (cfr. Gromier, *Prérogatives archiépiscopales*, Bruxelles (1924) p. 16).

These facts, though they be of little importance in themselves, can they be interpreted as a suggestion, an advance, a welcoming disposition? I do not know. In any case, they can serve, if not as a basis, at least as an excuse for the exposé which has been done along these lines.

Bibliography

Primary Sources:

UNPUBLISHED SOURCES

1. *Lambeth Palace Archives, London.*
The correspondence of Archbishop Randall Davidson. This correspondence was originally retained in five file boxes, but has been in process of re-classification.

Papers of J.A. Robinson: Mss. 2222, 2223, and 2224.

Bell Papers – on Church unity. Vol. 170. Bell Diaries 1921-23 No. 256, and 1923-25 No. 257.
My thanks to the archivist, Miss Melanie Barber.

2. *Westminster Abbey Archives, London.*
Some correspondence of J.A. Robinson, including a 21 page typescript/diary of Robinson's reflections on the Malines Conversations.
My thanks to Dr Richard Mortimer, Keeper of the Muniments.

3. *Archives of the Archdiocese of Malines, Belgium.*
Among the vast collection of correspondence and official papers of Cardinal Mercier, there are 12 Boxes of documentation referring specifically to the Conversations at Malines. This correspondence is roughly classified in a chronological order.
My thanks to the archivist, Prof. C. Van de Wiel.

4. *Archives of the Archdiocese of Westminster, London.*
The papers of Cardinal Bourne for the period of the Conversations at Malines are surprisingly few. There are included a good number of newspaper cuttings and articles from publications at the time.
My thanks to the archivist, Miss Elizabeth Poyser.

5. *Malines Papers of Lord Halifax, York.*
The whole correspondence of Lord Halifax on the Conversations is presently safeguarded in the Borthwick Institute of Historical Research, University of York. The files are classified chronologically in ten File Boxes.

6. *Mirfield Deposit, York.*
Among the documentation of the Mirfield Community, also retained at the Borthwick Institute in York, are about 300 letters of Walter Frere pertaining to his involvement in the Malines Conversations.

7. *Portal Papers, Paris.*
The personal papers of Abbé Fernand Portal are deposited with the Sisters of the

BIBLIOGRAPHY

Assumption (*Congrégation des Oblates de l'Assomption*), 203 rue Lecourbe, 75015 Paris. For many years these papers had been in the care of the religious group of women founded by Portal to work for reunion, *Dames de l'Union*, and kept in Aix-les-Bains. With the demise of this group, the Sisters of the Assumption in Paris have assumed the care of them.
The Portal Papers are unclassified, and contained in six large File Boxes.
Many of the letters refer to Portal's work with the Eastern Orthodox Churches, particularly the Russian Orthodox.
My thanks to the archivist, Sr Marie Clotide O.A.

8. *Jesuit Provincial Archives, Farm Street, London.*
A small but important number of letters from Cardinal Merry del Val to Fr Francis Woodlock SJ are contained in this archive.
My thanks to the archivist, Fr Geoffrey Holt SJ.

9. *Archives of the Congregation of the Mission, Paris.*
This archive is that of the mother-house of Abbé Portal's religious Congregation, at 95 rue de Sèvres, Paris. The bibliotheque contains all the published works of Portal, including those published under the pseudonym 'Fernand Dalbus'. There is no original correspondence of Portal kept here. Although remaining a member of the Congregation of the Mission, Portal had lived outside the community because of the nature of his apostolic work.
My thanks to the archivist Père Raymond Chalumeau.

Other archives consulted, such as that at the Abbey of Chevetogne, Belgium, did not have material pertinent to this thesis.

My thanks also to individuals consulted: M. Jean Guitton, 1 rue de Fleurus, Paris VIe.; Mgr Dumont, Centre Istina, 45 rue de la Glacière, Paris XIIIe

NOTE ON THE VATICAN ARCHIVES:

The one important archive pertinent to the Malines Conversations which remains unavailable is that of the Vatican. The *Archivio Segreto Vaticano* makes available documentation according to pontificates rather than the normal convention of a determined number of years. Presently, records are available up to the death of Pope Benedict XV, that is, 22nd January 1922.

The Protocol Registers of the Vatican Archives, however, include those for the whole of 1922, and for that year is noted three letters relevant to the Conversations;

(1) No. 2182; *'Malines' – 3rd April: Mercier to Holy See*
His discussions with Anglicans in trying to convert them. Includes comment 'dubbi'.

BIBLIOGRAPHY

(2) No. 3856; *'Malines' – 31st May: Mercier to the Holy See*
Documents and instructions about eventual attempts for union of Anglican Church and Catholic Church.
(3) No. 4994; *'D'Herbingy' – 20th June: D'Herbigny to the Holy See*
Results of the Conference for union of the Anglican Church.

All these Protocols are marked 'A/E', that is, *'Affari Ecclesiastici Straordinari'*, and are not deposited in the Vatican Archives but in the Second Section of the Secretariate of State for General Affairs.

With letters of recommendation from Bishop Cormac Murphy-O'Connor (Co-Chairman of ARCIC) and from Cardinal Edward Cassidy (President of the Pontifical Commission for the Promotion of Christian Unity), I requested permission to consult the Malines Conversations papers held by the Secreteriate of State, but permission was not granted.

My thanks, however, to Mgr Charles Burns of the Vatican Archives for his assistance in introducing me to the intricate protocol system.

I acknowledge also the helpful assistance of the following:
Sr Mary Peter of the *Centro Pro Unione*, Via S. Maria dell'Anima 30, 00186 Roma;

Revd Douglas Brown of *The Anglican Centre*, Palazzo Doria Pamphili, Via del Corso 303, 00186 Roma.

Mr Michael Wheaton of the *Venerabile Collegio Inglese*, Via di Monserrato 45, 00186, Roma.

PUBLISHED SOURCES

ABBOTT, Walter (Ed.), *The Documents of Vatican II*, (New York, Herder & Herder, 1966).

ARCIC, *The Final Report*, (London: CTS/SPCK, 1982).

AUBERT, Roger, *Le Saint-Siège et l'union des Églises, textes choisis et introduits*, Bruxelles, 1947.

AUBERT, Roger, *Problèmes de l'unité chrétienne*, (Éditions de Chevetogne, 1952).

AUBERT, Roger, *Bulletins de l'Académie Royale de Belgique*, (Bruxelles: Classe de Lettres, 1967).

AUBERT, et alii, *Commemorating Malines*, in *One in Christ*, Vol. III, 1967, No. 1.

BIBLIOGRAPHY

AUBERT, Roger, *A propos de la chaire dom Lambert Beauduin*, Revue Théologique de Louvain, 1970, I, pp. 76-88.

AUBERT, Roger, *Cardinal Mercier: A Churchman ahead of his Time*, (Antwerp, undated).

AUBERT, Roger, *Aux origines de la réaction antimoderniste. Deux documents inédits*, in *Ephemerides Theologicae Lovanienses*, No. 37, 1961, pp. 557-578.

AUBERT, Roger, *Le Cardinal Mercier dans le monde et l'Église de son temps*, in *Unité des Chrétiens*, No. 23, 1976.

AUBERT, Roger, *Un homme d'Église: Dom Lambert Beauduin*, in *La Revue Nouvelle*, 31 (1960), 241, t. XXXI, No.3

AUBERT et alii, *Dossier: Dom Lambert Beauduin (1873-1960)*, in *Unité des Chrétiens*, Paris, No. 29, January 1978.

AUBERT, Roger, *Cardinal Mercier, Cardinal Bourne, and the Malines Conversations*, in *One in Christ*, No. 4, 1968, pp. 372-379.

AUBERT, Roger, *Le Cardinal Mercier*, (Louvain-le-Neuve: Éditions Academia, 1994).

AUBERT, Roger, *L'Histoire des Conversations de Malines*, in *Collectanea Mechliniensia*, t. 52, No.1, 1967, pp. 43-54.

AVELING J.C.H./LOADES D.M./McADOO H.R., *Rome and the Anglicans*, (Berlin & New York: Walter de Gruyter, 1982).

BARLOW, Bernard, *The Conversations at Malines*, in *Louvain Studies*, Vol. IV, No. 1, (Leuven: 1972), pp. 51-72.

BEAUDUIN, Mgr. Édouard, *Le Cardinal Mercier*, (Tournai: Casterman, 1966).

BECK, G.A. (Ed.), *The English Catholics 1850-1950*, (London: Burns & Oates,1950).

BELL, G.K.A, *Christian Unity: The Anglican Position*, (London: Hodder & Stoughton, 1948).

BELL, G.K.A., *Documents on Christian Unity: The Anglican Position*, 3 vols. (London: Oxford University Press, 1924-1948).

BELL, G.K.A., *Randall Davidson, Archbishop of Canterbury*, 2 vols., (London: Oxford University Press, 1935).

BELLENGER, Dominic, *The French exiled clergy in the British Isles after 1789*, (Bath: Downside Abbey, 1986).

BIBLIOGRAPHY

BILL, E.G.E. (Ed.), *Anglican Initiatives in Christian Unity*, (London: S.P.C.K., 1967).

BISHOPS CONFERENCE OF ENGLAND AND WALES, *Response of the Holy See to the Final Report*, (London: C.T.S., 1991).

BOLTON, Anselm, *A Catholic memorial of Lord Halifax and Cardinal Mercier*, (London: Williams & Norgate, 1935).

BOSSY, John, *The English Catholic Community 1570-1850*, (London: Darton, Longman & Todd, 1975).

BOUDENS, Robrecht, *George Tyrrell and Cardinal Mercier. A Contribution to the History of Modernism*, in *Église et Théologie*, No.1, 1970, pp. 313-351.

BOUDENS, Robrecht, *Lord Halifax: An Impression*, in *Ephemerides Theologicae Lovanienses* No.60, 1984, pp. 449-453.

BOUDENS, Robrecht, *Kardinaal Mercier en de Vlaamse Beweging*, (Leuven: Davidsfonds, 1975).

BOWEN, Desmond, *The Idea of the Victorian Church*, (Montreal: McGill Press, 1968).

BRANDRETH, Henry R.T., *The Ecumenical Ideals of the Oxford Movement*, (London: S.P.C.K., 1947).

BRENDON, Piers, *Hurrell Froude and the Oxford Movement*, (London: Paul Elek, 1974).

BUTLER, B.C., *United not Absorbed*, in *The Tablet*, 7th March 1970, pp. 220-221.

CENCI, Pio, *Il Cardinale Raffaele Merry del Val*, (Roma and Torino, 1933).

CHADWICK, Owen, *The Victorian Church*, 2 Vols., (London: Adam & Charles Black, 1966).

CHADWICK, Owen, *The Church of England and the Church of Rome*, in *Anglican Initiatives in Christian Unity*, Ed. E.G.W. Bill (London: S.P.C.K., 1967)

CHADWICK, Owen, *The Secularization of the European Mind in the Nineteenth Century*, (Cambridge: Cambridge University Press, 1977).

CHADWICK, Owen, *The Mind of the Oxford Movement*, (London: Adam & Charles Black, 1960).

BIBLIOGRAPHY

CHURCH HISTORICAL SOCIETY, *Anglican Orders (English)*, (London: S.P.C.K., 1932).

CHURCH, R.W., *The Oxford Movement 1833-1845*, (London: Macmillan & Co., 1897).

CLARK, Francis, *The Catholic Church and Anglican Orders*, (London: C.T.S., 1962).

CLARK, A.C. & DAVEY C. (Eds.), *Anglican/Roman Catholic Dialogue*, (London: Oxford University Press, 1974).

COLLECTANEA MECHLINIENSIA, *The Commemoration of the Malines Conversations*, Mechelin, No. 52, 1967, No.1.

CONGAR, Yves, et alii, *Dossier: Fernard Portal, Lazariste (1855-1926): Une vie sur la route de l'unité,* in *Unité des Chrétiens,* No. 22, 1976.

CONGAR, Yves, *Chrétiens Désunis*, Paris, 1937. English Translation: *Divided Christendom: A Catholic Study of the Problem of Reunion*, (London: Geoffrey Bles, 1939).

CONGAR, Y., *Chrétiens en dialogue*, (Paris: Éditions du Cerf, 1964).

CONGREGATION FOR THE DOCTRINE OF THE FAITH, *Observations on the Final Report of the Anglican-Roman Catholic International Commission (ARCIC)*, (London: C.T.S./C.I.S., 1982).

COPPINS, Joseph, *Une lettre inédite de Lord Halifax*, in *Union et désunion des chrétiens*, Bruges-Paris, 1963, pp. 139-143.

CROSS, F.L., *The Tractarians and Roman Catholicism*, (London: S.P.C.K., 1933).

CWIEKOWSKI, Frederick J., *The English Bishops and the First Vatican Council*, (Louvain: Biblioteque de la Revue d'Histoire Ecclésiastique, 1971).

DALPIAZ, Viglio, *Cardinal Merry del Val,* (London: Burns, Oates & Washbourne, 1937).

DAUDUIN, E., *Le Cardinal Mercier et le Père Portal*, in *Unité des Chrétiens*, No. 23, 1976, pp. 12-14.

DAWSON, Christopher, *The Spirit of the Oxford Movement*, (London: Sheed & Ward, 1933).

DESSAIN, J., *Les progrès de l'oecuménisme: l'incident Mercier 1919-1922*, in *Revue Théologique de Louvain*, 1974, t.V, pp. 469-476.

BIBLIOGRAPHY

DESSAIN, J., *Le cheminement des Églises catholique romaine et anglicane vers l'union*, in *Nouvelle Revue Théologique*, 1977, t. XCIX, pp. 481-506.

DICK, John A., *The Malines Conversations Revisited*, (Leuven: University Press, 1989).

DICK, John A., *The Start of an Ecumenical Revolution: England and the Road to Malines*, in *Louvain Studies*, No.II, (Leuven: 1986), pp. 151-169.

DICK, John A. *English Roman Catholic Reactions to the Malines Conversations*, Doctoral Dissertation, Katholieke Universiteit Leuven, 1986.

DICK, John A., *Cardinal Merry del Val and the Malines Conversations*, in *Ephemerides Theologicae Louvanienses*, (Louvain: 1986) LXII, pp. 333-355.

DUBLY, Henry L., *The Life of Cardinal Mercier*, translated from the French by Herbert Wilson, (Cork: Mercier Press, undated).

EDWARDS, David L., *Leaders of the Church of England 1928-1944*, (London: Oxford University Press, 1971).

EVANS G.R, and WRIGHT, J Robert (Ed.), *The Anglican Tradition*, (London, S.P.C.K., 1991).

EVENNETT, Outram, *A Historian looks at Malines*, in *The Dublin Review*, No. 186, 1930, pp.243-265.

FABER, Geoffrey, *Oxford Apostles*, (Middlesex: Pelican Books, 1954).

FITZPATRICK, W.J., *Times and Correspondence of the Rt Revd Dr Doyle, Bishop of Kildare and Leighlin*, 2 vols., (Dublin: James Duffy, 1861).

FITZSIMMONDS, John, *Henry Edward Cardinal Manning*, (London: Burns & Oates, 1951).

FORBES, A.P., Bishop of Brechin, *An Explanation of the 39 Articles*, (Oxford: Parker, 1867).

FOUILLOUX, F., *Les catholiques et l'unité chrétienne du XIXe au XXe siècle. Itinéraires européens d'expression française*, (Paris: Le Centurion, 1982).

FOUYAS, Methodios, *Orthodoxy, Roman Catholicism and Anglicanism*, (London: Oxford University Press, 1972).

FRERE, Walter CR., *Recollections of Malines*, (London: Centenary Press, 1935).

GADE, John A., *The Life of Cardinal Mercier*, (London: Scribners, 1934).

BIBLIOGRAPHY

GASQUET, Aidan, *Leaves from My Diary, 1894-96,* (London: Burns & Oates, 1911).

GENERAL SYNOD OF THE CHURCH OF ENGLAND, *Towards a Church of England Response to BEM and ARCIC,* (London: C.I.O., 1985).

GOOD, James, *The Church of England and the Ecumenical Movement,* (London: Burns & Oates, 1961).

GOODALL, Norman, *A Decade of Change in the Ecumenical Movement: 1961-1971,* (London: Oxford University Press, 1972).

GOODALL, Norman, *The Ecumenical Movement (what it is and what it does),* (London: Oxford University Press, 1961).

GRATIEUX, Albert, *Le Père Portal serviteur de l'unité chrétienne,* in *Mission et Charité,* Paris, No. 15, July 1964.

GRATIEUX, Albert, *L'Amitié au service de l'union,* (Paris: Bonne Press, 1950).

GREENACRE, Roger, *Lord Halifax,* (London: Church Literature Association, 1983).

GREENACRE, Roger, *Rome et Cantorbéry: Contradiction ou Complémentarité?,* in *La Foi et Le Temps,* No. 16, 1986, No. 2, pp. 140-155.

GUITTON, Jean, *Le Père Portal initiateur,* in *Mission et Charité,* Paris, No. 15, July 1964.

GUITTON, Jean, *Dialogue avec les précurseurs,* (Paris: Éditions Montaigne, 1962).

HAAG, H., *Le Cardinal Mercier devant la guerre et la paix,* in *Revue d'Histoire Ecclésiastique,* 1984, LXXIX, pp. 709-783.

HALIFAX, Lord, *A Call to Reunion,* (London: Mowbrays, 1922).

HALIFAX, Lord, *Leo XIII and Anglican Orders,* (London, Longmans/Green, 1912).

HALIFAX, Lord (Ed.), *The Conversations at Malines 1921-1925, Original Documents,* (London: Philip Allan & Co., 1930)

HALIFAX, Lord, *The Conversations at Malines, 1921-1925,* (Oxford: Oxford University Press, 1927).

HEBBLETHWAITE, Peter, *John XXIII, Pope of the Council,* (London: Geoffrey Chapman, 1985)

BIBLIOGRAPHY

HEMMER, H., *Fernand Portal, 1855-1926: Apostle of Unity,* (London: Macmillan, 1961).

HENRIQUES, Ursula, *Religious Toleration in England 1787-1833,* (London: Routlege & Kegan Paul, 1961).

HENSON, H.H., *Retrospect of an Unimportant Life,* 3 vols., (London: Oxford Univ. Press, 1942-1950).

HILL C. & YARNOLD E. (ed), *Anglicans and Roman Catholics: The Search for Unity,* (London: SPCK/CTS, 1994).

HOLMES, J. Derek, *Cardinal Merry del Val – An Uncompromising Ultramontane: Gleanings from his Correspondence with England,* in *The Catholic Historical Review,* No. 60, 1974, pp. 55-64.

HOLMES, J. Derek, *Archbishops of Westminster and the Reunion Movement during the 19th Century,* in *One in Christ,* No. 8, 1972, pp. 55-68.

HOLMES, J. Derek, *More Roman than Rome: English Catholicism in the Nineteenth Century,* (London: Burns & Oates, 1978).

HOWARD, J.G.Morton, *Epistola ad Romanos,*(London: Council for Promoting Catholic Unity, Undated).

HUGHES, John J., *Absolutely Null and Utterly Void,* (Washington-Cleaveland: Corpus Books, 1968).

HUGHES, John J., *The Papal Condemnation of Anglican Orders: 1896,* in *Journal of Ecumenical Studies,* Philadelphia, Vo. 4, Spring 1967, No. 2.

HYLSON-SMITH, Kenneth, *Evangelicals in the Church of England 1734– 1984,* (Edinburgh: T. & T. Clark, 1988).

IUNG, N., *Bilan de l'oecuménisme contemporaine. Les Églises chrétiennes non romaines: la recherche de l'unité. L'action oecuménique de l'Église catholique. Points de divergence et d'accord,* (Paris: Mame, 1971).

JANSSENS, A., *Anglo-Catholicism and Catholic Unity,* in *Ephemerides Theologicae Lovanienses,* 1924, pp. 66-70.

JEDIN, Hubert (Ed.), *History of the Church,* Vol. VIII, *The Church in the Age of Liberalism,* (London: Burns & Oates, 1981).

KEATING, J., *Clearing the Air,* in *The Month,* No.143, 1924, pp. 97-105.

KEATING, J., *Malines and Corporate Reunion,* in *The Month,* No.144, 1924, pp.260-262.

KEATING, J., *Once more Malines*, in *The Month*, No.155, 1925, pp. 158-161.

KEATING, J., *A Last Word on Malines*, in *The Month*, No.149, 1925, p. 163.

KEMPENEERS, J., *Le Cardinal Van Roey en son Temps*, (Bruxelles: E.P.M., 1971).

KER, Ian, *John Henry Newman, A Biography*, (Oxford: Oxford University Press, 1990).

KLAUS, Robert J., *The Pope, the Protestants, and the Irish: papal aggression and anti-catholicism in mid-nineteenth century England*, (New York & London: Garland Publishing, 1987).

KNOX, Wilfred L., *The Catholic Movement in the Church of England*, (London: Philip Allan & Co., 1923).

KNOX, Wilfred L. and VIDLER, Alec R., *The Development of Modern Catholicism*, (London: Philip Allan & Co., 1933).

KOTHEN, Robert, *Catholiques et Anglicans – vingt ans après les Conversations de Malines,* (Lille: Editions Catholicité, 1947).

LACEY, T.A., *A Roman Diary and other Documents relating to the Papal Enquiry into English Ordinations*, (London: Longmans Green, 1910).

LADOUS, Régis, *Dom Lambert Beauduin et Monsieur Portal – veilleur avant l'aurore*, in *Colloque Lambert Beauduin*, Chevetogne 1978, pp. 97-133.

LADOUS, Régis, *Monsieur Portal et les siens (1855-1926)*, (Paris: Éditions du Cerf, 1985).

LADOUS, Régis, *Catholiques libéraux et union des Églises jusqu'en 1878*, in *Les Catholiques libéraux au XIXe siècle*, Grenoble, 1974, pp. 489-525.

LADOUS, Régis, *L'Abbé Portal et a Campagne Anglo-Romaine 1890-1912*, (Lyon: Université de Lyon, 1973).

LAHEY, R.J., *The Origins and Approval of the Malines Conversations*, in *Church History*, Chicago, XLIII, 1974, p. 366-384.

LAHEY, R.J., *Cardinal Bourne and the Malines Conversations*, in *Bishops and Writers*, by A. Hastings (ed.), (London: 1976).

LAVEILLE, A., *Le Cardinal Mercier*, (Paris: Editions Spes, 1927).

LEASE, G. *Merry del Val and Tyrrell: A Modernist Struggle*, in *Downside Review*, No.347, 1984, pp. 133-156.

BIBLIOGRAPHY

LEEMING, Bernard, *The Vatican Council and Christian Unity: A Commentary on the Decree on Ecumenism of the Second Vatican Council Together with a Translation of the Text*, (London: Darton, Longman & Todd, 1966).

LESLIE, Shane, *Cardinal Gasquet*, (London: Burns & Oates, 1953).

LOCKHART, J.G., *Cosmo Gordon Lang*, (London: Hodder & Stoughton, 1949).

LOCKHART, J.G., *Charles Lindley Viscount Halifax*, 2 vols., (London: Centenary Press, 1935).

MACQUARRIE, John, *What Still Separates Us From the Catholic Church? An Anglican Reply*, in *Concilium*, No.4, No.6, 1970,, pp. 45-53.

MASON, A.J., *The Church of England and Episcopacy*, (Cambridge: University Press, 1914).

McCORMACK, Arthur, *Cardinal Vaughan*, (London: Burns & Oates, 1966),

MERCIER, Cardinal D.J., *Les Conversations de Malines*, in *Oeuvres Pastorales*, No.7, 1924, pp. 288-305.

MESSENGER, E.C., *Epistle from the Romans*, (London: Burns Oates & Washbourne, 1933).

MESSENGER, E.C., *Rome and Reunion, A Collection of Papal Pronouncements*, (London: Burns Oates & Washbourne, 1934).

MIDDLETON, R.D., *Newman and Bloxam – An Oxford Friendship*, (Oxford: University Press, 1947).

MOELLER, C., *Dom Lambert Beauduin, un homme d'Église*, in *Unité des Chrétiens*, No. 23, 1976, pp. 22-23.

MOORMAN, John R.H., *A History of the Church in England*, (London: Black 1973).

MOYES, J., *What Does Lord Halifax Mean?*, in *The Tablet*, No. 146, 1925, pp. 74-75.

MOYES, J., *An Anglican 'Call to Action'*, in *The Tablet*, No. 145, 1925, pp. 617-619.

NICHOLS, Aidan O.P., *The Panther and the Hind*, (Edinburgh: T.& T. Clark, 1993).

NOCKLES, Peter B., *The Oxford Movement in context – Anglican High Churchmanship 1760-1857,* (Cambridge: Cambridge University Press, 1994)

BIBLIOGRAPHY

NORMAN, Edward, *The English Catholic Church in the XIXth Century*, (Oxford: Clarendon Press, 1984).

NORMAN, Edward, *Roman Catholicism in England from the Elizabethean settlement to the Second Vatican Council*, (Oxford: University Press, 1985).

OLDMEADOW, E., *A Layman on Malines*, in *The Tablet*, No. 144, 1924, p. 660.

OLDMEADOW, E., *Continuity Continued*, in *The Tablet*, No. 149, 1927, p. 573.

OLDMEADOW, E. *More About Malines*, in *The Tablet*, No. 143, 1924, pp. 168-169.

OLDMEADOW, Ernest, *Francis Cardinal Bourne*, 2 vols. (London: Burns Oates & Washbourne, 1940).

OLLARD, S.L., *A Short History of the Oxford Movement*, (London: Faith Press, 1963).

PARSONS, Wilfred SJ, *Canterbury and Malines*, in *America*, 5th April 1924.

PAWLEY, Margaret, *Faith and Family: the life and circle of Ambrose Phillipps de Lisle*, (Norwich: Canterbury Press: 1993).

PAWLEY, Bernard and Margaret, *Rome and Canterbury through Four Centuries: A Study of the Relations between the Church of Rome and the Anglican Churches, 1530-1973*, (London: Mowbray, 1974).

PHILLIPS, C.S., *Walter Howard Frere, Bishop of Truro: A Memoire*, (London: Faber & Faber, 1947).

PHILLIPS, C.S., *The Church in France 1848-1907*, (London, S.P.C.K., 1936).

PICKERING, William S.F., *Anglo-Catholicism – A Study in Religious Ambiguity*, (London: S.P.C.K., 1991).

PONTIFICAL BIBLICAL COMMISSION, *Unity and Diversity in the Church*, (Vatican: Liberia Editrice Vaticana, 1991).

POPE PIUS XI, *Consistory speech of 24th March 1924*, in *Acta Apostolica Sedis*, Rome 1924, t. XVI. pp. 121-132.

PORTAL, F., *Le rôle de l'amitié dans l'union des Églises*, in *La revue catholiques des idées et des faits*, December 1925, pp. 5-8.

PRESTIGE, G.L., *The Life of Charles Gore, A great Englishman*, (London: Heinemann, 1935).

BIBLIOGRAPHY

PRESTWICH, Menna (Ed.) *International Calvinism 1541-1715*, (Oxford: Clarendon Press, 1985)

PURCELL, E.S., *Life of Cardinal Manning*, 2 Vols., (London: Macmillan & Co., 1895).

PURDY, W., *The Search for Unity*, (London: Geoffrey Chapman, 1996)

PÜTZ, A. *Interkommunion und Einheit. Dokumente aus England*, Studia Anglicana, Vol. 3, (Trèves: Paulinus-Verlag, 1971).

QUITSLUND, S.A., *'United Not Absorbed' Does It Still Make Sense*, in *Journal of Ecumenical Studies*, No. 8, 1971, pp. 255-285.

QUITSLUND, S.A., *Beauduin: A Prophet Vindicated*, (New York: Paramus, 1973).

ROUSE, Ruth and Stephen C. Neill (Eds.), *A History of the Ecumenical Movement, 1517-1948*, (London: SPCK, 1967).

ROUSSEAU, O., *Le sens oecuménique des Conversations de Malines. Vue retrospective après cinquante ans*, in *Irénikon*, 1971, t. XLIV, pp. 331-348.

ROUSSEAU, O., *Les Conversations de Malines*, in *Unité des Chrétiens*, No.23, 1976, pp. 7-14.

ROWELL, Geoffrey, *The Vision Glorious: Themes and Personalities of the Catholic Revival in Anglicanism*, (Oxford: Oxford University Press, 1983).

RUPP, Ernest Gordon, *Religion in England 1688-1791*, (Oxford, Clarendon Press, 1986).

RYAN, H.J. and WRIGHT, J.R., *Episcopalians and Roman Catholics. Can they ever get together?*, (Denville, New Jersey: Dimension Books, 1972).

SANTER, Mark (Ed.), *Their Lord and Ours*, (London: S.P.C.K., 1982).

SAUDEE, J. Bivort de la, *Documents sur le Problème de l'Union Anglo-Romaine (1921-1927)*, (Bruxelles: 1948).

SAUDEE, J. Bivort de la, *Anglicans et Catholiques: le Problème de l'Union Anglo-Romaine, 1833-1933*, 2 vols., (Paris: Librerie Plon, 1949).

SCHYRGENS, J., *La destinée de Lord Halifax*, in *Vingtième Siècle*, February 1934.

SIMON, A., *Le Cardinal Mercier*, (Brussels: 1960).

SMITH, H. Maynard, *Frank, Bishop of Zanzibar*, (London: S.P.C.K., 1926).

BIBLIOGRAPHY

SNEAD-COX, J.G., *Life of Cardinal Vaughan*, 2 Vols., (London: Burns & Oates, 1910).

ST. JOHN, O.P., Henry, *The Malines Conversations: A Pioneer effort in Ecumenism*, in *One in Christ*, t.2, 1966, No.4, pp. 377-384.

ST. JOHN O.P., Henry, *Essays in Christian Unity*, (London: Blackfriars, 1955).

STEVENSON, Alan M.G., *Anglicanism and the Lambeth Conferences*, (London: S.P.C.K., 1978).

STUART, Elizabeth B., *R.C. reactions to the Oxford movement and Anglican schemes for reunion, from 1833 to the condemnation of Anglican Orders in 1896*, Unpublished D.Phil thesis, Oxford 1987. Bodlian Library Oxford, Western MSS. C. 7098.

SUENENS, Cardinal Léon-Joseph, *Présence du Cardinal Mercier*, in *Unité des Chrétiens*, No. 23, 1976, p. 3.

SUENENS, Cardinal Léon-Joseph, *Co-responsibility in the Church*, (Bruges: De Brouwer, 1968).

SWINDLER, L.J., *The Ecumenical Vanguard*, (Pittsburg: Duquesne University Press, 1966).

SYKES, S. & BOOTY, J., *The Study of Anglicanism*, (London: S.P.C.K., 1988).

TAVARD, George H., *Two Centuries of Ecumenism*, (London: Burns & Oates, 1961).

TAVARD, George H., *The Quest for Catholicity: A Study in Anglicanism*, (London: Catholic Book Club, 1963).

TAYLOR, T.F., *J. Armitage Robinson: Eccentric, Scholar and Churchman*, (Cambridge, James Clark, 1991).

THILS, Gustave, *Histoire doctrinale du Movement Oecuménique*, (Louvain, 1963).

VAN DYKE, Maria J., *Growing Closer Together,* (Slough, England: St. Paul Publications, 1992)

VAN DE POL, William H., *Anglicanism in Ecumenical Perspective*, (Pittsburg: Duquesne University Press, 1965).

VERHELST, D., *Lord Halifax and the Scheut Father Aloïs Janssens*, (Bruges: Desclée de Brouwer, 1967).

BIBLIOGRAPHY

VIDLER, A.R., *A Century of Social Catholicism*, (London: S.P.C.K., 1964).

WALSH, Walter, *The Secret History of the Oxford Movement*, (London: Church Assoc., 1899).

WEINER, Margery, *The French Exiles 1789-1815*, (London: John Murray, 1960).

WILKINSON, Alan, *The Church of England and the First World War*, (London: S.P.C.K., 1978).

WILLIBRANDS, J., *Diversity without Separation*, in *The Tablet*, No. 224, 1970, p. 92.

WOODLOCK, F., *Modernism and a United Christendom*, in *The Tablet*, 24th January, 1925.

WOODLOCK, F., *A Speech by Lord Halifax with Comments by Father Woodlock*, in *The Month*, No. 146, 1925, pp. 157-167.

WOODLOCK, F., *The Malines Conversations Report*, in *The Month*, No. 155, 1930, pp. 238-246.

WOODLOCK, F., *The Upshot of Malines*, in *The Month*, No. 145, 1928, pp.158-163.

WOODLOCK, F., *Le discours de Lord Halifax au congrès des 'Anglo-Catholiques'*, in *Études*, t. CLXXXIV, 1925, pp. 304-310.

WOODLOCK, F., *The Malines Conversations*, in *The Tablet*, No. 146, 17th October 1925, pp. 484-485.

WRIGHT, J. Robert, *Anglicans and the Papacy*, in *Journal of Ecumenical Studies*, No.13, 1976, No. 3, pp. 379-401.

YARNOLD, Edward, *The Church and the Churches,* (London: C.T.S./ S.P.C.K.), 1984).

Index

A Call to Reunion 82
A.P.U.C. 14–17, 18, 19, 20
A.R.C.I.C. 1, 2, 3, 5, 178, 188, 191, 193, 195, 213
Accademia dei Nobili Ecclesiastici 16, 206
Ad Anglos 34, 35, 38
Amay 175, 177
America 133
American Episcopal Church 50, 51
Andrewes Bishop L. 5, 114
Anglican Orders 27, 28, 30, 32, 37–44, 48, 49, 60, 70, 92, 95, 98, 105, 113, 121, 124, 130, 163, 167, 181, 197–199, 207, 211, 215–218, 222, 224, 230
Anglo-Catholic Congress 47, 110, 161
Anglo-Saxon chronical 119, 193
Apostolicae Curae 38, 40, 41, 43, 47, 70, 197, 200, 215, 218
Aubert, R. 147, 184
Avis, P. 186

Barnabo, Cardinal A. 13, 17
Barrington, Bishop S. 7
Batiffol, P. 111, 114, 115, 117, 118, 141, 142, 144, 154, 155, 157, 172–175, 182, 196
Beauduin, L. OSB 102, 147–151, 164, 177, 189–191, 202
Beauduin, Ed. 121, 122
Bell, G.K.A. 62, 76–81, 87, 105, 190, 213
Benson, Archbishop E.W. 36, 37, 105, 199
Berdiaaev, N. 201
Bishop, E. 58, 130
Bivort de la Saudée, J. 121, 136
Blackfriars 137, 207
Bloxam, J.R. 10, 11, 190
Boegner 201
Bonaparte, N. 22, 150
Book of Common Prayer 15, 92, 140, 143, 169, 172, 205
Bourne, Cardinal F. 57, 59–61, 78, 81, 82, 89–91, 110, 122, 125–133, 165–167, 169, 170, 172–175, 184, 208, 209, 246
Brent, Bishop C.H. 4

Capovilla, L. 214
Caroline Divines 5, 6
Catholic Eastern Churches (Uniates) 100, 149, 190, 192, 240–242, 245
Catholic Emancipation Act 21, 22
Cecil, H.R.H.G. 139, 140, 172
Cerretti, Cardinal B. 52, 170, 175, 176
Chadwick, O. 180
Charles I. 5
Chollet, Archbishop J.A. 170
Church Association 132
Church House 110
Church Times 161, 162
Church Union 24, 39, 42, 47, 53, 80
Congregation for Church Affairs 52
Congregation for the Doctrine of the Faith 2
Connolly, H. OSB 58
Consistory 136, 240
Contra Julianum Pelagianum 118, 193
Convocations 92, 123, 124, 205, 227
corporate reunion 12, 15, 16, 20, 28, 37, 38, 43, 113, 124, 133, 140, 141, 162, 179, 187, 207
Cosin Bishop J. 114
Council of Bari 238
Council of Brandenford 237
Council of Carthage 151
Council of Clovesho 119, 193
Council of Ephesus 154
Council of Nicea 18, 154
Council of Rockingham 237
Council of Trent 61, 64–66, 146
Cowley Fathers 130
Cranmer, Archbishop T. 236
Creighton, Bishop M. 44
Crosbee, B.F. SJ 12

d'Herbigny, M. SJ 74–81, 91, 208
Dalbus, F. (alias Portal) 30–32, 39
Darwin, C. 180
Davidson, Archbishop R. 47, 54, 57, 71, 73, 81–84, 88, 91, 93, 96, 101–105, 107–111, 113, 114, 121–124, 126, 128, 129, 136, 140, 141, 143, 158–161, 165, 167, 169, 171–175, 181, 186, 187, 190, 193, 199, 204–206, 208, 227

263

INDEX

de Llevaneras, C. 39
De Fide 103, 152, 154, 195
De Augustinus, A.M. sj 39
De Maistre, J. 155
Decree on Ecumenism 3, 191, 196, 214
Decree of Infallibility 94
Dessain, Canon F. 62, 166
Dick, J. 209
Drury, Bishop T.E. 113
Duchesne, L. 32, 39, 42, 111, 181

Edwardian Ordinal (1552) 40, 215
episcopè 195
Errington, Bishop G. 22, 23
Erskine, Cardinal 22
Études 164, 207
Evangelical revival 46
Evannett, O. 190

Faith and Order Conference 4, 48, 51, 94, 176, 188, 204, 206, 213
Ffoulkes, E.S. 17
Final Report of ARCIC I 1, 2
Fleming, D.H. 39
Flemish question 164, 202–204
Forbes, Bishop A.P. 14, 15, 65
Freemasons 33
Frere, W.H. 47, 48, 53, 58, 59, 63, 65, 69, 70, 72, 93, 96, 102, 105, 117, 119, 123, 126, 135, 142, 146, 150, 157, 173, 191, 221, 224, 225
Froude, R.H. 7
Further Considerations on behalf of Reunion 110

Garibaldi G. 183
Gasparri, Cardinal P. 39, 74–76, 79, 82, 88, 89, 122, 127, 129, 135, 136, 148, 162, 164, 184
Gasquet, Cardinal F.A. 38–40, 61, 122, 125, 129, 130, 138, 162, 164, 174, 176, 182, 184, 198, 203, 207, 218
Gerard, Bishop of Hereford 238
Gordon, J.C. 39, 218
Gore, Bishop C. 46, 57, 59, 104, 105, 110, 111, 114, 116, 118–121, 140–142, 144, 150–155, 157–159, 172, 177, 180–183, 188, 190, 191, 229
Guitton, J. 213

Halifax, 2nd Viscount Lord 5, 8
   Anglican Orders 24–44

Lambeth Appeal consequences 45–56
   First Conversation 57–92
   Second & Third Conversations 93–120
   Fourth Conversation 121–138
   Fifth Conversation & publication difficulties 139–158
   personality and influence 178, 179, 183, 187, 188, 197–201, 205–207, 214, 216, 221, 222, 224, 225, 231
Hemmer, H. 113, 115, 117, 119, 141, 142, 144, 145, 169, 172–174, 177, 208, 211
Henry VIII 3
Hensen, H.H. 181
High Church group 5, 6, 8, 12, 24, 32, 34, 58, 72, 112, 129, 178, 186, 187, 198, 205
Hill, Bishop C. 2
Hooker, R. 114

Immaculate Conception 113, 153, 154, 194–196, 202
Infallibility 152, 153, 194, 195
Institut Catholique 32, 111, 113
Irenicon 175
Iswolski, P. 111, 112, 201

Janssens, A. 152
Jarret, B. op 112, 113
Jenkins, Dr 113
Joachim IV, Patriarch of Turkey 29
Jones, L. osb 5, 6
Jure divino 104, 106, 110, 168

Kartachev 201
Keating, J. sj 132
Keble, J. 7, 8, 15
Kempeneers, J. 150
Kidd, B.J. 111, 113, 115–119, 121, 142, 144, 146, 174, 229
koinônia 195

L'Église anglicane, unie non absorbée 11, 102, 146, 177, 189, 233–246
L'Osservatore Romano 2, 136, 177
L'Univers 31, 32
La Science catholique 31
La Vérité 31, 32
La Semaine Religieuse de Paris 131
Laberthonniere, L. 201

INDEX

Lacey, Canon T.A.   39, 48, 53, 200, 217, 218
Ladeuze, Mgr   170
Ladous, R.   201
Lambeth Quadrilateral   186
Lambeth Appeal (1920)   45–47, 48, 49, 52–54, 62, 63, 68–70, 72, 76, 77, 86, 122, 123, 141, 197, 202, 204, 224, 229
Lambeth Conference   1, 43, 45, 68, 77, 86, 96, 99, 185, 204, 221, 222, 229
Lamentabili sane exitu   182
Lang, Archbishop W.C.G.   55, 59, 81, 86, 93, 105, 106, 108, 187, 200, 209
Langton, S. OSB   138
Laud, Archbishop W.   6
Le Monde   31, 32
Le Moniteur de Rome   32
Lee, F.G.   12–19
Leslie, S.   198
Lidden, Canon H.P.   24, 26, 181
Life and Work   48, 184, 213
Lockhart, W.   13, 62, 69, 94, 115, 169, 199, 203
Loisy, A.   42, 181, 182
Longley, Archbishop C.T.   185
Lumen Gentium   197
Lux Mundi   59, 111, 180, 181

Malta Report   188, 193, 196, 213
Manning, Cardinal H.E.   15–20, 23, 28
Maritain, J.   201
Mazzella, Cardinal C.   39
McNabb, V. OP   112, 137, 138, 207
Mercier, Cardinal D.J.   5, 11, 48–57, 59–61, 65, 67, 69, 70, 72–76, 78, 81–96, 100–102, 104–109, 111, 112, 116, 120–122, 125–129, 131, 133–144, 146–149, 151, 156, 158–170, 172, 173, 175, 177–179, 182, 184, 187–189, 191, 193, 201–204, 208, 209, 211–214, 224, 225, 227–230, 233
Merry del Val, Cardinal R.   38–41, 44, 50, 61, 91, 122, 125, 129, 162, 176, 182, 184, 200, 206, 207, 215, 219
Modernism   44, 112, 180, 181, 182, 207, 212
Mont Cesar   147
Mortalium Animos   176, 177
Mount St Bernard   10
Moyes, Canon J.   39, 61, 163, 207

Neill, S.   213

Newman, J.H.   7–9, 11, 12, 21, 29, 153, 155
Nicene Creed   193
Nickerson, H.   163
Nugee, G.   15

Oakeley, F.   7, 9
O'Connell, Cardinal W.   50
Oldmeadow, E.   60, 61, 91, 126–130, 133, 165, 166, 200, 207, 208
Ordination *sub conditione*   70, 105, 216, 217
Orientalium Dignita   34, 241
Orthodox churches   13, 15, 29, 31, 51, 69, 92, 100, 112, 124, 145, 153–155, 184, 192, 194, 201, 202
Oxford Movement   5–11 13, 16, 22, 28, 199

pallium   95, 98, 100, 102, 103, 144, 147, 149, 150, 191, 202, 223, 224, 235, 236, 239, 240, 242, 245, 246
Palmer, W.   7, 9
Panzani, G.   5
papal infallibility   143, 153, 167, 183, 194, 217
Parsons, W. SJ   133
Pawley, M.   20
Pascendi   182
Peter the Great   238
Petre, M.   110
Philipps de Lisle, A.   10–14, 18–20, 190
Pickering, W.S.F.   180
Pole, Cardinal R.   40, 215
Pontifical Biblical Commission   182
Pontifical Council for Promoting Christian Unity   2
Pope Alexander III   238, 239
Pope Benedict XV   50, 51, 73, 74, 184, 202
Pope Clement XI   39
Pope Eugenius IV   30
Pope Formosus III   237
Pope Innocent I   118, 193
Pope John Paul II   3
Pope Leo XIII   29, 30, 32, 33, 35, 40, 44, 49, 53, 60, 68, 70, 121, 122, 181, 197, 206, 207, 215, 216, 240–242
Pope Paul IV   40
Pope Paul VI   3, 178, 214
Pope Pius VII   150
Pope Pius IX   15, 22, 30

265

INDEX

Pope Pius X   182, 207
Pope Pius XI   74, 83, 87, 121, 167, 175, 176, 184, 202, 222, 245
Pope Urban II   238
Pope Vitalien   236
porrection   99
Portal, F.   5
   Anglican Orders   24–44
   Lambeth Appeal consequences   45–56
   First Conversation   57–92
   Second & Third Conversations   93–120
   Fourth Conversation   121–138
   Personality and Influence   178, 179, 182, 187, 188, 198–201, 205, 207, 211, 214, 221, 224, 225
Praeclara Gratiulationis   32, 33, 241
Prayer Book revision   92, 109, 171, 172, 175, 176, 199, 204
primacy   95, 103, 106, 108, 110, 114, 118, 156, 161, 168, 193, 194
primus inter pares   186, 194
Propaganda Fide   13, 17
Providentissimus Deus   181
Puller, F.W.   31, 39, 64, 200, 217, 218
purgatory   153, 180
Pusey, E.B.   7, 8, 24, 61, 65

Quick, Canon O.C.   113

Rampolla del Tindaro, Cardinal M.   33, 34, 38, 40, 42, 44, 122
Ramsey, Archbishop A.M.   3, 178, 214
rectification   99
requiem mass   180
Rerum Novarum   29
Revue Anglo-Romaine   42–44, 200
Revue catholique des Églises   47
Revue des Jeunes   136
Richard Cardinal F.M.   43
Robinson, J.A.   58, 59, 62–66, 68–72, 83, 93, 96–105, 115–117, 119, 139, 142, 143, 155, 156, 175, 189, 221, 224, 225
Roman Question   183, 184
Roncalli, A. (later Pope John XXIII)   213, 214
Runcie, Archbishop R.   3
Russian Orthodox   87, 111

San Anselmo   147
Satis Cognitum   40

Scannell, T.B.   39
Scots College   35, 206
Society for the Propagation of the Gospel   47
St Anselm   237–239
St Athanasius   144
St Augustine   118, 149, 193, 234–236, 245
St Cyprian   118, 151
St Dunstan   236
St Epiphanius   144
St Gregory the Great   119, 193, 234–236, 245
St Irenaeus   118, 193
St Peter   83, 103, 108, 110, 115–119, 161, 193, 219, 221, 234–236, 239, 245
St Stephen I   151
St Thomas à Becket   238
St Vincent of Lerins   153
Storr, Canon V.F.   113
Stuart, E.   10
Student Christian Movement   46
syllabus of errors   30

Talbot, Bishop E.S.   46
Talbot, G.   20
Temple, Archbishop F.   43
Theodore, Archbishop of Canterbury   236
The Guardian   31, 32, 110
The Month   132, 207
The Tablet   12, 43, 61, 90, 91, 122, 126, 128, 130, 133, 164–166, 207
The Times   58, 124, 125, 164, 166
The Union Review (The Union)   12, 15–19
The Universe   90, 122
Thirty Nine articles   8, 61, 64–66, 95, 132
Tractarians   5, 7, 9, 22, 180, 181
Tracts for the Times   7–9
transubstantiation   67, 114, 153, 193
Treaty of London   48
Tyrrell, G.   110, 182

Ubi arcano Dei   222
Ullathorne, Bishop W.B.   17, 20
Uniate Church of England   10, 11, 149, 150, 163, 190, 191, 209
University of Louvain   50, 59, 64, 201
Ultramontanism   16, 20, 21, 23, 37, 44, 187, 194, 207, 209